How the Workers Became Muslims

How the Workers Became Muslims

Immigration, Culture, and Hegemonic Transformation in Europe

Ferruh Yılmaz

University of Michigan Press
Ann Arbor

Published in the United States of America by the
University of Michigan Press
Manufactured in the United States of America
♾ Printed on acid-free paper

2019 2018 2017 2016 4 3 2 1

A CIP catalog record for this book is available from the British Library.

Library of Congress Cataloging-in-Publication Data

Yılmaz, Ferruh.
How the workers became Muslims : immigration, culture, and hegemonic transformation in Europe / Ferruh Yılmaz.
pages cm
Includes bibliographical references and index.
ISBN 978-0-472-07308-5 (hardback) — ISBN 978-0-472-05308-7 (paperback) — ISBN 978-0-472-12178-6 (ebook)
1. Muslims—Europe—Public opinion. 2. Immigrants—Europe—Attitudes. 3. Europe—Emigration and immigration—Public opinion. 4. Public opinion—Europe. 5. Islamic countries—Foreign public opinion, European. 6. Islamophobia—Europe. 7. Public opinion—Europe. 8. Xenophobia—Europe. 9. Islam—Public opinion. I. Title.

D1056.2.M87Y55 2016
331.6'2088297094—dc23

2015031991

For Soek-Fang
I wish you could have seen this book.

Preface

In early 2015, I went to a lecture by a European scholar about Islamophobia and the Far Right in Europe. As is the case usually, someone in the audience responded to the talk by "explaining" why the racist reactions against Muslim immigrants were justified: Muslims were culturally different and their culture was incompatible with European values. She garnered her "explanation" with vivid details of firsthand experiences with Muslim immigrants that she then generalized to the "evil" nature of "them." I commented on her generalizations and pointed at the racist implications of her "descriptions," to which she simply responded: "I am not racist, I am just talking about realities."

The more interesting aspect of this incident was the reaction of the moderator, who was a professor of European history: he did not like the accusations of racism, and he said that the person in the audience was expressing the genuine concerns of Europeans and we should allow people express their sincere sentiments. After the talk, I asked him whether he would have allowed her to say exactly the same things about Jews. He said no.

I certainly believe that her experiences were genuine and her sentiments were sincere but so were so many ordinary Germans' "sentiments" about Jews during the Nazi Germany. What has changed since then? The views or Jews?

I do not believe that the world can be experienced purely without the intermediation of language. Once language enters the process, it shapes our experiences through the identity categories that render the otherwise chaotic social world intelligible. It would be impossible to experience Jews or Muslims (or any other category) as entities if we did not catalog them with certain attributes. Since we cannot experience all Jews or Muslims at once, we need to connect our particular experiences to the entire category, the existence of which we can only know through the representations of those categories.

I have never been in favor of banning racist or hate speech. First, it is a complicated issue; racist messages and hate speech can be coded and packaged to avoid legal troubles. Second, rather than banning racist views or hate speech, they should be made unacceptable by banning them from common sense.

I am therefore more interested in studying how particular instances of bad behavior or violence are made to characterize an entire ethnic, racial, or religious category of people; how these generalizations come to be viewed as sincere and therefore acceptable and justifiable; and finally how these generalizations are particularized as reasonable with respect to just one particular group so that a translation between historical experiences becomes impossible (e.g., "this situation is completely different from the previous ones, because Muslims are essentially different"). In short, I am interested in how a professor of history can imply that there is an essential difference between Jews and Muslims without a second thought.

A quite young man was so distressed about the pervasive discrimination and persecution of his people with the same religious background that he bought a pistol, went to the building that symbolized the system that he so deeply hated, and assassinated a man who represented that system. His parents were poor immigrants without job and security. He himself had been treated as an outcast and dropped out of school in his teenage years and moved to another country. He became more religious than his parents or his uncle, who gave him shelter and helped him. He became more and more agitated and radicalized by the news about the constant discrimination and suffering of his own people. After the assassination, he declared, "I acted . . . because of love for my parents and for my people who were subjected unjustly to outrageous treatment." One of the leaders of the country he acted against fulminated: "This odious attack . . . once again deprives our people from attaining the peace and quiet they have so deserved" (Marrus 1988: 69).

This is not the story of Omar Abdel Hamid El-Hussein, a twenty-two-year-old man, who was born to Jordanian-Palestinian immigrant parents and raised in Denmark. On February 14, 2015, El-Hussein went to a public event called "Art, Blasphemy and Freedom of Expression," where Lars Vilks, who is famous for his drawings of the prophet Muhammed, was among the speakers and killed one of the participants. Later that night, he attacked the Great Synagogue in Copenhagen, killing yet another person before he was shot and killed by the Danish police. It was not El-Hussein who declared his act as a revenge for the "outrageous treatment" of his people, something that he could have done if he had been given the chance. But the Danish prime minister, Helle Thorning-Schmidt's, condemnation of the attack echoed the sentiments from the first story: "There are dark forces who believe darkness is stronger than light. . . . We stand united as Danes."

Nor is it the story of the two young men who attacked the French satirical weekly newspaper *Charlie Hebdo* and killed twelve people in January 2015. They, too, were said to be radicalized by the pervasive discrimination they suffered in France as well as the treatment of Muslims globally. The French president, François Hollande, called the attacks "an act of exceptional barbarism" and called for unity.

It is the story of Herschel Grynszpan, a seventeen-year-old Jewish boy who was born to Polish-Jewish parents in Hanover, Germany. On November 7, 1938, he shot the third secretary of the German Embassy in Paris and declared that it was an act against the "outrageous treatment" of Jews in Germany. It was Joseph Goebbels who declared that the attack deprived "our people" of "peace and quiet." The attack was used by Nazis to organize Kristallnacht pogroms against Germany's Jewish minority on November 9, 1938. The Nazis used the assassination to focus attention on "Jewish terrorism" and demonstrate the "Jews' responsibility for the outbreak of war in Europe" (Marrus 1998: 75). Many Jews at the time argued that Grynszpan's action worsened the conditions of Jews in Europe. Marrus (1988) is unconvinced that this is the case: the Nazis could have found another pretext to do what they did. Marrus describes Grynszpan as a frustrated and depressed young man who "sought a violent way out, and he was not the last person to find this kind of solution to an impossible problem" (79).

There is no way I can condone the heinous murders in Paris or Copenhagen. However, the similarities between Grynszpan's story and the stories of young "Muslim immigrants" who are agitated, radicalized, and retort to violence against those whom they see as symbols of the suffering of "their people" are striking. The irony is that while nobody would today hold Grynszpan responsible for the Nazis' actions, the treatment of Muslim immigrants is often justified by the actions of young Muslims. It has become perfectly sensible to argue that Muslims bring it upon themselves. History often repeats itself because we lack the framework within which stories and experiences can be translated into one another.

Acknowledgments

The book was written over a protracted period of time, and I accumulated many debts across the continents, but there are institutions and people who were involved in a more direct manner, and I would like to take this opportunity to express my gratitude to them.

First of all, this project would not have started without a scholarship from the Danish Social Science Research Council (now the Danish Council for Independent Research). Special thanks to the anonymous grant-reviewers who believed in my project. I hope they will like the result. A special thanks to the Danish Refugee Council, which granted me free access to its newspaper archive on immigrants and refugees and allowed me to photocopy more than ten thousand pages from the archive. The Council's contribution to this project has been invaluable. The Documentation and Advisory Center on Racial Discrimination and its leader, Niels-Erik Hansen, were very helpful with documents, office space, and practical questions; they deserve many thanks. Arly Christensen (RIP) and Bente Christensen gave me moral and practical support in Denmark.

During my fieldwork in the summer of 2001 in Denmark, every newspaper and media institution I contacted granted me access, allowing me to follow their news-making decisions and routines without any constraints. These media are *Ekstra Bladet*, *Jyllands-Posten*, *Politiken*, and *TV-Avisen* (Danmarks Radio). The journalists and management I met at these media were extremely helpful and friendly. Special thanks to the late editor in chief at *Politiken*, Tøger Seidenfaden, for his permission to use Pol-Info (now Infomedia), the electronic database for all newspapers in Denmark. Thanks also to Line Vikkelsø Slot for finding student interviewers in the Department of Sociology at the University of Copenhagen. They are Anders Hoff, Christina Viskum Lytken Larsen, Helle Kløft Schademan, Anne Marie Krag, Marius Sylverstersen, Rikke Kamstrup, and Camilla Rasmussen. Selma Atçeken transcribed some of my interviews.

One of the greatest influences on my intellectual development was my visit with the Discourse and Rhetoric Group at Loughborough University in the United Kingdom, where I spent several months participating in their weekly sessions on analysis and theory, and especially the sessions that focused on my project and transcripts. Special thanks to Jonathan Potter, Michael Billig, and Derek Edwards for the many face-to-face meetings and discussions.

I am grateful for the Fellowship in Media, Religion, and Culture from the School of Journalism and Mass Communication at the University of Colorado–Boulder. The seminars and comments from the participants have been very helpful. I especially want to thank Stewart Hoover and Lynn Schofield Clark for their feedback.

I truly appreciate the fellowship, office space, and support provided by the Center for Global Communication Studies (CGCS) at the Annenberg School for Communication, University of Pennsylvania, especially the director of the Center, Monroe Price. I thank Marwan Kraidy for facilitating my affiliation with CGCS and being a wonderful host in Philadelphia during an extraordinarily difficult time in my life.

Gayle Aruta, Sylvia Beauvais, and Rita Koryan provided invaluable logistic support in different phases of this protracted project.

Many people have commented on this work. I have been fortunate to have a wide network of scholars who generously shared their published and unpublished work and ideas with me and spent time discussing my ideas, chapters, and proposals. Michael Schudson, Robert Horwitz, George Lipsitz, Klaus Bruhn Jensen, and Yen Espiritu patiently read and commented on the first drafts of the manuscript and supported me throughout the process. Erik Larson helped me to find my way through SPSS. I want to thank Rikke Andreassen, Rebecca Atencio, Mohammed Bamyeh, Marie Demker, Bülent Diken, Nancy Fisher, Myria Georgiou, Kevin Gotham, Randall Halle, John Haslam, Radha Hegde, Peter Hervik, Stig Hjarvard, Christian Horst, Mustafa Hussain, Sara Jul Jacobsen, Tina Gudrun Jensen, Rene Elley Karpantschof, Arun Kundnani, Louise Lund Liebmann, Nancy Maveety, Elizabeth McMahon, Toby Miller, Benjamin Moffitt, Aurélien Mondon, Mahmut Mutman, Maria Oskarson, Radhika Parameswaran, Michael Nebeling Petersen, Kaya Şahin, Deniz Serinci, Annebelle Sreberny, Gavan Titley, Pradip Thomas, Thomas Tufte, Frank Ukadike, Margaret Wetherell, and Yasemin Yıldız for sharing their work and giving me advice and recommendations on drafts of chapters and ideas. Schirin Amir-Moazami and Frank Peter made it possible to present my research to international audiences at the Governmentalization of Islam in Europe conference in Frankfurt an der Oder, Germany, in 2009, and they were the editors for a special issue of *Current Sociology* where parts of the book material were published. Karina Horsti invited me to MigraNord conference in Helsinki, Finland, in 2010, and Kaarina Nikunen to the European Communication Research and Education Association's (ECREA) conference in Lisbon, Portugal, in 2014. I am also grateful to my colleagues in the Department of Communication at Tulane University for great intellectual, emotional, and logistic support.

The book-writing process has a lot of ups and downs, and I received much-needed support in various forms from Rod Benson, Gholam Khiabany, Vicki Mayer, Mehdi Semati, Ben Pitcher, Mauro Porto, Khaldoun Samman, and Ruth Wodak. These acknowledgments provide me with an opportunity to thank Daniel Hallin for his academic guidance, for his moral, practical, and intellectual support, for having faith in me, for his patience, precision, and timeliness, and last but not least for his friendship. Ernesto Laclau (RIP) deserves special thanks for being a great intellectual mentor and inspiration. I cannot overstate his contributions to this book. He truly believed that this book provided a multidisciplinary contribution to hegemony theory. He promised to write a foreword for this book but passed away before he could do it.

Aaron McCollough, my editor at the University of Michigan Press simply is the person who made it possible to publish this book. I truly appreciate his patience, timeliness, and support.

Finally, I do not know how I would keep my sanity if not for my wife, Esra Özcan, who was beside me listening to my frustrations and ideas, reading all of my papers for language and providing logistic support and love.

New Orleans, May 2015

Ferruh Yılmaz

An earlier version of chapter 1 was published in *Journal of Language and Politics* 14, no. 6 in 2015 with the title "Analyzing Variations and Stability in Discourse: Hegemony, Nation, and Muslim Immigrants." It is reproduced here in expanded form with permission. Parts of this book were used in previously published articles: "From Immigrant Worker to Muslim Immigrant: Challenges for Feminism" in *European Journal of Women's Studies* (22, no. 1 [2015]), and "Right-Wing Hegemony and Immigration: How the Populist Far-Right Achieved Hegemony through the Immigration Debate in Europe" in *Current Sociology* (60, no. 3 [2012]). The materials from the articles are reproduced in this book with permission.

Contents

Introduction

> Unless we expel the Jewish people soon, they will have judaized our people within a very short time.
>
> —Adolf Hitler, from a speech at Nuremberg, January 13, 1923
>
> (Jäckel 1981: 52)

> There may be second, third, fourth generation [of Muslim immigrants in Europe], they don't consider themselves part of that country. They're actually going in there to colonize, to overtake the culture.
>
> —Bobby Jindal, governor of Louisiana
>
> (Diamond 2015)

> My grandparents came of age in France in the 1930s. Then as now, disquiet abounded about the impact of immigration from the East, on jobs, on the social order, on a venerable civilization. It was a different East (Europe instead of Middle), and it threatened Judaization instead of Islamification. Then as now, ordinary and well-meaning people believed that they had legitimate reason to be afraid of others who were not like them. Then as now, ordinary and well-meaning people were seduced by demagogues playing to the all-too-human tendency to generalize and categorize. [. . .] I am not safe as "a Jew in France." Nor are any of the "Muslims" here. No one can ever be safe in a category. (Mouillot 2015)

The whole world was shaken by the terrible attacks on *Charlie Hebdo* magazine and the Jewish supermarket in Paris and against the public event "Art, Blasphemy, and Freedom of Expression," in Copenhagen a few weeks later. In a show of solidarity and unity, 3.7 million people marched in France, the largest demonstration ever in France. Over forty presidents and prime ministers, including leaders from Britain, Germany, Spain, Israel, and Palestine, joined the demonstrators. The *New York Times* noted that "Jews, Muslims, Christians, atheists and people of all races, ages and political stripes [responded to the attacks and] swarmed central Paris beneath a bright blue sky, calling for peace and an end to violent extremism" (Alderman and Bilefsky 2015). CNN called the marches "a gesture of unity" (Fantz 2015). The general sentiment, that the Paris attack targeted "our core values," was summed up in the student column in the International Communication Association's newsletter in March 2015: "Terror attacks targeted not only citizens but also democratic values—starting with freedom of speech and freedom of religion."

The killings in Paris were an appalling offense to human life and dignity. But the suggestion that violence by self-proclaimed jihadists is the biggest threat to freedom of speech and democracy in Western societies indicates a curious, selective amnesia. Journalists and citizens are often killed or imprisoned all over the world—including the Western world—for exposing corruption and illegal government activities. When Michael Page, a white supremacist and U.S. Army veteran, attacked a Sikh temple in Wisconsin on August 5, 2012, and killed six Sikhs, probably because he thought they were Muslim, it did not attract the same kind of attention and worldwide condemnation as an attack against freedom of religion. Neither did the numerous attacks on French Muslims, nor other, ongoing instances of horrific carnage around the world (e.g., Central African Republic, Nigeria, Gaza, Pakistan) committed in the name of religion. In France, and in many other nations whose leaders participated in the demonstrations, people are arrested and prosecuted for making comments deemed to be anti-Semitic or encouraging terrorism; most countries in the Western Hemisphere formally limit free speech. Furthermore, I assume that most of the demonstrators would not accept the kind of insulting speech that *Charlie Hebdo* stood for if the speech was directed at other minorities.

The massive demonstrations indicate that the attacks signify something bigger than the horrific killings: that Muslims and their actions in the name of religion constitute a greater threat to our basic freedoms and values in the West. And inversely, the reactions to the attacks also create a sense that despite "our internal differences" we in the "West" share some core values such as freedom of speech and democracy.

European countries do not go in panic mode only when there is a massacre of this caliber. Denmark, for example, went into overdrive in the summer of 2013 about the importance of pork meatballs to Danish culture and identity. Switzerland had a referendum on minarets (of which there are few in that country); Sweden and Germany were each shaken by the murder of a young woman, which was labeled as "honor crime," a peculiar form of violence against women that is deemed to be rooted in Muslim culture. European public sentiment is often in high alert over highly publicized issues such as female genital mutilation, gang rapes, forced marriages, veils, girls who are not allowed to attend swimming classes, parallel societies—all presented as signs of a "creeping Islamization" that threatens basic norms and values. The media frenzies around these issues are so intense that it is difficult not to feel alarmed, even if one wants to distance oneself from the often racist and Islamophobic overtones of the debates. The result is a sense that there was a time when members of society lived in peaceful coexistence that has been broken by the newcomers. The constant incitement to discourse on Islam and Muslim immigrants ontologizes Muslims vis-à-vis "us."

I went to Denmark in 1979 as a young, left-wing activist who had no idea what the term "identity" meant. Within two decades, I became a "Muslim": by the mid-1990s, I was answering yes when people asked me if I were a Muslim. I said yes despite the fact that I have never identified myself with anything religious. On the contrary, my political formation had made me think of religion as the opium of people. I also "learned" not only about the term "identity" but that identity is anchored in culture as a set of traditions, norms, and values, although they never made sense to me: I did not share more traditions, norms, and values with people from the same ethnic background than with my Danish friends.

My "conversion" had nothing to do with religion but with the central place immigration took in the public debate, which increasingly organized public and private talk around immigration and its impact on society. Not only did immigration move into the center of public debate, it also influenced how we talked about it and how we positioned ourselves in the debate. In my first years in Denmark, I lived in a progressive commune with a small group of people. We talked a lot about politics; our political views and values bound us together and made us part of the same collectivity (i.e., identity). The ethnonational or other differences between us were mere nuances that did not matter much in the grand scheme of political divisions. In the early and mid-1980s, we protested the new right-wing government's assault on labor unions and its dismantling of the welfare system; the Soviet invasion of Afghanistan; Saddam Hussein's use of chemical weapons against the Kurds; and the Turkish military regime's brutal oppression and violation of human rights. We protested against violations of rights hard-won through decades of struggles.

My friends' or my political views and values did not change much over the course of the two decades I lived in Denmark, but we started to talk first about refugees and then immigrants more and more as cycles of controversies and moral panics kept the issue on public agenda. The controversies and moral panics were first about the number of refugees, but the focus quickly changed to the immigrants and "their culture." A story about a "forced marriage" among immigrants would quickly be echoed in the mass media and become amplified in public consciousness. The steady stream of these stories about immigrants' cultural values and practices would force us to discuss the cultural characteristics of immigrants, which did not seem to fit with our progressive outlook. By the mid-1990s, our political conversations would generally concern immigration, racism, and culture; these issues no longer bound us against a common political opponent. The conversations about immigrants constantly interpellated me as an immigrant and my friends as Danes although they did not see me as part of the category of immigrants whose "cultural values"—now in focus—were regarded as alien. Outside my social and political circles, I had always been an immigrant. The slightest variation in your accent gives you away in Denmark. Although in the beginning I was interpellated with an ethnonational label whose signification was more ambiguous vis-à-vis the political configuration of society and did not lead to questions about my culture; in the 1990s, the less ambiguous label was "cultural-religious" (i.e., Muslim). Yet I did not act like other Muslims as generally portrayed in the media. People would ask me questions: "Why do you drink beer? Are you not Muslim?" To resist the implied categorical attributions, I started to respond with "Yes, I am Muslim." Any other answer would confirm my status as an exception to the rule. This is how I turned into a Muslim a decade and half after my arrival.

My story is not unique. During my early years in Denmark, immigrant organizations were generally national or ethnic (e.g., the Moroccan Association in Denmark) and often affiliated with political organizations on the Danish left. The Union of Workers from Turkey was known to have connections to the Communist Party; others were affiliated with Social Democrats or groups on the New Left (e.g., the Organization of Workers from Turkey). The immigrant organizations defined themselves by their class positions. By the time I left Denmark, ethnonational worker associations had been replaced by cross-national Muslim associations.

As Saunders (2012) notes, when the first immigrants came to Europe, they were not Muslims—they were Turks, Arabs, Indians, Pakistanis, or North Africans.

> Islam may have been the religion of these twentieth century arrivals, but in general their faith was just part of the background of their lives. It wasn't the way they thought of themselves, it wasn't something they sought out in others. Despite their religion's claims to universality, they felt more affinity with non-Muslim immigrants from

> their birthplace than they did with Muslims from other countries. And most were too busy struggling to find work and housing to think much about religion. (139)

They faced discrimination as Turks, "Pakis," or Arabs. The second generation joined the antiracist movements of the host countries. As political parties, journalists, and activists started to call them "Muslims," young people started to embrace Islam as "a way to hold their heads up in a country that had belittled and humiliated them" (Saunders 2012: 140). They began to call themselves Muslims, or Danish, German, or British Muslims, not Turks, Pakistanis, or Arabs. Islam was indeed an essential part of "integration." It means, as Fernando (2014) notes, that the Muslim being hailed by the majority is not the same Muslim that "Muslims" inhabit.

The story of how I (and other immigrants) became Muslim illustrates the main analytical points of this book, which tells a story about the culturalization of discourse and the production of Muslim immigrants as a distinct ontology that displaced the old hegemonic structure in Denmark and elsewhere in Europe. Although this book is about Denmark, the mechanisms through which political discourse is culturalized and pushed to the right are similar across Europe, so that this book is a case study that can be used to understand the dynamics and state of European public discourse(s) on European/national identity and immigration.

Far-Right Hegemony

In their seminal work *Hegemony and Socialist Strategy*, Laclau and Mouffe (2001) explored the possibilities for a revised socialist strategy under new fragmented political and social conditions. Two and half decades later, we can note that it is not the socialist movement but the populist Far Right that has shown an ability to adopt a successful strategy, which has led to the reconfiguration of internal fault lines in European societies. This book anatomizes such a reconfiguration through a case study of what has been taking place in Denmark since the mid-1980s. Examining the intervention strategies of the populist Far Right, which has achieved an unprecedented influence on mainstream politics and changed the parameters of political discourse, may provide clues about why the Left is unable to provide a viable alternative vision and is in a deep crisis. This in turn can open up new ways of thinking about progressive politics.

That Europe has been moving to the right over the question of Muslim immigration has become commonplace, even in mainstream media. *The Economist* wrote that the Netherlands had turned sharply to the right after the far-right, anti-immigrant, anti-Islam Freedom Party had come in third in the summer elections of 2010. Similar comments were made when in 2007 Nicolas Sarkozy defeated Socialist Segolene Royal after an explicitly anti-immigrant, anti-Muslim campaign, and again in 2010 when far-right Sweden Democrats entered parliament for the first time, and when in 2014 when the far-right Danish People's Party, the French National Front, and the UK Independence Party (UKIP) finished first in European Parliament elections. *Der Spiegel* summed it up on September 28, 2010: "All across Europe, right-wing populist parties are enjoying significant popular support . . . they are exploiting fear of Muslim immigration and frustration with the political establishment—and are forcing mainstream parties to shift to the right."

Although the fear of Muslims is sometimes linked to the September 11 attacks (e.g., Fekete 2009), the common assumption is that the turn to the right reflects tensions about globalization, demographic changes, and the increasing number of immigrants—anxieties that the Right has been able to capitalize on. Too often, social scientists view social change as a mechanical result of agentless structural changes, to which political forces respond but are not decisive in determining their direction. To describe political articulation as reaction or response to structural changes is to assume that tensions around immigration are natural, prepolitical reflexes, an orientation that closes down theoretical and analytical avenues that might allow for a fuller grasp of the nature of the Right's interventions as well as the nature of the social and political change in Europe.

I argue that the Right's ability to adopt a successful hegemonic strategy has led to the reconfiguration of the internal fault lines in European societies, that is, to a shift in what Laclau and Mouffe (2001: xiv) call the "ontology of the social." This book is an anatomy of that reconfiguration in Denmark. Although the populist Right's strategy is crucial in the analysis of the reconfiguration traced here, this book is not a study of the dynamics of the Far Right or of populism in Denmark.

There is no consensus about what term to use to describe the far-right parties that have become central players in European political discourse during the last three decades. Some scholars opt for the term "extreme right" (Bornschier 2010; Fekete 2009; Hainsworth 2008; Ignazi 2003; Klandermans and Mayer 2006; Schain, Zolberg, and Hossay 2002), others for "radical right" (Givens 2005; Kitschelt 1995; Mouffe 1995; Norris 2005; Rydgren 2004, 2013; Williams 2006) or "populist radical right (Betz 1994; Mondon 2013; Mudde 2007; Rydgren 2010), or "far right" (Ellinas 2010) or "right-wing populism"

(Berezin 2009; Betz and Meret 2013) or just populism (Panizza 2005; Taggart 2000) or neopopulism (Betz and Immerfall 1998). Berggren and coauthors (2007) prefer to call these parties "fascist." Whichever term is used, they generally refer to parties and groups that focus on an identity politics of immigration and generally participate in the electoral process.

Although there are various explanations for these parties' success—for example, popular anxieties around Europeanization (Berezin 2009), changing social structures such as postindustrialization and globalization (Ignazi 2003; Andersen 2004; Rydgren 2004), the disappearance of political difference between left and right and the void left by the Left's inability to adopt to the new epoch (Betz and Meret 2013; Mondon 2013; Mouffe 1995), and the change in balance from the salience of economic (class) cleavages to cultural cleavages (Rydgren 2004; Bornschier 2010)—almost all explanations point to the fact that the mobilization of far-right "movements and milieus today is closely related to the anti-Islam and anti-Muslim issue" (Meret 2011: 256).

The latter set of explanations, which draw attention to the discord between West European party systems (which are historically organized around class cleavages) and the new sociopolitical space that emphasizes cultural cleavages, sound similar to the explanations set forth in this book. According to these explanations, the economic cleavage dimension, which is about the degree of state involvement in the economy, pitted workers against capital, whereas the cultural cleavage dimension, which is mostly about issues such as immigration, law and order, and abortion, puts workers against left-libertarian positions. It is argued that it is the increased salience of the cultural cleavage dimension that created optimal conditions for populist far-right forces to effectively mobilize working-class voters against libertarian elite and their "treasonous" immigration policies.

This explanation, however, is inadequate when we consider the transformation of both mainstream and far-right parties, which adopted gay-friendly and antimisogynic rhetoric (as opposed to the "homophobic and misogynic Muslims"). Moreover, it refers to "structural changes" as the background for the political shift as if the structural changes preceded the political articulations of those changes—an assumption at odds with the theoretical orientation of this book (see below).

A more suitable explanation is that the mainstream Left's adoption of neoliberal orthodoxies created a political void where discontent with the system was no longer represented in the mainstream political system (i.e., crisis of representation). The populist Far Right successfully articulated this discontent in terms of a new antagonism "which has shifted the understanding of politics in the minds of the *classes populaires* from a class struggle, in the Marxist sense of the term, to a struggle of race and 'civilization'" (Mondon 2013: 159).

As the entire political spectrum was pushed to the right through the discourse on Muslim immigration, the formation of what Gramsci (1971) called a "historical bloc" is observable in the alliances forged across the political spectrum around what are posed as "core values," virtually none of which had been considered universal (or even common) before their juxtaposition with Muslim immigrants. The concept of class has become marginal in political representation. Likewise, the positions of feminists, gays, environmentalists, and human rights activists are gradually being disarticulated from the progressive politics with which they had traditionally been aligned, as strategic demands once borne by conjunctural political articulations are being elevated to universal values that are articulated as aspects of national or "Western" culture. Many left-wing activists align themselves with right-wing political forces in their defense of what are purported to be established, long-held common values, such as women's emancipation, gay rights, or freedom of speech. In this epistemic collusion between the Right and the Left, the figure of Muslim immigrant helps create the very social cohesion that is presented as preexisting and under threat. The assumption is that social cohesion is anchored in cultural sameness, but this assumption itself is produced by references to an ethnically homogeneous past, not only in the populist imagination but in all kinds of discourse including "progressive" academic research. The common understanding of the past as ethnically and culturally homogenous and therefore harmonious is indicative of the populist hegemony. The projection of cultural cohesion into the past is one of the major ways in which the new hegemonic vision is established.

A Short History of Immigration to Denmark

To realize that neither immigration nor negative attitudes toward immigrants are new phenomena, one only needs to watch the much-praised movie *Pelle the Conqueror*. The movie is about the life of Swedish immigrants in Denmark. The Danish historian Bent Østergaard (2007) argues that immigration has always been part of Denmark's (and Europe's) history. Germans, Swedes, Poles, Russians, Jews, Roma people, Hungarians, the Dutch, and many other ethnic groups settled in Denmark. The common assumption is that the earlier immigrants were culturally similar and were easily assimilated into host societies, whereas the new non-Western (especially Muslim) immigrants with their essentially different culture threaten the core values of

Western liberal democracies. Both Østergaard (2007) and Lucassen (2005) challenge this common assumption: Østergaard argues that all immigrants have contributed positively to the economic and cultural development of society, whereas Lucassen shows that earlier immigrants such as the Irish in England, the Poles in Germany, and the Italians in France were also considered inherently different and were seen as cultural/religious threats.

The main argument of this book in this context is that the new immigrants were relabeled as "Muslims" after the 1980s as the result of political articulation. They did not arrive as Muslims, nor did they identify as such; they were part of the labor force in Denmark.

The contemporary phase of immigration in Denmark is usually seen as beginning in the second half of 1960s when groups of "foreign workers" from Turkey, Yugoslavia, Spain, Morocco, and later from Pakistan began to work in Danish factories and farms (Mikkelsen 2001; Jensen 2000; Madsen 2000; Gaasholt and Togeby 1995; Østergaard 2007). At first, the flow of a foreign "workforce" did not happen in an organized fashion in the sense that they were not recruited systematically in their country of origin but received work permits if they found jobs while in Denmark. The first restrictions—which made it necessary to apply for work permits from abroad with an actual job offer—were introduced in 1970 and in 1973 when the oil crisis led to economic stagnation, the Danish parliament (*Folketinget*) imposed a complete ban on the immigration of foreign workers.

However, the law was not effective in stopping immigration, which continued in two distinctive forms: First, "guest workers" did not return to their countries of origin. Instead, they were joined by their spouses and children in Denmark, and because of family reunion laws the number of immigrants continued to increase. The second form of immigration was, after 1984, through political asylum with the arrival of large refugee groups from Iran, Iraq, Lebanon (Palestinians), Bosnia, Albania, and Somalia, as well as, the latest, from Syria. As a result, the debate since the mid-1980s centered on asylum and family reunion laws, which have been continuously tightened since that time. According to the figures from Statistics Denmark (2015: 4), foreigners and their descendants make up 11.1 percent of the population in Denmark, and approximately 58 percent of foreigners come from so-called non-Western countries. It is the non-Western part of the immigrants—rather than Germans or Americans—who are the objects of the intense debates. Because the authorities do not classify immigrants according to religion, it is difficult to know the precise number of "Muslim" immigrants. Although not all non-Western immigrants are Muslims, the word "immigrant" would automatically trigger "Muslim" in the minds of Danes.

The first two decades (1964–84) of debate on the latest immigration phase showed many similarities to the last century's debate on Swedish immigrants: concerns about wage suppression, working conditions, criminality, the burden on welfare system, and immigrants' social problems. Culture, ethnicity, and religion, although present in discourse, were not the dominant themes, at least quantitatively. In 1970, there were only 14 (out of a total 448) newspaper stories that focused on cultural problems (Madsen 2000). By 2015, Danish newspapers were even discussing whether Danes would buy halal chocolate candy (e.g., *Ekstra Bladet* had a poll on the issue where 87.13 percent of those who voted said no).

Theoretical Framework: Heterogeneity of the Social and Empty Signifiers

Two important views of language offer ways to think about the discursive nature of social life. The Swiss linguist Ferdinand de Saussure proposed a fundamental distinction between language and the reality it purportedly describes. He challenged the status of language as a relatively transparent medium between things and meaning by pointing to the constitutive nature of language. In my context, the important aspect of his theory is the distinction between "signifier" and "signified." The meaning of a sign is produced through the differential system of language: words (signifiers) gain their meanings not from what they signify (signified) but through their difference from other signifiers. Saussure argued that the meaning of a word—for example, "dog"—is produced by its place in a paradigmatic and syntagmatic chain rather than by the thing itself.[1]

When we talk about a more complex sign, such as culture, or under that sign, a signifier such as "Dane" or "Danish," what are we talking about? A common definition would be that someone Danish (i.e., a Dane) was born in Denmark, as opposed to an immigrant. Is that sufficient? What about being born abroad to Danish parents? What about those born in Denmark but to non-Danish parents? It is evident that the meaning of the signifier "Dane" becomes immediately vague and contested as soon as we begin using and then attempting to definitively capture the meaning of the term. Once we put the meaning of the sign into the exigencies of human communication, "Dane" becomes even more complicated and polysemic: people use the word to signify a wide variety of features, some of which may be contradictory. Danes may be simultaneously described friendly and unfriendly depending on the rhetorical context of the utterance. Of course, the signifier "native" (i.e., Dane) cannot signify a clear concept of a thing, person, or group. The meaning of the signifier "Dane" is, therefore, arbitrary to the extent that it is almost empty, an important point I will examine in chapter 1. What is important for the current discussion is that the meaning of the sign "Dane" may be temporarily fixed at a concrete moment of communication, which limits the possibilities of proliferation. On the other hand, total closure is never possible because the local premises that limit proliferation of signification change from context to context and can always be contested. In this temporary fixity of meaning, Danes talk about themselves, and are talked about, as if Danish culture is the most natural and given entity in the world, as if there is a clear definition of a group of people who have something in common, regardless of the myriad problems with pinpointing what that common essence is.

Starting from the view of language not as *langue* (i.e., a structural system in Saussure's sense), but as *parole* (i.e., actual acts of speech), Bakhtin's ideas about dialogism, heteroglossia, and the centripetal/centrifugal forces of language offer useful ways to think about culture and discourse. According to Bakhtin (1981), "The dialogic orientation of discourse is a phenomenon that is, of course, a property of *any* discourse" (279). Moreover,

> A unitary language is not something given . . . but is always in essence posited . . . and at every moment of its linguistic life it is opposed to the realities of heteroglossia. But at the same time it makes its real presence felt as a force for overcoming this heteroglossia, imposing specific limits to it, guaranteeing a certain maximum of mutual understanding and crystallizing into a real, although still relative, unity. (270)

Thus, "Every extra-artistic prose discourse . . . cannot fail to be oriented toward the 'already uttered,' the 'already known,' the 'common opinion' and so forth" (279). But the already uttered, the already known, and the common opinion (e.g., Danish culture) is not an element of discourse fixed once and for all. Instead, it is inherently heteroglot in nature, such that meaning can only be fixed in the concrete context of utterance. But any concrete context of utterance is already embedded in the matrix of heteroglossia, wherein centrifugal forces continuously attempt to disperse meaning away from the center whereas centripetal forces attempt to centralize and unify the language—that is, exert a homogenizing and hierarchizing influence.

Bakhtin's conceptualization of the processes of heteroglossia is similar to what Laclau and Mouffe refer to as the "heterogeneity of the social," in which any systematic language is an attempt to suppress heterogeneity by imposing specific limits to it, by making its own language "common sense," that is, the center toward which all other utterances are oriented. I argue that this center is not a patterned discourse—or articulation of differences in an equivalential[2] link, as Laclau and Mouffe (2001) would argue—but ontological categories that are persistently referred to and that can only be apprehended through empty signifiers.

Rhetorical Texture of Society: Discourse and Heterogeneity

This book does not depend on a distinction between discourse and reality. The ontological structure of society is not something already given in nature or in economic relationships among members of a society, but is created through an articulation of relations. As such, they are political relationships. The identity of a social formation such as the working class, for instance, does not originate in objectively identifiable material interests but in the articulation of particular interests common to a group of people. In this sense, there is no difference between the ontological category of "working class" and the articulation of it with reference to their common interests. Those interests have been, as we have seen throughout history, articulated in different ways while keeping the category of "working class" intact. What kept "working class" intact was not the consistent ontic content of the category but the experienced gap between its members and capitalists. The continuing political representation of "working class" interests as opposed to capitalists is what once sustained the ontological structure of society in class terms.

I do not use the term "working class" ironically here, just as I do not use the term "Muslim" ironically unless there is a specific contextual reason for it. To do so would be to indicate some kind of false consciousness, which amounts to taking ontological changes as inaccurate reflections of a real world whose composition is given in the relations of production prior to political articulation. It would suggest interpreting the focus on Muslim immigrants as a new form of racism masking a social division based on class distinction—a reality to which I, as a leftist intellectual, might perhaps have privileged access—narrows down the analytical venues one can take. Instead, I consider class, as much as Muslim immigrants, the result of particular political articulations that have ontologizing effects. As a hegemonic construct, the ontological category of class has its own organizations, political parties, labor unions, and cultural institutions. It makes no sense to discuss the falsity or reality of this construct because the social is always the playground of political articulations that have the power of turning the same ontic content into a different ontological category. Yesterday's foreign workers are now largely represented through religiously oriented organizations and therefore have truly become Muslim immigrants.

Following Laclau and Mouffe (2001), I take discourse as the human meaning-making process in general, including both linguistic and nonlinguistic elements,[3] offering as an example Wittgenstein's concept of language games, which "include within an indissoluble totality both language and the actions interconnected with it. . . . The linguistic and non-linguistic elements are not merely juxtaposed but constitute a differential and structured system of positions—that is, a discourse" (108). In other words, the whole social space is discursive. It is a vast argumentative texture through which people construct their reality.

For Laclau (2014), the rhetorical nature of society means that society does not have an objective referent (substance or essence). We can therefore only approach it by using metonyms, metaphors, allusions, or analogies that give us a sense of what society is like, for example, a statistical chart that takes parts as indicators of the whole. The intelligibility and stability of discourse on society is the result of the repetition and regularity in dispersion in discourse (Bowman 2007).

In my theoretical universe, the rhetoricity of society has as much to do with the inherently fragmented and disjointed nature of the social world. The relative stability of our sense of the social world and our place in it has much more to do with the commonsensical way we imagine the ontological structure of society than regularity in dispersion in discourse. Like Laclau and Mouffe's (2001: 125) understanding of society as a figuration without an essence, I take the ontologies of the social as empty categories that cannot be apprehended objectively because every statement about the ontic content of an ontological category may be contradicted by a concrete example, a testimony, a statistic, or a label. The following example illustrates the heterogenic and rhetorical nature of human world.

While we were walking on the busiest pedestrian street of Copenhagen, my friend's mother wanted to eat sausage from one of the street vendors. My friend warned her that it was made of pork. "If God created it, I don't mind eating it," she replied. His father, on the other hand, did not want to eat pork because, he said, he did not like the taste (even though he had never tried it before). My friend's mother was relatively pious Muslim and observed the religious rituals, whereas religion was not part of his father's life at all. Yet it was the pious mother who chose to eat pork and used a religious language to justify it, while his secular father, who refused to eat pork, justified his choice in "secular" terms. The interesting point here is not only that "the meanings of a single religious sign or practice may be multiple and inconsistent, and may change as a particular sign is used to work on the world and the self" as Orsi (2003: 172) argues, but also that the inconsistencies are nevertheless informed by a sense of our place in the world.

In our dealings with the social world, we are much more goal oriented than we may recognize and we draw on many different—sometimes contradictory—ideas to fit the demands of the rhetorical situation. As an example related to the discussion above, Eliasoph's (1998) ethnographic study among members of a country club demonstrates that expressions of racism cannot be taken at face value as reflections of racist minds, but as markers belonging to the context in which they are uttered. Eliasoph argues that the group atmosphere in the country club was more racist and sexist than most of its individual members, and that the same person could tell racist jokes "just to keep the tone right" in social gatherings while seriously expressing nonracist attitudes in more private settings, a discrepancy she explains with reference to Goffman's (1959) distinction between backstage/frontstage in interactional needs (Eliasoph 1998: 100–103). The implication is that beliefs, attitudes, and cognitions are not entities separable from interaction, but are constructed and managed during interaction (Potter 1998; Potter and Wetherell 1987; Edwards and Potter 1992) in an essentially heterogeneous social world. This implies that our utterances about the world should not be taken as reflections of our mental picture of the world; we may say different things at different moments about the same piece of reality depending on the situation and those with whom we are speaking. This is not about impression management techniques, which imply a distinction between sincere and insincere, but about the inherently fragmented and episodic character of our relationship with the world, which renders our accounts of it variable and inconsistent.

Social scientists have long been aware of inconsistencies in people's expressions of opinions and attitudes, especially in opinion poll and survey questions, often explaining it with reference to ambivalent feelings toward objects of discourse. Acknowledging the ambivalence in people's attitudes toward the world, however, is based on the assumption that the world is readily there independent of our accounts of them.

If all discourse is contextual and thus rhetorical, the critical question becomes: How can we make sense of ontologies of the social that appear to be stable constructions? In other words, once we begin to conceive the social world in terms of indefinite series of linguistic possibilities, which can be realized in a wide variety of ways and that are continually reformulated in the course of an ongoing interpretative process, how do we account for the fact that we all speak about "society," for instance, as a stable entity and seem to understand each other? How do we speak about "culture" and understand each other? How do we even begin to conceptualize politics that deal with putative structures such as culture if discourse is heterogeneous, fragmented, and episodic?

We enlist categories as if they are independent, self-contained, and stable entities with which we orient ourselves and about which we express our views because, in fact, they enable us to speak about the world, interact with one another, and allow us to associate ourselves with collectivities, however contingent they may be. In this book, these categories are understood as discursive resources that help us to organize and talk about the world, rather than evidence of mental reflections of objective structures whose meanings are given through their place in a real world of objects. They help us to construct our subjectivities through positions in and about the world; they help us apprehend ourselves as subjects distinct from one another as well as from the objects with which we deal.

It is within this general framework that we can consider a major conceptual category on which this study hinges—culture—and the process I have referred to as "culturalization."

Culturalization, Culture, and Identity

In 1986, an Iranian refugee in Denmark tried to kill his wife. The incident, reported on the inner pages of national newspapers among other local crime stories, was attributed to the husband's jealousy. There is no mention of culture or cultural background as an explanation for a husband's emotions or motives or his crime of domestic violence. By the end of the decade, the discussion was all about culture as the background for whatever immigrants might be doing.

In the early 1990s, I was called by a journalist colleague from the Danish Broadcasting Corporation to comment on a murder case in a live radio broadcast. An older Turkish man had killed his grandchild and injured his daughter-in-law with a cooking pan. I was invited to explain what in Turkish culture might have made him commit the murder. "He must be out of his mind," I cried out. "What is there to explain?" I was invited to the studio to say just that, but one of station's correspondents had already made a report that aired immediately after my interview. His narrative techniques surrounded the murder with cultural mystery and mystique: the Turks in the town acted suspiciously and were not willing to talk about the murder or the murderer. Later it turned out that there was no story, no cultural explanation: the Turkish man was mentally ill and had previously been in mental institutions. There was nothing to talk about after all.

The question is this: Would there be a story worthy to be discussed in a news/actuality program if the murderer had not been an immigrant? Certainly not: murder stories do not normally find their way into "serious" media such as radio or TV news unless the murder has a larger impact on society (e.g., the victim or the murderer is a public figure or the murder is part of a "trend"). What made it a notable story was not so much the murder itself but who committed it. What is the implication of reporting on a murder case when an immigrant commits it? The media does not report on events as they happen; they ascribe significance to events. In the minds of the journalists, a murder committed by an immigrant is more significant than an "ordinary murder" because of the assumed alterity of it.

The radio program was but one of a long series of media stories about a deviant act as reflective of "their culture." These stories produce "immigrants' culture" as a meaningful category through single acts of deviance woven into parts of the same overall category. A murder committed by an immigrant is metonymically made to stand for the entirety of culture. Through the constant focus on the cultural difference, "immigrant" became a cultural/ethnic/Muslim object to be examined, debated, and policed.

The term "culturalization" is central to this book, but I do not use the terms "culture" or "cultural" as a way of classifying people or their identities. Raymond Williams describes culture as "a description of a particular way of life which expresses certain meanings and values, not only in art and learning, but in institutions and ordinary behavior" (quoted in Hall 1993: 351). In this anthropological sense, culture is understood a symbolic meaning-making system in the same way as ideology (Geertz 1973).

It is clear that this sense of culture conflicts with the notion of the social as a heterogenetic space. If we use symbols flexibly to meet the rhetorical demands of a particular context, it is difficult to map out a systematic way of producing meaning; our enunciations in different contexts will be inherently unsystematic and inconsistent and will not reflect a "particular way of life" or shared values. In my theoretical universe, values are flexible resources people draw on to do various things. In other words, culture is the totality of the symbols available for discourse. It is a fragmented domain in which inconsistent and episodic references to values and categories are made and established. What makes the fragmented discursive resources appear to be articulated in systematic ways in particular historical and political conjunctures are the pervasive juxtapositions with ontologies of the social, not the built-in systematicity of culture, as I will discuss in chapter 1.

The same goes for the term "identity." The term is used, even in its vernacular form, as an academic abstraction: one's attachment to a collectivity. But the attachment to a particular collectivity in everyday life is flexible; even during a particular conversation we may identify ourselves as a dancer, and then as the focus of the conversation shifts, we may express our belongingness in terms of the neighborhood we live in, the food we share, the music we listen to, our annoyance with a particular group of people, and so on. But if "identity" triggers references to cultural (ethnic or national) categories of belongingness, it is because the social and political ontologies are often interpellated through cultural indicators and cultural resources (i.e., norms and values) are articulated in relation (or attached) to these ontologies. In the Danish context, for example, the continuity of "nation" is now continuously linked to identity projects that present culture as the politically necessary precondition for functional homogeneity. It leads to the culturalization of politics in which political values "are *talked about* as culture either in the sense of being linked to nationally specific and favorable historical traditions or ways of life (including, in the Danish case, secularized religion)" Mouritsen (2006: 73). These values are usually opposed to the so-called immigrant or Muslim culture, which generally refers to internalized religious norms and values about family, gender relations, punishment forms, food (halal), and so on, which are assumed to determine Muslims' behavior. Muslim culture, in this sense, is considered to be in opposition to Danish culture, which is described as either inherently secular or inherently Christian (or alternatively as secularized Christian).

This book argues that it is the culturalization of discourse—that is, the pervasive references to culturally interpellated ontologies of the social—that turns a right (e.g., a political value such as freedom of speech) into a cultural value. In other words, it is the purported existential connection between freedom of speech and a nation that owns it as a cultural value. It is clear that political values that were originally conceptualized as rights "do not have their origins in processes of cultural evolution but have come about as the result of major conflicts and sharp breaks with the past" (Chanock 2000: 16). Even in anthropology, "culture" did not come into widespread use until the 1960s (Jenkins 1997) and the notion of culture was not central to the sociopolitical imagination until the mid-1980s (Schierup 1993).[4] By the late 1980s, culture had become a commonsense frame for organizing, managing, and explaining the world. According to Fredric Jameson (1991), this "universal" trend expands "culture throughout the social realm, to the point at which everything in our social life—from economic value and state power to practices and to the very structure of the psyche itself—can be said to have become 'cultural' in some original and as yet untheorised sense" (48).

Thus, "culturalization" means that the sociopolitical world is predominantly understood as defined by differential norms and values: culture, as Soysal (2009: 5) noted, has "become the predominant mode of addressing citizenship, security, and even economy, which were conventionally considered to be distinct from culture." It is important to note that in everyday (or political) discourse actors do not always use categories in the same analytical and distinctive way as academics (e.g., Roy [2010] makes a clear distinction between culture and religion). Rather, these categories are used flexibly and interchangeably: "Muslim" can mean a racial category as well as deracialize immigrants; it can be used in the place of culture or to deculturize an act. It is the persistent references to culture that ontologize cultural-religious categories whereby social and political problems are explained by reference to the incommensurable nature of cultural differences. The culturalization of discourse has changed the understanding politics as the site where problems caused by cultural encounters are handled (see also Lentin and Titley 2011).

Race, Racism, and Islamophobia

For readers of this book, it will increasingly become clear that I generally refrain from using the terms "race," "racism," or "Islamophobia." If we define "racism" broadly as the discrimination of individuals or groups of people on the basis of ethnic, cultural, or color differences, then racism is the pervasive feature of European countries including Denmark. The term "cultural racism," understood as ways of talking about immigrants' traditions, norms, and values as inferior to those of the host country, would be particularly appropriate to describe the discourse on immigrants because statements from leading politicians, intellectuals, journalists, and experts generally refer to "immigrants' culture" as an inferior category that needs to be changed and made compatible with the norms and values of the host country. Because of the xenophobic and nationalist tone of the debate on Muslim immigrants, many scholars considers the new phenomenon as the good old racism in new clothes with labels such as Islamophobia or cultural, differential, or symbolic racism (see, e.g., Balibar 1991; Blaut 1992; Modood 2005; Wren 2001).

This book's focus is, however, not on racist discrimination of immigrants but more generally on how the culture, understood as a totality of traditions, norms, and values, is used to ontologize immigrants—an ontologization that reshapes the social horizon and realigns various social and political groups in relation to a new ontological structure of society. The culturalized category of "immigrant" signifies the disintegration of the harmonious cohesive past by culturalizing the past via today's obsession with cultural values. Focusing on cultural racism and Islamophobia as racism in new clothes distracts from the broader implications of the culturalization of discourse. For the same reason, I do not use the term "Islamophobia" to describe a negative representations of Muslims, although the way Muslims are talked about and policed fits the definition of Islamophobia as "the fear of Islam." I refrain from using the term for two reasons: first, it would be analytically difficult to categorize a statement as Islamophobic that encourages Muslim immigrants to "acknowledge the historical superiority of democracy, acknowledge women's competences and gender equality; acknowledge reason and science as the foundation for human interaction" (Villy Søvndal, the previous leader of the Socialist People's Party in Denmark, quoted in Andreassen 2012: 152). Second, the term "Islamophobia" narrows down the analytical focus to negative attitude expressions (of which there are plenty) about Islam.

A further problem is that the terms "Muslim," "ethnic minority," "immigrant," "immigrant culture," and "Islam" are often used synonymously and interchangeably, which makes it difficult to pinpoint Islamophobic statements in discourse. My argument is that even when people do not engage in fear-mongering around Islam and express sympathetic "attitudes," the new ontological horizon constrains the way they navigate the new social landscape, often leading to epistemic collusion between Left and Right (as can be seen in Søvndal's statement).

Hegemony

The obvious methodological challenge in examining the culturalization of immigration discourse is how to generalize the hegemonic character of the cultural paradigm. Demonstrating that references to culture in the immigration debate are widespread does not necessarily prove that there is new type of hegemony in Denmark (and, by extension, in Europe). Hegemony is first and foremost a theoretical construct, and I can only make a qualified argument about a new type of hegemony: a new historical bloc is formed around "common interests" now understood as shared values that secure social cohesion (and subsequently the welfare system). As my discussion above indicates, it does not mean that this is merely predicated on culture; it means that the welfare system (or democracy) is now presented as anchored in a "cultural sameness" whose continuity becomes the political goal. Erased is the traditional notion that the welfare system and democracy are the result of the social democratic consensus based on class politics.

I take as my starting point the theory of hegemony as proposed by Gramsci (1971) and extended by Laclau and Mouffe (2001). For Gramsci, hegemony is about a political force gaining

> the upper hand, to propagate itself over the whole social area—bringing about not only a unison of economic and political aims, but also intellectual and moral unity, posing all the questions around which the struggle rages not on a corporate but on a "universal" plan, and thus creating the hegemony of a fundamental social group over a series of subordinate groups. (Gramsci 1971: 181–82)

This is not to say that the dominant group dupes the masses into buying its messages; it means that the dominant group aligns its own interests with the interests of subordinate groups thereby forming what he calls "a certain compromise equilibrium" between the dominant and subordinate groups. Gramsci calls this formation a "historical bloc." For Gramsci, this formation happens first and foremost ideologically: "The realization of a hegemonic apparatus, insofar as it creates a new ideological terrain, determines a reform of consciousness and methods of knowledge . . . when one succeeds introducing a new morality in conformity with a *new conception of the world*" (Gramsci 1971: 365–66; emphasis added). As Hall (1977: 332) unpacks it,

> Ideology provides the "cement" in a social formation, "preserving the ideological unity of the entire social bloc." This operates, not because the dominant classes can prescribe classes (they too, "live" in their own ideologies), but because they strive and to a degree succeed in *framing* all competing definitions of reality *within their range*, bringing all alternatives within their horizon of thought.

Reality is framed, in my words, within the ontological horizon of society. Although the role of the political leadership and ideology in the formation of hegemony is crucial for Gramsci (1971), he nevertheless sees "the material forces of production [as the] basis for the emergence of the various social groupings" (180).

This is where Laclau and Mouffe part with Gramsci, who insisted on material reality as the terrain where social classes are formed. As discussed above, for Laclau and Mouffe—and for this book—a class does not exist independent of the political articulation of its existence. Gramsci recognized the fragmented and disjointed character of popular thought (i.e., common sense) and understood it is the terrain that hegemonic projects attempt to master, but he saw inconsistency as a flaw and weakness. Working-class consciousness, for example, had to be brought in line with its "real" interests, becoming conscious of its own social being, strength, tasks, and becoming (Gramsci 2000: 196). For Laclau and Mouffe, the openness and incompleteness of the social as a field open to articulatory practices is a precondition to the hegemonic articulation of a sociopolitical identity. There is no difference between consciousness and "real" interests as if the latter are readily available prior to linguistic articulations of them. In this sense, ideology is no longer a useful concept as a representation of an objective reality because reality is always/already a discursive construction. For Laclau and Mouffe (2001), hegemony is "a political *type of relation, a form* . . . of politics; but not a determinable location within a topography of the social" (138). In other words, the ontological structure of society is not given prior to political articulations of it but rather is the very result of those articulations of the relations between social forces.

It is important here to clarify the distinctive poststructuralist vocabulary Laclau and Mouffe employ to discuss hegemony. They make a distinction between discourse and the field of discursivity. Their understanding of discourse is similar to that of Foucault.[5] "A discourse is an attempt to fix the elements of discourse into a web of meanings in a particular domain of discourse (e.g., the medicinal discourse) and therefore "an attempt to dominate the field of discursivity, to arrest the flow of differences, to construct a center" (Laclau and Mouffe 2001: 112).

There is a general field of discursivity, wherein free-floating elements are transformed into "moments" in an articulatory practice, a moment being the temporary fixity of the meaning of a single element articulated in a chain of equivalence. Laclau and Mouffe (2001: 113) use the term "floating signifier" to designate any signifier that has not yet been "captured" in an articulation that partially fixes its meaning in relation to other signifiers. The signifier "body" would, for example, mean different things for different people and can be considered a floating signifier. It is only by its place in a chain of equivalence that is articulated in an antagonistic relation to another chain of equivalence that the floating element is transformed into a discursive moment. For example, the meaning of "body" is fixed in a particular way in medical discourse, where it becomes a "nodal point," as opposed to alternative treatment.

Discursive formations are constituted around nodal points—points of condensation of a number of social relations. Nodal points function as "magnetic" focal points that pull different elements of discourse into a formation, an articulated totality of its differential elements. If we use Laclau and Mouffe's perspective, signifiers such as gender equality, freedom of speech, or tolerance for gays would be articulated as parts of a totality that could be articulated around the nodal point "socialism," as opposed to "capitalism," which is presented as a purveyor of patriarchal, oppressive, homophobic practices. In current hegemonic articulations, these elements are partially fixed as parts of the common cultural repertoire of the Danish nation (or the West), as opposed to Islam, which subverts these ideals.

However, my understanding of partial fixity of meaning is slightly different from that of Laclau and Mouffe. The contribution of this book is its reconceptualization of the articulation process not as the articulation of elements (i.e., values) in a consistent discourse but as the persistent juxtaposition of elements with an ontological entity. In other words, the partial fixity of a signifier is related to its use in conjunction with an ontological category rather than as parts of a totality in an equivalential chain because the meaning of a particular signifier is constantly subverted in written and spoken discourse. As an example, a headscarf—even as Muslim garb—can signify a number of different things depending on the rhetorical situation. When used in conjunction with the category of Muslim immigrant, however, its meaning is partially fixed to signify a cultural/religious ontology. The proliferation of possible meanings of the signified is limited when it is situated as an element that signifies an ontological category rather than a particular meaning (e.g., oppression of women). Thus, "headscarf" becomes a signifier of ontological difference. In another example, we do not attach a particular ontological meaning to, say, gang rape. But when used in conjunction with Muslim immigrant, it becomes a deviant act that threatens "our way of life." Thus, "gang rape" comes to signify the antagonistic relationship between opposing social forces. The idea that social harmony existed prior to Muslims' arrival becomes a nodal point around which the cultural identity of the Danish nation as something that binds "us" is forged politically.

The last point indicates that "the hegemonic articulation of meaning and identity [collectivity] is intrinsically linked to the construction of social antagonism, which involves the exclusion of a threatening Otherness that stabilizes the discursive system [i.e., the ontological structure]" (Torfing 2005: 15).

Moral Panics and Crises

If discourse is full of variations, inconsistencies, and contradictions, how can a political force intervene in discourse and successfully articulate relatively coherent and stabile identities?

Gramsci argues that change occurs when a situation of well-being is threatened and the normality of the situation can no longer be sustained by hegemonic forces. During these hegemonic crises, social groups become detached from their traditional political parties, which are not capable of adapting themselves to new tasks and new epochs—a situation that is evident in the rapid dissolution of traditional working-class social democratic parties and the increasing support for the populist Far Right. However, as will become clearer, this process is not about a shift in "previously existing disposition of social forces" (Gramsci 1971: 178), but the transformation of the identities of social forces. In other words, it is not classes that become detached from their traditional representatives but the very ontological basis on which the parties are formed shifts, causing an identity crisis for the traditional parties.

The interesting question that does not get proper attention in abstract treatises on discourse theory is how the displacement from one ontological structure (class) to another (culture) actually happens and how new ontologies are produced in political life. This book's answer is that deliberately provoked, sustained moral panics maintain public focus on "folk devils" who over time become ontologized vis-à-vis society. I will discuss the role of moral panics in hegemonic interventions in detail in chapter 2; suffice it to note here that continual crises and moral panics around immigrants' "cultural or religious [Islamic] practices" function to sustain public focus on Muslims as an antagonistic force that threatens the unity and harmony of the nation. The unending problems with Muslim immigrants create an impression of an impending danger, and the presentation of Muslim immigrants as an impending cultural threat creates an sense of cultural sameness across the sociopolitical spectrum vis-à-vis Muslims. The creation of the feeling of cultural unity is similar to what Gramsci calls the creation of a new historical bloc.

Data and Analysis

There is a consensus among scholars that Denmark experienced a swift right-turn in the immigration debate in the mid-1980s, although they have varying explanations for the turn (Andersen 2004; Gaasholt and Togeby 1995; Rydgren 2004; Schierup 1993; Østergaard 2007). Danish historian Bent Østergaard (2007) considers the new immigration law of 1983 as the turning point that made the opposition to immigration a permanent fixture in the Danish political landscape. Østergaard describes the years between 1983 and 2001 as the period that would shape the immigration debate for years to come. I know from my own experiences as a journalist who covered the immigration debate from the early 1980s that a right-wing intervention in 1986 played a decisive role in turning the focus in the immigration debate from issues related to rights and humanitarian help to cultural issues. I therefore chose to examine the period before and after this intervention (1984–87) and included media coverage from 2001 to see how much culture had become the defining feature of the immigration debate before the 2001 elections fundamentally changed the political landscape.

The data for this project come from two major sources: newspaper articles from five major Danish daily national newspapers (*Politiken*, *Berlingske Tidende*, *Jyllands-Posten*, *Ekstra Bladet*, and *BT*) taken from a set of three-month periods. I chose to focus on newspaper clips from September through November 1984, 1986, and 1987. The fourth set of clips is from June through August 2001. The newspaper clips come from the Danish Refugee Council's media archive, which is the only media archive in Denmark with an entire collection of newspaper clips on immigrants and refugees dating back to the early 1980s.[6] I photocopied almost eleven thousand pages of news and feature stories, background articles, editorials, and letters to the editor from the newspapers mentioned above.

The stories examined in this study should be understood to represent a critical part of a media environment in which the newspapers were the main source of information along with only two TV channels (one of them began broadcasting in 1988).

The newspapers are politically and stylistically different, and none have direct political affiliations, although most have clear political leanings.[7] *Jyllands-Posten*, the largest with a daily circulation of 150,000,[8] was established in 1871 as a regional paper for the Jutland (Jylland) Peninsula and now has two daily sections for local news of Copenhagen and Aarhus. The paper is known for its right-wing views. This was the paper that caused the "cartoon crisis" by publishing drawings of the prophet Mohammed to teach Muslim immigrants that in a democracy they have to accept being ridiculed.

Politiken, established in 1884, is the second largest newspaper with a circulation of 129,000, and can be said to reflect "social liberal" political values at the opposite end of the spectrum from *Jyllands-Posten*. *Politiken* had the most consistent "immigrant-friendly" line throughout the project period. It had been affiliated with the Social Liberals but lost its direct links with political parties during the second half of the twentieth century.[9]

Berlingske Tidende, established 1749, has circulation close to that of *Politiken* and is known for its conservative views and is considered the voice of corporate business, in contrast to the values of *Jyllands-Posten*, which is traditionally linked to agricultural sector.

Ekstra Bladet and *BT* are sensationalist tabloids published respectively by the *Politiken* and *Berlingske* publishing houses. Both have circulations around 100,000. Despite great similarities in coverage and style, *Ekstra Bladet* had a reputation as the voice of "the little man," including immigrants, and took an aggressive, antiracist line at the beginning of the study period, whereas *BT* was considered more conservative. In 1987, however, *Ekstra Bladet* had a sudden shift with reference to "Danes' real concerns" and, during the 1990s, ran several aggressive campaigns against immigrants and immigration. In 1986, *Ekstra Bladet* called Søren Krarup "the black priest" but a decade later offered him a column. *BT*, on the other hand, always had an anti-immigrant sentiment albeit without aggressive campaigns.

My first objective for the analysis of the newspaper data was to quantitatively map out the themes, topics, categories, metaphors, and frames (cultural or humanitarian) commonly deployed in public debate. I did a content analysis to paint a broad picture of shifting trends over time. Since this methodology can only identify manifest content and not capture contextual information or intricacies of discourse, content analysis was supported by textual analysis of some newspaper stories to better explain the points made about the statistical data.

My second objective was to map out the rhetorical strategies of Søren Krarup, a key figure in the Far Right's 1986 intervention. He rearranged the discursive landscape with two remarkable advertisements in September 1986. He can be characterized as the ideological father of one of the largest and most influential far-right parties in Europe, the Danish People's Party, for which he was a member of the *Folketinget* (the Danish Parliament) between 2001 and 2011. He also had a column in *Jyllands-Posten* and later *Ekstra Bladet* for decades. Krarup's discursive intervention required a type of analysis that could focus closely on how he managed to shape the premises for debate. With the exception of Engelbreth Larsen (2001) and Yılmaz (2000), there has been little research on his intervention.

The second data set comes from qualitative interviews conducted in the summer of 2001 with thirty-nine ethnic Danes. They were ordinary Danes in the sense that they were not in positions of power or members of organizations particularly engaged with immigration, such as the racist and populist Danish Association or antiracist movements or organizations. The interviewers (myself and sociology students from the University of Copenhagen) were told to include people from various backgrounds in terms of age and occupation, for example, teachers, students, retirees, nurses, academics, and workers. Immigrants were not included in the sample because I wanted to analyze how ethnic Danes spoke about immigrants.

The interviews were done in private homes and took the form of relaxed, loosely structured conversations. Participants were encouraged to speak about Danishness, Danish culture, Denmark's place in the world, immigrants, immigration, and related issues. Each interview lasted about an hour and was analyzed qualitatively. The quotations from these interviews used in this book are my translations.

The theoretical orientation set forth above necessitates some explication of the interpretive approach to both newspaper data and what interviewees said. A qualitative method widely used by scholars involves grouping similar statements and presenting them as their analytically derived categories. This method enables discussion of representations of social groups, ideologies, or discourses as easily recognizable categories. Often, of course, the social groups, ideologies, or discourses are conceptualized prior to the analysis and the analytical work focuses on finding the linguistic evidence of these entities. The impulse is to select parts of the data that fit the analytical or theoretical constructs. The challenge to this approach is to treat social groups, ideologies, or discourses not as categories existing prior to the discourse but as categories to which people orient themselves and about which they talk in flexible and often inconsistent ways. To do so, we need to make clear distinctions between our own analytical categories and the categories used by the participants in our sample. Our concept of the "working class" or "culture," for instance, and the way articles or the participants' remarks deploy "working class" or "culture" may be quite different.

If the starting point for analysis is that discourse is inherently dialogic, contextual, and episodic, it is far more difficult to conclude from any series of examples that a given utterance signifies a larger construction. If we focus on discourse as social action in which people orient themselves in creative ways, it is, in fact, all too easy to come across utterances that point in contradictory directions, and it is inadequate to simply treat them as anomalies. Analysis sensitive to the context in which utterances are made promises more insight into potentially different versions of reality that statements might be trying to establish or rebut. Even repetition across interviews does not necessarily mean that there is a pattern because each statement may be connected to other, possibly contradictory, signs and may be used to achieve differing and sometimes conflicting outcomes. What looks like patterned ways of speaking may actually be the effect of the researchers' attempt to create analytical categories of attitude patterns. It is not sufficient to simply take similar statements out of their immediate contexts and put them together in abstract analytical categories presented as conclusions (see chapter 1).

The analytical solution in this book is to combine three different methodologies: content analysis, discourse analysis, and rhetorical analysis. Content analysis usually means determining the presence of certain words or concepts within texts and counting them. In this approach, words and concepts are taken to be indicative of the categories that researchers are seeking in the material analyzed. Researchers quantify these words or concepts and make inferences about the relationship between the words and the messages (or broader categories such as ideologies). My approach is, however, a bit different. Rather than counting words or concepts, I read all stories at least twice and tried to determine the perspective(s) from which a story was written. If there were more than one perspective, they were coded as such. I also coded the newspaper data for topics, sources, tone, labels, and metaphors.

I draw on discourse analysis, which related to discursive psychology (which, in turn, is influenced by rhetorical analysis, constructivism, and ethnomethodology). My approach relates mainly to the rhetorical analysis tradition in Michael Billig's (1996) sense, which emphasizes the action-oriented nature of discourse and sees categorical distinctions such as human and nonhuman, artificial and natural, child and adult, and representation and reality as resources people use to say contentious things about the world, to claim and dispute things, to describe and account for how things are, or to justify change or continuity (see also Edwards 1995; Edwards and Potter 1992). It means that in discourse, categorical distinctions are deployed according to the purpose of the talk rather than as abstract entities that are valid across contexts.

My main concern for the research was to examine the culturalization (and therefore ontologization) of immigrants by far-right political forces in a complex interplay with other actors, how the Far Right's framing of immigration as a cultural issue has become the main way the media cover immigration, and how culturalized discourse enables certain kinds of talk about immigrants (as evidenced in the interview material) while simultaneously constraining the social horizon in terms of how people navigate the social landscape.

Chapters

This book is concerned with social change. I am interested in how, in fewer than three decades, political discourse in Denmark moved to the right via the question of immigration. This was made possible by redefining the main social antagonism as one between incommensurable cultures rather than classes. In other words, the way the structure of society is envisioned changed from class ontology to cultural ontology, rearticulating other divisive issues (e.g., gender, sexuality, democracy, and welfare) around a new antagonistic frontier that takes cultural values and norms as the touchstone for social harmony in postwar Denmark and Europe.

The first chapter takes as it starting point the rhetorical nature of meaning. People "give shifting, inconsistent and varied pictures of their social worlds" (Wetherell and Potter 1992: 171) because they use language to act upon the world rather than simply express what they think about the world. In other words, what they "think" about the world changes as the discursive (rhetorical) context changes. That the world can be described in a wide variety of ways in ongoing interpretative activities makes it difficult to conceptualize hegemony, which requires some level of fixity of meaning across the rhetorical contexts. To identify how and where that fixity happens is the first goal of this chapter. My argument is that although the meaning of an element is only fixed in its immediate context, the meaning of social categories repeated across contexts can only be fixed if they are emptied of content. It is the empty signifier, the empty character of a social category, that provides a basis for constructing and maintaining the distinction upon which social antagonisms depend. The second goal of this chapter is to demonstrate how a fine-grained analysis of utterances can shed light on the ways in which hegemonic articulations may be reflected in discourse as people orient themselves to social-ontological distinctions using available—and constraining—discursive resources. Qualitative interviews provide material for a rhetorical interpretation (using tools provided by discursive psychology and Toulmin's argumentative analysis) that shows the likely presence of a hegemonic formation operating around the antagonistic signifiers "Dane" and "Muslim immigrant."

Chapter 2 begins to explore the nature of discursive change, examining events in the mid-1980s to identify the social and political dynamics that opened the way for new articulations about immigration and immigrants that had the potential to disrupt both discursive order and political consensus. Shortly after the 1983 consensual passage of a humanitarian law granting immigrants extensive rights, a complex interplay among actors with access to public discourse—particularly state actors from the mainstream

Right—resulted in publicity that created a moral panic concerning refugees seeking asylum in Denmark. The chapter presents an analysis of the press conventions and the particular rhetorical strategies that made refugees a focus of increased interest and a challenge to taken-for-granted humanitarian assumptions. It also examines the more diffused utterances found in letters to the editor, indexing not only conflicted discourse regarding immigrants but links to dissatisfaction with the mainstream political order, that is, an incipient crisis of representation.

Chapter 3 continues the examination of discursive change by presenting a close analysis of the nature and effects of a single discursive moment in September 1986. It argues that Søren Krarup's two advertisements in a national newspaper and the responses they sparked had a decisive impact on consolidating a new set of discursive resources that culturalized the debate on immigration in general. Krarup successfully created a huge controversy by calling for a boycott of an iconic humanitarian fundraising campaign. Krarup's bold rhetorical strategy sheds light on the ways in which his populist rhetoric managed to turn the brewing moral panic around asylum seekers into a hegemonic crisis by articulating discontent with Denmark's immigration policy as discontent with the representational system (i.e., the political and cultural elite). His intervention did more than bring immigration to the center of attention: it created a powerful discursive ground onto which many actors intentionally entered just to defeat him. During the battle, Krarup's premises that the future of the nation was the primary worry of the Danish people, that alien Muslim immigrants posed a threat to the Danish nation, and that the political order no longer represented the Danish people went unquestioned. Analyses of newspaper reports show how even Krarup's opponents acknowledged that the Danish people were deeply concerned about the future of the nation and conceded that "we have to listen to people." They also acceded to a culturalized discourse that took for granted his claim about the unbridgeable cultural difference between immigrants and Danes. This chapter also examines the period after Krarup's intervention in which the new family reunification laws became the new battleground. The shift in focus from refugees to immigrants meant a simultaneous shift from humanitarian considerations (for or against refugees) to cultural issues (positive or negative about immigrants) and therefore contributed immensely to the culturalization of the immigration debate. By the end of 1987, the debate about immigration was largely made up of arguments about the significance of cultural differences.

Chapter 4 takes up the question of how we know the culturalized ontology of the social discussed in previous chapters had become hegemonic by

2001 and traces how power now operates through a culturalized discursive system that antagonizes Muslim immigrants vis-à-vis the Danish nation and structures the social field along a divide that reorganizes the political spectrum.

As noted above, many consider 2001 the turning point: a right-wing government came to power after an explicitly anti-Muslim immigration campaign and immediately placed immigration at the center of its politics by replacing the Ministry of Interior with a new Ministry for Refugees, Immigrants, and Integration. The new ministry was tasked to create policy initiatives to reinstate the cohesive force of society, which was claimed to be broken by the cultural practices of Muslim immigrants. The mainstream Left, which was rapidly losing its voter base over the question of Muslim immigration to the populist Far Right and the Liberal Party (which had also adopted the populist rhetoric of the Far Right), responded by adopting a similar populist rhetoric on cultural values. The immigration debate rapidly displaced traditional class-based struggles with attention to culture. Values and norms were presented as the glue that keeps society together. In other words, the immigration debate produced a new kind of historical bloc. The hegemonic displacement that has taken place has disoriented the mainstream Left, which is now in complete disarray.

The chapter also analyzes how the new social imaginary not only shifted the focus in mainstream political discourse, but also transformed populist forces from economically ultra-neoliberal positions to a modified welfare defenders, albeit only for ethnic Danes; from being misogynic and homophobic to becoming defenders of gender equality and homosexual rights. One of the central arguments of this chapter is that gender and sexuality have become central signifiers of core Danish values and therefore the symbols of the antagonism between the Danish nation and Muslim immigrants. In the process, immigrants' own representations also changed from workers associations affiliated with progressive parties to religious or cultural associations.

The chapter concludes with a section that demonstrates the limits the new hegemonic formation imposes on political subjects even when they try to oppose its ideological propositions. In the new political environment, both the political establishment and those who claim to challenge the populist Right's vision of society nevertheless base their arguments on the same ontology of the social, creating an epistemic collusion between right and left and even imprisoning the critique within the boundaries of the new ontology of the social.

CHAPTER 1

Discourse and Hegemony

A heated public debate about Danish culture and Muslim immigrants erupted during "cucumber time"[1] in the summer of 2013 and prompted Denmark's Social Democrat prime minister, Helle Thorning-Schmidt, to issue a public statement that "Danish traditions furtively sneak away out of our institutions" (*Berlingske Tidende*, September 13, 2013). The debate, dubbed the "meatball wars," was about the importance of pork meatballs to Danish culture and identity. It began after newspapers reported that some day care centers served only halal meat because the overwhelming majority of the children were Muslim and did not eat pork. The populist far-right Danish People's Party (DPP) complained about such discrimination against Danish food culture. This was just one recent event in a chain of continuing fierce debates on Muslim immigrants' impact on Danish culture and identity.

Preoccupation with the threat to Danish national culture is normally considered the DPP's political turf but, in fact, it has been populated by actors from the Left and Right for a long time. As many scholars have observed, Islam and Muslims have become an imminent threat to the "core values" of European nations, bringing together diverse groups from across the political spectrum.[2] Denmark is undoubtedly one of the most notable examples of the preoccupation with the threat posed to national identity (Akkerman and Hagelund 2007). The Left and Right "converge on the more or less explicitly stated suspicion that religious Muslims remain outside of a civility shared by majority of society" (Henkel 2012: 353).

A closer look, however, may complicate the neat image of Danish culture that such generalizations elicit. For instance, ethnically Danish Anne Vang, the Social Democratic mayor for children and youth in Copenhagen, argued that "there are many other ways of being Danish than shoveling meatballs into your mouth," whereas Latifa Ljørring, a Muslim city council candidate for the right-wing Liberal Party, argued that she defended meatballs in all institutions because "we live in Denmark" (*Berlingske Tidende*, September 13, 2013). It is clear that the sides in the meatball debate did not themselves neatly correspond to a divide between Danes and Muslims. It is not only public arguments that complicate the purported cultural divide; the way people talk and write about "us" and "them" is generally so full of variations and contradictions that a picture of stable patterns fails to emerge.

This state of affairs raises questions about how to reach conclusions about local, national, or global discourses about "us" and "them." How can we identify who "we" and "they" are—that is, demarcate social or cultural groups on the basis of belongingness or otherness—when worldviews, beliefs, and characteristics attributed to either side of the equation defy dichotomous classifications? As scholars from different disciplines have argued, putative reality—the very objects of discourse—is not as stable as it may seem and the social is inherently heterogeneous. Yet we manage to talk about the world in a meaningful way. How can we explain that we talk about society and politics as more or less stable categories? And, of key interest in this book, how is it possible to begin conceptualizing hegemony that presupposes some degree of stability of the social world and the identity categories embedded in it?

These are basic questions for this chapter, which seeks to understand if and how meaning can be fixed within the heterogeneity of discourse, and to propose a framework that brings theories of hegemony and signification into relation with fine-grained empirical analysis in order to illustrate that "immigrant" has become a culturalized category of common sense and identify how hegemony seems to work in concrete instances.

Empty Signifier: Common Sense

I argue that if we are able to talk about the world in terms of stable entities and relate ourselves to one another socially and politically, it is because the terms and concepts that define those entities are emptied of content. We use them as empty signifiers. In other words, signifying stability is not a matter of dichotomous constructions of "us" and "them" with corresponding binary representations but of relatively abstract ontological distinctions that limit the discursive resources available for navigating the social landscape.

There is, however, more to this argument: although the ontological entities are emptied of content when used to generalize across individual instances of an entity, they can be overdetermined by a limited number of features from a particular field of discourse, for example, economy or culture. "Working class" is mainly an economic category[3] that can be described by its location within relations of production, limiting discursive resources for talking about the working class. "Immigrant," on the other hand, can be an economic or cultural category or both, depending on concrete contexts of utterance. Nevertheless, in certain historical conjunctures the discursive repertoires for imagining the category "immigrant" may be limited to the field of culture through repetitive moments of discourse that direct attention to culture as the determining field of discursivity.

We can talk about various entities as the most natural things in the world as long as we keep them at an abstract level and treat them as shared knowledge or, more simply, common sense. For example, we talk about Danes and Danish culture as commonsensical entities. But as soon as we start talking about Danes, Danish culture, or Danishness in concrete terms, we find complication and polysemy: people use the words to signify a wide variety of features, some of which contradict others. The meaning of the sign seems to be only temporarily fixed at a concrete moment of communication. This limits the possibility of proliferation of the signified. Thus, if a durable category is to be signified across concrete occasions, its content needs to be fairly abstract to fulfill this function.

By emptying a category of specific content, we are able to use it to refer to something beyond our immediate grasp. In this way, "Danish" does not signify a determinate group of people with particular characteristics common to the group but "the presence of meaning in opposition to its absence: a specific institution which has no positive, determinate function—its only function is the purely negative one of signaling the presence and actuality of social institution as such" (Žižek 1999). The signifier needs some external reference, which cannot, for the same reasons, have positive content. "Danish" and "Dane" each signify a distinction from something else, depending on concrete context of utterance. For instance, in a rhetorical context Danes could be distinguished from Germans by assigning opposite characteristics (e.g., free-mindedness vs. authoritarianism). Neither vague characterization in and of itself signifies Danes or Germans. They are simply associated with Danes and Germans in that particular context; in another context they could apply interchangeably. The terms *signal the distinction*, an antagonistic relationship between two categories, Danes and Germans, constructed as two incompatible categories by association with incompatible characteristics flexibly articulated from case to case. The ontological constant is the antagonistic divide. What the empty signifier—"Dane," "Danishness," "Danish culture"—marks is the divide itself, which does not consist of objective relations between two positive entities.

In this book, these categories are taken as common sense, where common sense is understood as a discursive resource appealed to and managed interactionally in concrete instances, not as something identified as a discursive structure.[4] Commonsense talk requires some emptying of the signifiers that mark ontological categories such as "Danish" and the concepts associated with these categories in order to treat them in a taken-for-granted manner. It is the empty character of the category that stabilizes its meaning but only to the extent it is treated as taken for granted. As soon as the meaning of "Danishness" is concretized, however, it becomes contestable. That points to continuous hegemonic struggle. Each utterance invests "Dane" with a particular meaning that subverts its emptiness and makes impossible its closure.

Richard Jenkins's 1999 study of how Danishness was invoked in political debate about the European Union offers clues as to how the process of speaking about Danes at an abstract level works when each moment of utterance renders it open to destabilization. He studied letters to the editor in a small-town newspaper during the referendum debate on the Treaty on European Union. He found that many contributors easily referred to Danishness as if everybody knew what it was. "On closer inspection, however, they did not always agree about what it was that they had in common. It is the assumption of Danish cultural homogeneity—and the mobilization of that idea as a political and rhetorical resource—that we are talking about here, rather than its actual existence" (Jenkins 1999: 131). He showed not only how differently—and in contradictory ways—Danishness could be described but also how many characteristics assigned to Danishness could be used to argue either for or against the European Union. The commonsense character of "Danishness" was maintained despite its inherently polysemic nature through some external reference that helped to sustain Danishness as an ontological category. As Jenkins observed, various external threats to Danishness (Germany, immigrants, cultural and political elites) were conjured up regularly for both sides of the argument (133).[5] It is not the assignment of specific characteristics that comprises the category of Danishness but its difference: it is the antagonistic relationship between some external categories and Danes. This enables people to speak generally about it.

To exist, Danishness needs an externality. At the same time, the necessary external threat prevents Danishness from being full and in harmony with itself. It can never achieve complete closure or positivity. As Laclau and Mouffe (2001: 125) argue, the antagonistic other prevents me from being totally myself, as it cannot achieve a full presence: "Its objective being is a symbol of my non-being and, in this way, it is overflowed by a plurality of meanings which prevent its being fixed as full positivity." Michael Nebeling Petersen (2013) suggests, for example, that homosexuality has become one of the symbols of Danish cultural identity, but the social coherence that is supposed to be therefore marked cannot fully be achieved because of the threat from homophobic Muslims. It is indeed because of the imagined threat that homosexuals came to be included in the collectivity. In other words, Danishness is the name of the desire to constitute a totality rather than the totality itself. This explains Jenkins's observation about the great emphasis on the cultural homogeneity of Denmark.[6] Danishness is the name of the attempt to constitute a cultural homogeneity that can never be achieved because it can only negatively be signified through the presence of an other that prevents the fullness of the Danish identity. Without an other, there would only be Danes, and Danishness would lose its meaning. The antagonistic other constantly threatening the social formation has to be continuously produced in discourse.

There is, of course, also no positive content attached to the social other. As this study will show, the antagonistic divide, once established, can be maintained and naturalized through politico-rhetorical moves that repeatedly reproduce the divide through a persistent focus—via repetitive chains of putative crises—on the alien cultural practices of immigrants. The dichotomized social space around two poles, "us" and "them," functions as a magnetic focal point, pulling certain meanings toward itself and leaving others, potentially subversive, out of what Laclau and Mouffe (2001) call "equivalential chains." As Laclau (2008: 74) argues, "All social elements . . . locate their identities around either of these two poles, whose internal components . . . [are] in a mere relation of equivalence."

Laclau and Mouffe rarely get their hands dirty with hands-on analysis of how their theory of hegemony and discourse applies to what is happening. On the other hand, the discourse analytical approaches, particularly discursive psychology, that influence this study's analyses of empirical material rarely lift the gaze from the immediate to look at how larger contexts (e.g., the social imaginary of the ontological structure of society) not explicitly formulated in the course of interaction may enable or constrain talk or text. Yet Laclau and Mouffe's theory of discourse shares many basic assumptions of discursive psychology concerning the nature of interaction, language, and social life, including a rhetorical approach to language and meaning. While discursive psychology tends to focus on the here and now of discourse, Laclau and Mouffe focus on how social life is organized around certain moments of discourse that both produce and constrain the way social identities are envisioned and talked about. They are interested in the structuring effects of power, a virtual absence in discursive psychology.[7] Conjoined with the discourse analytical approaches, Laclau and Mouffe's discourse theory offers a theoretical model that attempts to understand how movements, classes, and other types of social identities are established and sustained over time as relatively stable entities despite the inherently rhetorical and contingent nature of discourse, which they refer to as "the openness of the social" or "radical relationalism."

Because discourse is episodic and full of variations, is it possible to analyze hegemonic formations through an analysis of written or spoken texts? My answer is a careful yes. The ways in which hegemonic articulations are stabilized and institutionalized are reflected in discourse in the sense that people orient themselves to the abstract socio-ontological categories their arguments refer to. They talk about social division both in concrete and in abstract ways. While concrete talk is full of variations, speakers often resort to abstract discourse to fix the meaning of a social division. In this process, some discursive resources are more readily available than others or are considered more appropriate because they are repeatedly used in the media. An analysis that is sensitive to variations can demonstrate which discursive resources are treated as more appropriate in which kinds of situations, and how they may indicate hegemonic articulations.

Heterogeneity and Culturalized Discourse

An analysis that is attuned to Laclau and Mouffe's framework, and that is sensitive to the contexts of utterances, offers insight into different versions of reality embodied in stretches of discourse, and therefore also offers insight into hegemonic articulations as they actually play out. "Hegemonic articulation" in my theoretical universe means the consistent ways in which we imagine social and political identities and the relationships between them. My particular concern here is the way a culturalized ontology of the social simultaneously enables and constrains the discursive repertoire for talking about society.

In a study with many affinities to this one, Hervik (2004; 2011) notices that a key feature of neoracist discourse, as expressed in interviews with Danes, is the construction of a rigid dichotomy between Danes and foreigners, to the point that it is unbridgeable.[8] The cultural distinction between "we" and "they" is present in all interviews even when the question is about a specific person. When one participant is asked about Wilson Kipketer, the

Kenya-born, black track-and-field athlete who won the 800-meter world championship for Denmark, he leaps automatically into "we" and "they," as if everyone would know which people he is referring to: "*They* can do something *we* can't. *They* are, *they* are good at playing cricket and *we* don't even know the rules" (Søren, 27, carpenter/student) (Hervik 2011: 96; emphasis added). When the same person is asked about the headscarf, he switches from a gendered pronoun to the unspecified "it": "I think it doesn't make sense. This is about keeping '*it*' [cultural difference] within the four walls of the home" (96). Hervik concludes that the tendency to treat "we" and "they" categories as taken-for-granted common sense is salient in most interviews, as in a statement by a young teacher: "Even when *they* try their hardest to do like the Danes do—in order to be accepted, then that is still never sufficient. *They* can't all of sudden have blond hair like the *Danes*" (Helle, 25, teacher) (97). Hervik notes that regardless of the concreteness of the questioners' terms, participants immediately turn to the general, abstract stock of "they" without specifying who "they" are, indicating commonsense reasoning. Such findings are completely in line with this analysis and replicate the experience with my interview sample, where categories such as "Danes" and "immigrants/Muslims" are persistently used as empty commonsense entities able to function as points of reference for identification.

Hervik makes an unwarranted leap, however, to a broader conclusion that the categorical distinction operates through two sets of mutually exclusive characteristics. To support his argument, he uses a table from Ulla Fadel (1999) that shows the dichotomous character of the distinction (see table 1.1).

I am not sure that Hervik's data support such a conclusion, because I do

TABLE 1.1. Danish and Non-Danish Attributes

Foreigners (immigrants)	Danes
Group-oriented	Individualist
Live in large families	Live in nuclear families
Have many children	Have few children
Exploit society	Contribute to society
Dirty/smell bad	Clean/do not smell
Loud/bad-tempered	Quiet/calm
Fight/kill each other	Talk/compromise
Poor upon arrival	Rich before immigrants arrived
Submissive to religious and moral doctrines	Casual relationship to religion
Traditional, old-fashioned	Modern
Suppress women	Women emancipated
Women wear headscarves and long dresses	Women wear bikinis or go topless on beaches

Source: From Hervik 2011: 97.

not have access to the interview material. A closer look at the three excerpts above, however, reveals them to be responses to specific questions, which means that they cannot be readily generalized to the overall ontological categories except by taking them out of context. The first statement equates "them" to sportsmen precisely because the question was about the athlete Wilson Kipteker. The respondent seems to describe "them" positively by assigning the cultural competence of knowing rules. Taking such statements out of their interactional contexts makes it difficult to see the rhetorical work a respondent is accomplishing. It is, therefore, difficult to see what triggers the leap to talking about "their" competence in cricket when the question is about an athlete. In the second excerpt, the same respondent is asked about the Muslim headscarf. Instead of talking about the category of "they," he switches to using "it" to signify the headscarf in the first use, cultural difference in the second. This is probably a choice that makes his negative evaluation less connected to the group than to the practice itself. What is clear is that he is not talking about the same category of people in the two excerpts. Black athletes from Kenya or cricket players from India have nothing in common with Muslim women with headscarves. What binds them together is the topic itself (immigrants). The same kind of variation is also evident in the third excerpt, which describes "them" in a positive manner as victims of racial discrimination. In this context, "they" are the ones who have a darker skin (or hair) color.

There is nothing that binds these three notions of "them" into a category except the pronoun "they" knitting together the category. It is clear that there are Danes who have competence in sports or cricket and many immigrants have never heard of cricket. The three notions of "them" are produced in interaction. If both "they" and "we" are filled with particular content when uttered, the particular content cannot defensibly be taken out of the interactional contexts to appear as generalizations about immigrants and Danes, respectively.

I produced a table with the same dichotomous division of characteristics using my own sample of semistructured qualitative interviews with ordinary Danes conducted in the summer of 2001 (see table 1.2).[9]

The statements in table 1.2 are not generalized in the same way as in Fadel's table because it was difficult to turn contextually responsive utterances into abstract general opinions about immigrants or Danes. The statements were made answering questions and responding to cues the interviewer provided in an ongoing conversation. For instance, the statement "Muslim women in Denmark are not allowed to do many things on their own" was uttered in a context in which the respondent was trying to explain why crime rates were relatively low among Muslim women, and functioned to *avoid* a sweeping generalization about immigrants by a respondent invested in questioning the representation of immigrants as linked to high crime rates. Without statistics to hand, knowledge of the low representation of women was a resource useful for challenging statistics, as extract 1 shows.

Extract 1

> Uhm, you gradually become so affected by all those statistics you get thrown at you. One of the things I pay closer attention to, it is that the least criminal group in Denmark, it is the Muslim women. It goes, of course, without saying that it is so, (.)[10] what shall I say, (.) so strict regulations for what they are culturally allowed at all to do on their own, but, but this is something you seldom hear, isn't it? This is one of those things that you can look up for, like, weird, isn't it? But you hear (.) you [*long pause*] . . .
>
> (Birgitte, Ph.D. in natural sciences, researcher in a research institute; translated by the author)

TABLE 1.2. Statements about Immigrants and Danes

Immigrants	Danes
Do not speak Danish properly.	Language is important for Danish identity.
Youth give themselves Danish names to avoid discrimination (on the phone, implies that "they" speak Danish fluently).	It is difficult to understand Danes from the west coast.
A Turk is more open.	It is not in Danish culture to discriminate.
They are reserved, maybe because of religion.	We are tolerant and hospitable.
They speak loudly and are noisy.	We are not open to other cultures.
They don't respect women in general.	We are open to the world.
Women in family are valued highly.	We close our doors and don't even speak with our neighbors.
Muslim women in DK are not allowed to do many things on their own.	We are discreet and restrained.
In Danish view, Islam and culture are the same.	Danes respect and understand people.
They want to do something with their lives.	We have sexual emancipation.
They do not want education.	Christendom binds us together in European culture.
They have a very strong faith (religion).	They want to do something with their lives.
We have to remember that where they come from people are not as law-abiding and decent as us.	We have free will, we are rational.
They don't pay taxes.	We are law-abiding and not corrupt.
	We don't pay taxes either but avoid them less than other Europeans.

I will return to this interview in detail below, but for now it is important to note that the statement about Muslim women is not a generalized statement about their nature but a reflexive moment that assesses the strength of the speaker's argument. It is brought in as a rebuttal to a potential objection to her premise that culture does not make immigrants criminal. As such, it has a clear rhetorical function in her account, even though it is not a well-thought-out or well-executed rhetorical move but introduced in a haphazard manner, just as the pauses indicate. The speaker, Birgitte, is challenging the idea that immigrants are culturally conditioned to be criminal, but she immediately weakens her own argument by culturalizing her own rebuttal by referring to what Muslim women are "culturally allowed to do." The repeated "but, but" indicates that she has problems relating back to her main argument that culture does not make immigrants criminal once she has offered her own cultural explanation.

It is clear that descriptions and attributes are used in a flexible manner to establish one's ethos, support or undermine claims, or defend or criticize actions or practices; they are not direct reflections of what one "really" may think about a group or an issue. Even this little extract offers contradictory postures on culture: on the one hand, it is a tacit challenge, deducible from the context, to the idea that culture determines behavior; on the other hand, it is an explicit argument that reculturalizes and essentializes immigrants to explain why immigrant women may not be as criminal as immigrant men.

Further, unlike Fadel's table, mine shows that the same characteristics can be attributed to both groups and that opposite characteristics can be used to describe the same group. Danes and immigrants are simultaneously described as reserved and open, immigrants as respectful and disrespectful of women, capable and incapable of speaking proper Danish.[11] One of the respondents explained that language is important for Danish identity when asked about Danish culture but expressed, during the same interview, a desire for subtitles when Danes from the west coast are interviewed on television.

The only way to construct a binary table is by taking single phrases or sentences out of their rhetorical contexts to present them as general descriptions of the categories of Danes and the immigrants. My sample is full of what one easily could recognize as "prejudiced"[12] expressions. One respondent says: "You think of criminality, you think of immigrants," but unlike Birgitte, who attributes this tendency to the selective nature of statistics and media repetition of these statistics, this respondent explains immigrants' criminality with conditions in their homeland: "I also think that we should remember where they come from—a place where they are not as law-abiding and decent as most of us Danes are." According to another interviewee, "They have to learn that you do not steal and you do not rape young women." One respondent says, "Here we don't kill [people]. We don't do such things in Denmark. It is illegal and it is punishable." As discussed below, Birgitte makes a similar statement about values: "My set of values tells me that you don't kick down an old lady."

In most cases, these utterances are not challenged by the interviewer, either for interactional reasons or because they sound commonsensical. If they were challenged, it is difficult to imagine that the interviewees would insist that all people who are not Danes are law-breaking, rape young women, or kill people, and that these acts are legal in their home countries, all the while insisting that Danes never commit such criminal acts. It is easy to see how tempting it is to read expressions of a prejudiced mind-set and present them as dichotomic constructions of Danes and immigrants. What is there to talk about, after all, if we can only understand people's statements in their local contexts, which are episodic and ultimately subversive to the notion of generalized categories of the social? I believe that the need to generalize about discourse is behind this common practice of attributing opposite characteristics to both sides of the equation of "us" and "them." As Hervik notes, respondents easily turn to "us" and "them" and do often present accounts as generalized statements about these categories. It is the persistent use of "they" and "we" distinction that creates the appearance that people always express their opinions about the general category of immigrants and Danes.

For many social scientists, the production of social power is assumed to be predicated on representations of social groups on the basis of race, ethnicity, nationality, religion, gender, sexual orientation, or social class, and the analytical focus is on clarifying the links between particular linguistic realizations and larger constructs such as ideologies or dominant discourses.[13] My perspective makes it difficult to take the particular linguistic realizations (e.g., words, terms, renditions, or categorical statements) at face value as indicators of power relations or a hegemonic formation. I suggest instead an eclectic analytical approach that pays more attention to how the imagined ontological structure of society enables as well as limits the availability of discursive resources for talking about social identity categories. My argument in this book is that in the discursive environment that developed in Denmark after 1986, social divisions came to be imagined as based on essential cultural differences often articulated in contradictory ways in actual discourse. The identity categories can only be stabilized across contexts if emptied of content.

A longer extract from the interview with Birgitte enables us to see her statement about immigrants' violent nature—surely recordable as racist and prejudiced on a dichotomous list—in its larger context, providing a deeper understanding. This interview took place not long after publicity about a violent attack against an old Danish woman by young men identified as immigrants. Concrete cases reported in the media, such as this attack, are powerful factual resources for talking about immigrants in general terms because these cases, often explained with reference to immigrants' cultural background, produce immigrants as an abstract cultural category as opposed to Danes, rather than as concrete human beings in various types of relationships with their surroundings. This is part of the context imported into the response to the fourth question.

Extract 2

Q1: But when we speak about problems and all those things, do you think of them [immigrants] altogether or do you think of particular ones?

R: But then again, I think this problem is related to a particular social group. And it is not the average. I am sure that it isn't a coincidence who have the good social opportunities and who have the bad social opportunities. I believe an American who comes here with a medical education has better opportunities, also for better social terms, whereas if you have an equivalent background from Bosnia, there you don't have as good opportunities.

Q2: It is about discrimination, you think?

R: Prejudice. I think again it is self-perpetuating. Again something like, how many of them are there? I think so. How much have we heard of problems with American migrants, and how much have we heard of problems with second-generation Pakistani, Turkish migrants? [. . .]

Q4: You said "those halal hippies" [a derogatory term coined by the immigrant politician Naser Khader meaning politically correct but irresponsible liberals]. That's what I wanted to ask you, that they have "phobia against conflict." For instance, they don't want to discuss whether refugees and immigrants should be expelled when they commit criminal acts. Who did you think of there? Did you think of someone who seeks asylum or the youths in Vollsmose [a neighborhood in Odense with a concentration of immigrants] or—

R: I am thinking especially those youths in Vollsmose, where there were two groups of opinions about how it should be handled, right? One of them, it was we simply shouldn't touch this at all— "away, on a deserted island, home, away from this country!" Or "Just decapitate them!" This was one side of it. The other side it was "Send them on holiday, a holiday of adventure of one month in the Bahamas with some pedagogical support and let's convert them!" Right? I mean, there are somehow these two sides. On the one side you have the hawks [those who advocate tightening immigration policy], and then you have those Naser Khader calls halal hippies on the other side.

Q5: I understand it so that halal hippies wouldn't debate at all whether they should be expelled.

R: Not that they won't debate, but they just take— they have just the fear of contact to sanction.

Q6: How do you think one should sanction?

R: [Sigh]. Again, it is difficult to have the right answer to this. I again think that you have to look at what they would respect. What is it— again in their set of cultural values, which is also mixed? There are things that are Danish, there are things they have gotten from their parents and grandparents during their upbringing at home. What is it that they would respect? What is it that would make them behave properly? I can't judge it. There isn't of course an easy answer to that. Or so somebody would have found it, and done it. But (.) It wasn't an especially clear answer.

Q7: Can you expel them, for instance?

R: I think it is difficult to expel some young people who if their parents stay here in the country, and they are maybe eighteen years old or seventeen, they cannot be expelled, children whose family is in this country. I mean, it is difficult. On the other hand you have to sanction strongly, especially if it is repeatedly and you have— I mean also that you must— we have some rules that you have to submit yourself to. My set of values says that you don't kick down an old lady. That is, there are, there are some— I can understand that groups of seventeen-year-old Danes and immigrants may fight over, what do I know, their attitude toward girls or something else. But that you— [long pause]

Q8: Do you think it has something to do with their ethnicity?

R: No, I don't think it has. I think it has something to do with being really, really deprived. Of course, you also have Danes who do such things. But there are probably— there it is pushed to the extreme because they are under pressure from forty sides. That's what I mean them— if you have immigrant background, you are under pressure on many fronts. It isn't just skin color or language, your name in itself. I mean, if you call— if you call with your name and want to rent a room, it is easy for Niels Hansen [a typical Danish name] to rent a room than it is with your name to rent a room. It is so simple. There is— there have been research on this that I have seen, [laughs].

Q9: You said that it is maybe their culture [unclear]. Where do you see the biggest difference?

R: On what? (.) There, I mean if you are a second-generation migrant, that is, you grew up in this country and—then you have a culture that is mixed.

Q10: I know that. But what is the Danish, what is the non-Danish for you?

R: It depends again on what the non-Danish— what it is the background they come from? Again, I don't think you can generalize. I mean, I believe also that, heh, there may be— of course individual within families. I mean, there will be families where you (.) have another— after two generations in a country have another cultural standpoint than other families that have lived here in two generations. It is extremely difficult [long pause] to express a simple formulation on, "Well, bilingual background, then you have those and those cultural problems!" I don't think you can say that.

My first observation is that the interview moves in a circular and contradictory fashion. Contradictions and the circularity are results of the limits of the social imaginary. The respondent is intellectual and reflexive; she is tuned in to the notion of prejudice and often reflects upon what might possibly be seen as her own prejudices with short anecdotes during the interview. Although reflexivity may be heightened by my presence as an immigrant and social researcher, it also helps construct Birgitte's ethos as a rational person who is able to distinguish between her own possible prejudice and real problems in the world. It is in the description of that reality that talk becomes circular in the sense that, despite attempts to deconstruct immigrants as a culturally defined group, she cannot move out of the realm of culture.

The extract is taken out of a larger discussion about "real problems" and what one can do about them. The real problems, taken to be independent of the speaker's mind, are criminal acts by second-generation immigrants.[14] In answer to my first question, she defines immigrants as a social group characterized by their marginalized position within society. Marginalization is caused by Danes' prejudices,[15] a view she repeats later (in response to Q8) with confidence. Both answers are direct responses to my questions that encourage her to denounce cultural definitions that otherwise might imply prejudiced thinking that link criminality to people's ethnic background. A question such as "Do you think it [criminality] has something to do with their ethnicity?" would in most cases cue the respondents to become sensitive to the issue of prejudice. That is what happens here.

Despite her deliberate efforts to deculturalize criminality among young immigrants, Birgitte reverts to cultural explanations in her answer to question 7, where she says, "My set of values says that you don't kick down an old lady." Why the circularity and contradiction, as she simultaneously denounces cultural explanations and explains a violent incident with immigrants' value system as the main culprit?

The answer may be in the dilemma she creates for herself. On the one hand, she deconstructs criminality statistics by adjusting them for other factors, which implies that the problems with criminality are not related to culture or ethnicity. On the other hand, we have a "real problem" and real problems need real solutions. The problems, however, have been repeatedly defined as cultural in Denmark's public discourse. The dilemma is produced because she wants to be able to talk about these real problems and sanctions against this group of youngsters without being identified as prejudiced, as her phrase "fear of contact" (Q5) indicates. To achieve this effect, she constructs a dichotomy between hawks (i.e., prejudiced people who want to expel these youth groups) and "halal hippies."[16] The dichotomy enables her to distance herself from both sides and establish her position as a balanced, moderate one.

Talk is flexible. What one says to establish one's ethos in one context may work against one's position in another. When I ask how one can sanction this group of youths (Q6), the dichotomy creates a problem: Birgitte has to produce a concrete answer that is moderate and properly distanced from both sides of the debate as constructed by her, and one that is not linked to culture. She has put herself into a difficult situation. She cannot say immigrants should be sent "away, on a deserted island, home, away from country!" which would put her in the same category as prejudiced persons; on the other hand, she needs to produce something more concrete than those who say, "Send them to the Bahamas with some pedagogical support," avoiding discussion of the real problems. Because of the dilemma, she has tremendous difficulty suggesting any concrete solutions.

I suspect the challenge of proposing concrete but noncultural solutions is related to a second dilemma, which is not as explicit as the first. Her definition of the problem as rooted in social conditions (i.e., deprivation, in response to Q8) presupposes social solutions. "Immigrant youth," however, is a cultural demarcation, and a cultural category demands cultural solutions specific to the group persistently defined by cultural characteristics. Thus, it is the category "immigrant youth" that forces the conversation into a circular pattern difficult to break out of. First, Birgitte relates criminality to marginalization and discrimination (in response to Q1)—parameters external to the group. If one accepts this as the premise, then the focus should stay on social structures, but this could put her in the "halal hippie" category, those who often are accused of finding excuses for immigrants in the name of tolerance. At the same time, she insists that something should be done ("You have to sanction strongly," in response to Q7).

Something should be done about what? Crime or immigrants? It is precisely here that discourse on immigrants becomes tricky and slippery, not only in the context of this particular interaction but in general. Once paired with immigrants, crime becomes more than simple crime; it refers back to its predicate, which renders it a specific phenomenon. Specific problems require specific solutions. But when Birgitte tries to avoid defining immigrants by their culture, she has a problem. If criminality is related to external social factors such as poverty and discrimination, how can we sanction against the group instead of focusing on the social and political structures that the problem is rooted in or make them respect rules and behave properly (Q6)? She is aware of these contradictions, as indicated by her last sentence in this response: "But (.) it wasn't an especially clear answer." It would be a great help if the transcription were able to show intonation, here indicating an attitude of having given up.[17] Birgitte's feeling for the dilemma becomes clearer in the next answer (Q7), which ends with an interrupted sentence and long pause immediately after she implies some fundamental cultural differences with reference to values.

The statement "My set of values says that you don't kick down an old lady" has to be understood in the context of this dilemmatic situation rather than as a simple reflection of a "prejudiced" mind. Rather, it seems to be a resource brought in while navigating between hawks and halal hippies. However, once the focus is on the group and their actions, solutions also need to be related to the group because there is no other commonsense way of imagining immigrants other than as a cultural group, culturalizing discourse regardless of one's intentions.

Birgitte's statement about values responds to a well-publicized incident around the time of the interview. In the ensuing public debate, many putative experts weighed in with cultural explanations about violence by immigrant youth. Reference to the incident pushes Birgitte back into the sphere of cultural explanations. She immediately becomes aware of it, as indicated by the interrupted sentence: "That is, there are, there are some— ." That young Danes or immigrants fight over girls is understandable, but violence against an old lady does not fall within the definition of ordinary youth culture. It must be something specific to that group.[18]

The tension between Birgitte's attempts to deconstruct the cultural category of immigrants and the difficulty of describing them in other terms is the predicament of the hegemonic social imaginary. The cultural category of immigrants is not only the result of the particular interaction. It is a pervasive feature of the discourse on immigration to the point that cultural inflection has become the common stock of the social imaginary in general. Demarcating a social group with specific problems—social, cultural, or medical—implies a targeted effort focused on roots of the problem specific to this group. As I will show, the discursive resources for the demarcation are often limited to a repertoire of cultural characteristics made pervasive by recurrent public debates around particular incidents consistently linked to immigrants' cultural background. Attempts to counter the cultural explanations of criminality bounce back from the notion of immigrants as a cultural category.

We may say that criminality is a social problem, but if the sole access to the social is through the cultural ontology of the social that limits the social horizon, we immediately face an impasse. That is what is happening here. What makes "kicking down an old lady" into a specific cultural phenomenon is not the act itself but the fact that it is locked into a relationship with an ontological category that produces its meaning. If challenged, Birgitte would likely rebut the conclusion: no culture makes one kick an old lady, and Danish youth might well do the same thing. In the following, Else (67, retired) refers to the same incident:

Extract 3

R: Now what I am saying here is not coming out anywhere, is it?
I: No, it's not.
R: That I won't suddenly have a lot of Turks standing here— and beating me up?
I: [Laughs]. You don't have to be afraid of it. No— because Turks are that kind who beat people?
R: What?
I: Are Turks the kind who beat people?

R: No, but you don't have to say much to them, those young people. But the Danes are also like that. Then they get involved in fights. Take Vollsmose. The police become afraid. They couldn't cope with it.

I: *Is it a particular incident you are thinking of in Vollsmose?*

R: It was that thing that they— they knock on the door and then just walk in and then steal from an older lady. And then they kick the door in— Well, I could tell you about many incidents. It hasn't been so fun out there, but they are about to gain control over it now. Then there was somebody who got beaten up dead, not dead but was almost dead— had to escape, go underground. And it doesn't look like anything, when it is our country.

In this rare example, the interviewer challenges the respondent about the prejudiced implications of what she is saying. The response is a rejection of the implied conclusion, "No, but you don't have to say much to them. . . . Danes are also like that." In this case, however, reflexivity falls short of retracting what was said before. Instead, the concrete incident is used to explain why she is afraid of "those young people." Concrete incidents are taken to produce factual data and enable respondents to speak about prejudice-relevant issues without appearing prejudiced. In this extract, the concrete incident is used to justify the generalized conclusion that immigrants, as an abstract category, have a violent nature. In fact, in the next extract from the same interview, Else becomes more reflexive:

Extract 4

R: Why should we have them [immigrants] all here and feed? We— others, we have been working, earning money, and paying taxes all these years, and what do they do? It pours down with cuts and cuts on us— because they [immigrants] come here.

I: Do you have any personal experiences with it?

R: No, on the contrary I only have positive [experiences]. Because I go to a night school, and there are many of them, too, and they want to do something with their lives. And they are very competent.

The sudden change in the characterization of immigrants from negative to positive happens several times during the interview. But it is not only the characterization of the category that changes but the very category of immigrants itself. The first is an abstract category of immigrants as a burden on the welfare system, which Else takes those she considers real Danes to have created. The second is a concrete category of people in night school, who have personal perseverance and competence. The negativity of the first category is tied to the economic consequences of immigrants' presence in Denmark rather than to their character. The interesting part is that in her first answer, Else describes immigrants as an antagonistic category: undeserving aliens, they prevent Danes from enjoying the system they have built up; they cause Danes' welfare benefits to be constantly eroded. It is only at this abstract, conceptual level that Else can treat immigrants as a force preventing enjoyment of harmony and rewards. The antagonistic "they" indeed creates in reverse and sustains the pure idea of a "we" whose communitarian fullness is absent as the result of that subversive force (Laclau 1996: 42). Laclau and Mouffe (2001: 7) argue that this hegemonic identity alludes to an absent totality rather than signifying any positive content. Of course, depending on the rhetorical context of a given speech act, abstract notions may be brought in to describe individual cases and vice versa.

In Danish political discourse, as I will show in chapter 4, the immigrant threat to the welfare system is repeatedly articulated as a matter of cultural differences by the Far Right and by the mainstream Left and Right. The welfare system itself is often associated with a mythical Danish cultural homogeneity. Thus, the welfare system is presented as the result of historicized ethnic solidarity rather than as the result of decades-long political struggles based on class solidarity. As a consequence, the erosion of the welfare system is not tied to the neoliberal policies of the various coalition governments since the 1980s but to immigration associated with the destruction of the national state, in a signifying structure where immigration is symptomatic of globalization and Europeanization. As extract 3 demonstrates, this is only possible when "immigrant" is an abstract category functionally associated with preventing the Danish nation from living in harmony with itself. When it comes to the concrete, individual immigrants, the attributes are not as clear-cut as at the abstract level.

What makes interactions flow as if speakers are talking about the same category is the use of the pronoun "they." It is the naming that binds heterogeneous and contradictory elements within a single category. Else's "they" shifts as the result of the different local contexts in which immigrants are the topic. The first context is general political debate, where she has sympathies for the populist far-right Danish People's Party. The second context is her own immediate connections, where her orientation is not toward political discourse.

As Wetherell (1998: 401) observed, the flexibility and openness of the social arise "because of the reflexivity built into social interaction and the emergent and transformative properties of that interaction." This type of seamless shift from one categorization to another is a typical feature of any text, making it problematic to generalize about categories across texts. This is not an argument against the common observation that racism and Islamophobia are widespread phenomena in Denmark and elsewhere. On the contrary, we can analyze the function of these seamless shifts that, in particular texts, may display consistent patterns, including justifications of discrimination. Rather, my argument is that the stability of the categories is not a matter of binary representations but the effect of abstract ontological distinctions that limit discursive resources available for navigating the social landscape.

Another example from my interviews elaborates this point. In this excerpt, immigrants' cultural values are explicitly tied to their violent nature. If discourse is inherently rhetorical (i.e., goal-oriented rather than expressing mind-sets), we should be able to analyze the argumentative texture of the social fabric through an analytical model that explicates the basic premises that license the kind of inferences that can be made. Such basic premises are usually treated as established, commonsense knowledge, which does not need further discussion. To this end, I introduce an argumentative model by Toulmin (1958). His model enables us to detect how discourse on immigrants is informed by basic assumptions about the essential role of culture in immigrants' conduct.

Toulmin's model is built upon the Aristotelian syllogism, which has three components: a minor premise (singular premise), a major premise (universal premise), and a conclusion. The classic example is the following:

Socrates is a man (minor/singular premise).
All men are mortal (major/universal premise).
So Socrates is mortal (conclusion).

In this example, we have information for all three components of the schema. According to the model, the major premise provides a certainty that proves the truth-value of the argument.

Toulmin suggests instead a fourfold model, called a T-schema, where the conclusion (C) remains but the major premise is replaced by the term "warrant" (W), and the minor premise by "data" (D), and "backing" (B) is the fourth component. The difference from Aristotle's model is that "warrants" are not like premises that provide the facts for the argumentation but are themselves subject to questioning and have to justify their authority. A warrant is an inference-license that legitimizes the step from data (D) to conclusion (C) but is relatively local and cannot necessarily be carried over to the next argument, where it may be that an opposite warrant is used to link evidence (data) to conclusion. "Backing," in turn, is used to support and explain the warrant and may be carried out by referring to taxonomic classifications, statutes, laws, or statistical statements that are more readily accepted and can be used at a more general level. With this model in mind, let us look at an example that would not be considered controversial if only the conclusion were explicit:

Whales give birth (D).
Mammals are birth-giving animals (W).
So whales are mammals (C).

The argument can be set up in a following T-schema (fig. 1.1).

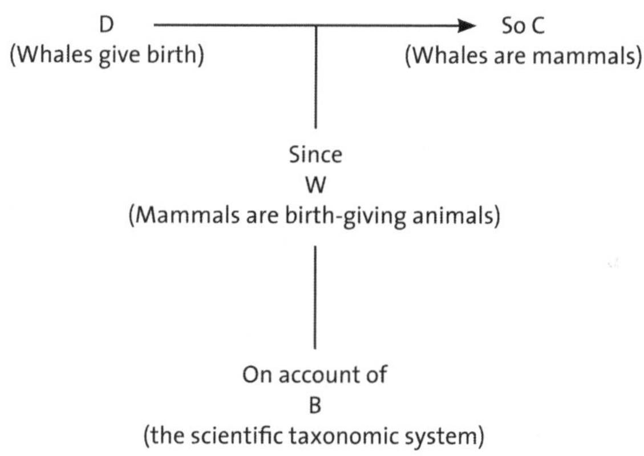

Fig. 1.1. T-schema (Whales = mammals)

Backing is not explicated here, but it would be a reference to an encyclopedic entry or a taxonomic classification in a biology book. There is, of course, nothing wrong with this reasoning as long as the warrant is unquestioned. In fact, warrants are often conceded without challenge and their backing is understood. However, not only the warrant but also the very category of mammals can be challenged as a valid taxonomy to classify living organisms.

In three-line argument above, the warrant has a scientific authority about it and would almost never be disputed. Yet even a slightly different dictionary definition of mammals can make this otherwise robust argument unstable.[19]

According to Toulmin, the rationality of an argument cannot be assessed by its truth-value. Rather, rationality is field-variant and depends on the possibility of establishing inference-warrants in the relevant field, or, in other words it depends on "to what extent there are already *established* warrants in science, in ethics or morality, in law, art-criticism, character-judging, or whatever it may be; and how far the procedures for deciding what principles are sound, and what warrants are acceptable, are generally understood and agreed" (Toulmin 1958: 176).

In the following extract, Mikkel (32, student) describes immigrants as aggressive and violent people. The established warrant that makes the inference about immigrants' violent nature on the basis of a single episode of violence would be the essential role culture plays in human conduct, or, in other words, culture determines behavior. This warrant is supported by the cultural ontology of the social, without which it would be difficult to navigate the social landscape. My analysis also draws on terminology from discursive psychology in addition to Toulmin's terms.[20]

Extract 5

I: Did you experience problems with immigrants?

R: Nooo, I can't say I did. I mean, no, I didn't. It— it, uh, it was, no! Then I would have remembered it, right? It— it is— but there is much, some of them are a little dominant in the streets, right? Yeah, I mean, I did, I didn't, it wasn't myself, right? And it . . . I wouldn't want to judge anybody in that case, but I was in a dance club where there was, uh, a friend of mine. He knew, uh, yeah, he knows a biker, right? And uh, this biker and some of his friends, they had probably provoked some Turks, right? And then, uh, one of the Turks, he hit the biker on the head with a bottle, right? And it it was, you know, it was, I am not saying that there is something he can't, I mean, I am not on the biker's side here, okay, not at all, but I am just saying it is such a typical reaction from an immigrant, or I just feel so, right? When they are out, you know, then they are very aggressive, like, and they by definition they are not afraid of anybody. They, they have, like, their honor. . . . I would never dare hitting a biker on the head with a bottle, so, uh, or there are some people who just scare me, right? But it is as if it

> doesn't apply to them. They just don't, they just don't care, so, they were only two, the Turks together, right?

Mikkel describes immigrants as violent people—a characterization that points to press stories about "immigrant youth" appearing during the interview period in addition to being prevalent in Danish discourse about immigrants for decades. Although he says he never had any problems with immigrants, he immediately begins a complex argumentative discourse that constructs immigrants as violent. His language is not simply referential, merely indexing the event (a fight) and the social categories he is speaking of (immigrants/Turks, bikers) and then telling his opinions. The categories and his views of them are tightly woven together. The problems that can be deduced from his description of the event are not presented as his personal views about immigrants, which in this case would indicate prejudice against immigrants. Instead, the problems are tied to the immigrants' own nature, and this conclusion is supported by testimonial evidence and commonsense reasoning.

The argumentative scheme seems simple: if you dare hit a biker on the head with a bottle, then you must have an aggressive nature because, as we all know, everybody else would be scared of bikers. The use of honor as a value system provides the link from the two individual Turks to the generalized category of immigrants (and Muslims). To support his conclusion, Mikkel uses a variety of rhetorical devices, including categorization (Turks are immigrants, "typical reaction from immigrants"), particularization (bikers do not equal Danes and bikers' violent behavior does not represent Danish norms), and a combination of vivid ("they hit the biker") and systematically vague formulations ("And it it was, you know, it was, I am not saying that there is something he can't, I mean, I am not on the biker's side here")—narrative techniques that bind events, categories, and arguments together. He invokes commonsense knowledge through the repeated phrases "you know" and "right?" Mikkel talks about "they" doing this and that but uses the pronoun for both the two Turks and the entire category of immigrants.

The rhetorical devices operate to present an unprejudiced mind without opinions about immigrants prior to the interview question but coming to the negative conclusion reluctantly through rational inferences, step by step, which are explicated for the interviewer. All this helps construct the realism of his descriptions and the truth-value of his conclusions. In Shotter's (1993) words, "It is by the use of such rhetorical devices—as reference to 'special methods of investigation,' 'objective evidence,' special methods of proof,' 'independent witness,' etc.—that those with competence in such procedures can construct their statements as 'factual statements,' and claim authority for them as revealing a special 'true' reality behind appearances" (25). Such factual versions are constructed not only to make an argument but also to undermine alternative versions often absent from the explicit argumentation (Billig 1988; 1991). Mikkel, for instance, leaves out an obvious comparison: bikers also operate with a strong code of honor.

For my purposes, the most important components of Mikkel's argumentative scheme are the warrant and the backing. Both make the connections between different parts of his argument possible, but these parts are left out as commonsense knowledge: the role of culture in human conduct (culture determines the Turks' behavior), the backing for which is the unspoken cultural ontology of the social. A T-schema of the argument makes the structure clearer (fig. 1.2).

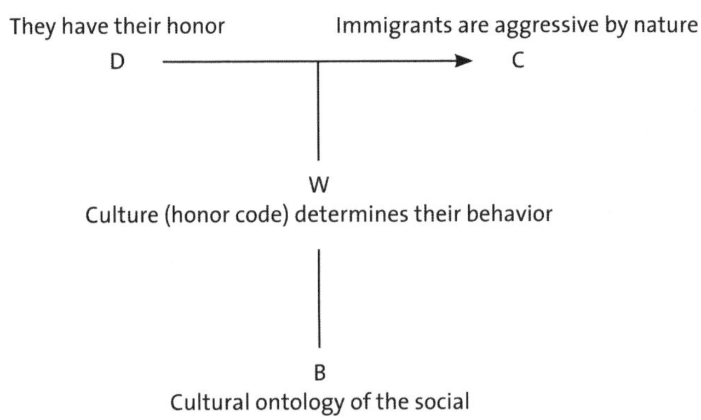

Fig. 1.2. T-schema (honor)

We do not need the T-schema in order to analyze this feature of discourse, but the model enables us to analyze systematically the complex argumentative organization of the utterance and explicate hidden premises that warrant the conclusions. Mikkel does not make the warrant explicit in the interaction, but the implicit categories treated as common sense have a built-in quality about them and can be inferred from the logical organization of the local argument.[21] There is usually no semantic need to make basic propositions explicit except for interactive purposes. The quality of "sharedness" is what renders implicit the common knowledge propositions. Explicating the basic premise might, in the hierarchical organization of the overall argument, move it into a C (conclusion) position, which may open it up for contestation.

The perfection with which this argument corresponds to the T-schema is not often found in natural conversation. What we are dealing with here resembles a theoretical discourse more than a practical discourse (e.g., who is going to take garbage out). I connect the theoretical character of the response to the specific interactional character of the interview situation: Mikkel is questioned by a social researcher in whose presence he probably feels a need to justify not only his specific claims but also their rationality. One way of establishing rationality is to explicate all the inferences one is making. As Edwards (2003) demonstrates in his analysis of a similar discourse, the speaker displays a sense of inferential carefulness through expressions of epistemological concerns ("as if," "it wasn't myself") and by appeals to common knowledge ("yeah," "you know," "right?"), which are not necessarily expressions of what a speaker actually thinks is common knowledge.

The culturalized ontology of the social that belongs to the backing is also important. This makes the whole argumentative chain intelligible. It is the basic proposition that holds together the various elements of discourse because it tells us about the object of discourse. We may differ in how and what we conclude about that object, but we do not differ in regard to the premise that the basic object is cultural.

A caveat here may prevent a possible misunderstanding. If rationality is localized, contextualized, and shaped by the goals of particular argument, we cannot speak of a single logic that always leads to the same conclusion out of the same set of data and warrants. In our analytical example, Mikkel might have employed the same backing, the same essentialist cultural paradigm that culture determines behavior, yet ended up concluding how wonderful and respectable immigrants are because of their culture. Or he might have advanced both arguments at once. The important point for our purposes here is that the question about immigrants orients the respondent toward the cultural repertoire readily available for talk. The interviews offered many examples of the fluid use of resources present in the discursive environment. One respondent, for instance, stated, "We don't punish with the death penalty and such things in Denmark and Europe," a reference to a controversy of June 2001. A member of the Social Liberal Party (Det Radikale Venstre), identified as a Muslim, allegedly refused to condemn the death penalty. Although it was revealed that fellow party members, identified as Danish, were also sympathetic to the death penalty, they were never questioned about it in the media, nor did the newspapers indicate any public debate about them, in contrast to the extensive coverage and debate around the Muslim candidate. In essence, the controversy was not so much about the death penalty as about how much "we" can tolerate "their" culture. In this environment, the respondent's statement, "We don't punish with the death penalty" should not be taken as a reflection of what she may actually think but as an example of the death penalty functioning as a useful, flexible rhetorical tool in apprehending cultural dichotomy. The concrete attributes clearly do not hold up under even slight scrutiny. The respondent's utterance actually indexed Western culture in general as opposed to "their Muslim culture," but the dichotomy cannot survive the simple observation that the United States has the death penalty and Turkey does not.

A variety of statements from my sample—"Here we don't kill [people], we don't do such things in Denmark, it is illegal and it is punishable"; "They have to learn that you do not steal and you do not rape young women"; "We should remember where they come from—a place where they are not as law-abiding and decent as most of us Danes are"—need not be taken as interviewees' firm beliefs. Few would say that murder is legal in immigrants' home countries or that theft and rape are acceptable. In fact, most respondents might deny such propositions if their statements were challenged or they were questioned in a different context. Such statements should be read as attempts to apprehend an otherwise ungraspable antagonistic relation between "my being" and the other's threat to it through publicized, concrete acts. I think this is, I assume, what Laclau (2014) means when he writes that "there is no ontic content that, by itself, has a precise ontological signification" (115). "If I identify with a certain content, the latter ceases to be mere content; it is invested in such a way that it becomes a symbol of my own being. That is, it comes to fulfill a different ontological role. But this new role is only possible insofar as another 'positive' content becomes a threat to my own identity" (113).[22]

Thus, the interviewees' utterances above, whatever ontic content they may have (i.e., whatever content they attribute to a category), indicate an affective investment in the ontological role the statements play. In particular, they indicate the constitutive divide between Danes and immigrants, two antagonistic social formations defined by cultural incompatibility. The actual, opposing attributes change with the rhetorical situation, but the place assigned to the category of immigrants is repeated across instances of discourse, within and beyond interviews. It is the abstract and empty quality of the signifier "[Muslim] immigrant,"[23] rather than the concrete use of it, that allows meaning to be fixed and appear as a stable entity across contexts.

Does my focus on the context of interviewees' utterances mean that their seemingly "prejudiced" utterances do not have racist and discriminatory implications? Certainly not. On the contrary, even apparently positive, nonprejudiced statements can be recruited to discriminate against people of different race, ethnicity, religion, or sexual orientation. Racism, in my theoretical universe, is not an ideology or discourse that guides people's understanding and evaluation of other social groups. I use the term "racism" as discriminatory practice on the basis of "perceived"[24] ethnic, cultural, or racial differences.[25] People deploy ethnicity, culture, religion, and race as flexible resources to signify difference per se. Discrimination does not require racist intent or negative evaluation of a group. A number of studies that pay attention to the intricacies of discourse argue that there is an enduring tendency to justify discrimination even when people display egalitarian and antiracist sentiments.[26] As we have seen in the analysis of the interview extract with Birgitte, a person may end up justifying discourses that have discriminatory implications despite attempts to argue against discrimination on the basis of culture, when the only "realistic" and viable access to describing immigrants is through a cultural ontology, which provides a readily available repertoire of cultural designations for making sense of a social world structured by cultural divisions.

Racism, of course, is not dependent on culturalization; it has been practiced since time immemorial. As will become apparent, however, the culturalization of discourse on immigration in Denmark has made racism widely acceptable and one of the cornerstones of the new hegemonic order. First, culturalization has made racism almost invisible by displacing skin color and focusing on the immigrants' cultural background as the marker of difference. The most important function of the shift has been lumping together all immigrants into a larger civilizational category, "Muslim," a term that functions to mark anxiety and threat. As Yıldız (2009: 475) argues in German context, "As 'Muslims' . . . they can be imagined as being part of a much larger and much more globally extended community than before. Without a change in actual numbers, this indexical function alone multiplies their size in the dominant social imaginary." The instances of violence I discussed earlier, repeatedly linked to the category of Muslim, are therefore taken to be indicative of the threat posed by Muslims to "a homogeneous Danish culture, perceived as a historically rooted asset of traditions" such as gender equality, tolerance toward homosexuality, and freedom of speech (Wren 2001: 148). The perceived immediate threat to such common achievements can bring together diverse groups in defense of some imagined shared cultural values. The convergence of left and right creates a new sense of commonality—a commonality that can constitute the basis for a new "historical bloc" in Gramscian sense (1971).

This chapter has sought to identify a cultural antagonism that forms a critical dividing line through which society is envisioned. When society can be imagined in the cultural terms identified here, such divisions are equally available for institutionalization (e.g., in representation systems, laws, political platforms, and schools) and subjectification processes. All these mark a hegemonic formation that can come to subordinate other antagonisms along the main dividing line. Specifically political articulations, often themselves hegemonic projects pursued through public discourse in the media, attempt to naturalize class, ethnic, religious, gender, or other differences as a basis of the social divisions on which their own representations rest. In the case at hand, culture is the naturalized site of antagonism. It is important to understand that these are "only the *possible* differences among actors who populate the social; they do not naturally carry a political valence" (De Leon, Desai, and Tuğal 2009: 194). It is through the work of political forces that some differences gain particular political valence—in this case, that a culturalized antagonism becomes hegemonic.

Hegemony is never complete because of the heterogeneous nature of the social. Thus, it demands a constant struggle to keep the ontological order in place. In the following chapters, I turn to the milieu in which the hegemonic project of the political right was initiated in the mid-1980s, the political moment of the key rhetorical intervention that bent signification along certain lines, and the ways in which a culturalized hegemonic order has been established and is now sustained in politics, institutions, public discourse, and subjective identifications.

CHAPTER 2

Crisis and Hegemonic Displacement

The previous chapter concluded with a quote from De Leon, Desai, and Tuğal (2009) in which they argue that cleavages do not in themselves have a political valence. It is through the work of political forces that cleavages gain political valence and shape the social horizon. The question is, How do cleavages come to carry political valence and become hegemonic? In particular, how did cultural cleavages acquire so much political valence that they dislocated more traditional socioeconomic cleavages and transformed old political identities in Denmark, reconfiguring the political landscape? These are the leading questions discussed in the next two chapters. In this chapter, I analyze how the Danish justice minister from the Conservative Party and his accomplices within the police and immigration services created a moral panic in an already anxious economic and political environment in the mid-1980s. The moral panic destabilized the political representation system and created an opportunity for an intervention by the populist Far Right that managed to become a permanent fixture in political discourse. Their vision has become the basis for the hegemonic social imaginary (i.e., the ontological structure of society). I analyze the complex interplay among various political actors in the creation and capitalization the moral panic that opened up the space for this populist intervention.

The Mid-1980s: A Turning Point

There is a general agreement among scholars that a fundamental shift in immigration discourse occurred in the mid-1980s:[1] the focus shifted from immigrants' social problems to their (problematic) culture, which was mainly expressed in terms of the "Muslim threat." Gaasholt and Togeby

(1995: 162) argue that the rhetoric on immigration changed character during 1984–85. At the beginning of the 1980s, the focus was on "respectful integration of immigrants" and "immigrants' rights"; in the second half, Danes discussed "making demands of immigrants," "refugees of convenience," and "the Muslim threat." Madsen (2000: 87) points to a remarkable jump in the polls of Danes' views on "whether immigrants constitute a threat to our national character": 23 percent declared agreement with the statement in 1985, whereas that figure jumped to around 40 percent in 1987 and 42 percent in 1998. In 2010, 54.9 percent said they regard Islam as a problem for the cohesion of Danish society.[2] Thus, "immigration as a threat" to national identity became a permanent sentiment among Danes. "Immigrant" also became synonymous with "Muslim immigrant."

Not only has the focus shifted in immigration discourse; immigration gradually became the most important and salient issue. In the 1970s and 1980s, Danes were concerned about economic questions such as taxes, public spending, and unemployment; during the 2001 election, however, two interrelated topics dominated opinion polls: welfare services and immigration (i.e., the perceived strain on the welfare state caused by immigrants; Togeby 2003). In 1987, only 4 percent of the voters mentioned immigration as the most important issue affecting how they vote, but by 2001, 20 percent of the voters considered immigration the most important issue, and about half of all voters named immigration as one of the most important issues for their decision about how to vote (Andersen 2004; Rydgren 2004; Togeby 2003).

Depending on their field and the object of their study, scholars have different explanations for the shift in immigration discourse and the salience of immigration in public discourse. According to some scholars of immigration, the salience of the issue reflects people's reactions to demographic changes, that is, the increasing numbers of immigrants (Gaasholt and Togeby 1995; Hervik 2002; Necef 2001). Others, especially scholars of the Far Right,[3] point to structural transformations such as postindustrialism, globalization, and Europeanization as the background for anxieties around immigration. According to these scholars, conflict in the industrial era was largely structured by the socioeconomic left-right dimension (i.e., socioeconomic cleavage), and cleavage structures in the postindustrial period are informed by the value dimension with immigration as the central sociocultural issue (Andersen 2004; Bjørklund and Andersen 2002; Rydgren 2004, 2010, 2013). And immigration became one of the central issues of our time; it became politicized following the sudden increase in the numbers of refugees beginning in 1984.

Although these scholars relate the centrality of immigration to the rise of the populist Right, immigration is understood as the new dimension of the center-periphery conflict, that is, the most visible representation of globalization that threatens the level of welfare services that workers enjoy (Andersen 2002; Rydgren 2013) as well as the result of the decrease in the salience of the socioeconomic cleavage dimension (Rydgren 2004: 495). This explains the strong "working class" basis of the populist far-right parties and the shift in ownership of the welfare issue from social democracy to the Far Right.

According to Rydgren (2004: 489), contemporary Western European countries are characterized by two major conflict dimensions: economic (i.e., workers against capital) and cultural (e.g., immigration, law and order, abortion). Economic conflict dimension structured the political landscape until the 1980s, after which cultural conflict became more important even though welfare remained a salient issue. The Western European party systems that had been frozen within the structure of economic conflict began to fracture, voter profiles of the parties started to change, and this led to the parties redefining themselves in terms of the cultural/value dimension (Andersen 2004; Betz and Meret 2013). In Denmark, where the conflict between labor and capital (i.e., class struggle) was predominant, the displacement of this conflict dimension has meant the breakdown of the social democratic hegemony, which was based on an openly redistributive welfare system fueled by high taxes. The Social Democratic Party (SDP), although it never gained an absolute majority in the *Folketinget* (the Danish Parliament), monopolized power between 1953 and 1968—a period of increasing prosperity as well as the development of the welfare state. Even during a nonsocialist coalition government (Social Liberal Party, Conservative Party, and Liberal Party) between 1968 and 1971, taxes continued to increase and the extension of the welfare state continued (Rydgren 2004).

In short, the issue of welfare and the nature of the welfare state had long been situated in the framework of class struggle around questions of how to redistribute wealth and how to reform the capitalist system. In the 1960s and 1970s, working-class organizations, stripped of an earlier internationalism, were well established as modern trade unions whose demands had been incorporated into the hegemonic political system. Danish society was articulated in terms of the welfare state; working-class demands were advanced through negotiations rather than confrontations; and wage increases were linked to increasing productivity even during the economic crisis that began in the early 1970s.

This hegemony began to fall apart in the early 1980s after the new right-wing coalition government[4] took over in 1982 and immediately began to implement neoliberal economic policies: although Denmark's progressive tax system has one of the highest rates in the world, social benefits and unemployment payments were reduced, wages were frozen, and job security was undermined through "restructuring" and "optimization" as a solution to the economic crisis[5] and as a response to globalization (i.e., making Denmark more competitive in an increasingly globalized world), yet tax rates were lowered for businesses. These policies led to large-scale protests and strikes by labor unions, but the government responded with an assault on the unions' negotiating powers.

There was also a general ideological push for a shift from social democratic/left positions (that unemployment and poverty were the result of an unjust capitalist system that could not generate enough work for everybody) to the neoliberal idea that unemployment was a question of incentives: the high levels of unemployment and welfare payments did not provide sufficient incentives for people to seek jobs.[6]

The Social Democrats responded to these developments by adopting neoliberal positions on the economy and welfare under the guise of a "third way" (Betz and Meret 2013: 110). The party seemed to accept the basic proposition of the neoliberal paradigm: expansive welfare services are not sustainable in a globalized world. The gradual erasure of the classic left-right distinction increasingly frustrated the "working class," whose "interests" were supposed to be represented by the Social Democrats. These moves set in motion a reconfiguration of the political landscape and opened up space for populist forces to fill the political void and articulate new types of social and political conflicts with an emphasis on cultural values.

Although there is a general agreement on the culturalization of discourse,[7] explanations of the culturalization process depend on theoretical and disciplinary approaches being used. Political analysts have a tendency to see the disappearance of class identities as the result of the macrostructural changes and the prominence of cultural cleavages as a "natural" consequence of structural changes that, among other changes, led to the emergence of a vast middle class and to the party system's attempt to adapt to the new constituencies that do not define themselves by class. In addition, the rise of the populist Far Right has been explained as "an effect of the decreased salience of the socio-economic cleavage dimension" (Rydgren 2004: 490).

This is, however, not a natural process: the emergence of political identities does not depend on a priori social rationality. On the contrary, politics is central to the formation of political identities, which is contingent upon the intervening forces' successful articulations. As Mouffe (1995) explains, "Politics aims at the creation of unity in a context of conflict and diversity;

it is concerned with the formation of a 'we' as opposed to a 'them'" (502), but who "we" and "they" are is not given a priori. More specifically, I argue that the transformation of "we" and "they" of class ontology into "we" and "they" of cultural ontology (e.g., the people vs. Muslim immigrants) is not the result of an independent, objectively observable macrostructural transformation but that of a hegemonic intervention by the populist Far Right, whose articulations shaped the very sociopolitical landscape and identities embedded therein.

In this sense, analyzing the populist Right's ability to capitalize on popular anxieties about the erasure of the welfare state and its ability to turn these popular sentiments into a crisis of representation is crucial for a more operationalized understanding of the resulting hegemonic displacement.[8] I argue that the Far Right's capitalization, management, and provocation of crises around immigration have played a central role in this process. In other words, immigration did not become an important issue because of the number of immigrants or the ensuing diversity but because its centrality benefits the populist Far Right so that it was able to dominate the debate on immigration. By managing and performing cycles of crises around immigration, they were able to insert themselves as one of the primary protagonists in the ensuing controversies. They succeeded in turning immigration from a labor issue into a cultural issue and then pushing the debate to the center of the discourse where the cultural antagonism shapes the social horizon.

Crisis and Political Intervention

Many scholars of populism emphasize the importance of a crisis for opening up a space for the emergence of new discourses and political interventions. Stavrakakis (2005: 247), for example, argues that "the emergence of new discourses and new identities is always related to the *dislocation* or crisis of previously hegemonic discursive orders. It is a certain failure of previous identifications that forces subjects to seek refuge in a new discursive attachment and investment." In other words, "New relations of representation . . . become possible because of dislocations of the existing political order" (Panizza 2005: 3). For Laclau (2005), "The crisis of representation . . . is at the root of any populist, anti-institutional outburst" (139) and "The institutional system has to be (again, more or less) broken if the populist appeal is to be effective" (177). Mouffe (2005: 80) argues that "populism arises as the result of a crisis of representation, as a response to either the incapacity or the refusal of elites to respond to people's concerns. There is some evidence to support this view. The populist right often exploits xenophobia to swell its ranks and disqualify (other) professional politicians."

Moffitt (2015: 191), on the other hand, notes that all these approaches see a crisis as an external trigger of populism and argues that "populist actors actively participate in the 'spectacularization of failure' that underlies crisis, allowing them to pit 'the people' against a dangerous other, radically simplify the terms and terrain of political debate."

My analysis of the Danish case shows that the relationship between populism and crisis goes in both directions: A crisis opens up the political terrain for interventions by fringe forces such as populists, but once they have gained access to the discourse and have become successful, their existence depends on the perpetuation of crisis—which they continuously perform.

A crisis about a particular issue (e.g., a moral panic around immigration) can, if successfully capitalized on by populists, be presented as an indication of a deeper crisis in the hegemonic order. The populists' success, on the other hand, depends on the existence of an external threat to "the people"; the feeling that there is a continuing external threat can only be upheld by a constant focus on the external group and their actions; otherwise, the categories of identification (e.g., the people, immigrants/Muslims) will fade away in the messy waters of the discursive sea. A continuous series of public controversies and moral panics of varying scope are necessary for producing the experience of an ongoing crisis, and the far-right actors are often—though not always—the initiators of these crises around the target group.

"Crisis" is a vague term that refers to a phenomena of differing scopes and time spans. Laclau (2005), for example, speaks of "crisis of representation" in a Gramscian sense where social groups do not feel their interests are represented within the system. "Crisis" is also used to describe moral panics, political stalemates, and other intense public controversies.

I use the term "crisis" broadly to refer to a situation where there is a sense that the issue at hand urgently needs to be addressed; in my use, the term "crisis" includes "moral panic"—a term I use to refer to a more specific situation and period (short or long term) in which a well-defined group of people (e.g., "folk devils") are demonized and presented as a threat to society's moral values and interests (Cohen 1972). For analytical purposes, I use the term "controversy" to refer to a heated public debate on an issue or topic (e.g., health-care reform). I also use the terms "crisis of representation" or "hegemonic crisis" to describe a widespread public sentiment that the system as a whole is broken.

Moral Panics

Krinsky (2013: 1) defines a moral panic "as an episode, often triggered by alarming media stories and reinforced by reactive laws and public policy, of exaggerated or misdirected public concern, anxiety, fear, or anger over a perceived threat to social order." However, there is a great deal of disagreement among social scientists about how to define a moral panic, and even the terms used to describe the phenomena vary significantly (e.g., moral panic, rumor-panic, panic, menace, craze, scare, crisis). They also disagree about the causes: some see moral panics as initiated by the public and spread by the media, whereas others lean toward the elite-engineered model; the most common approach is, though, an interest-group perspective, in which "rule creators and moral entrepreneurs launch crusades, which occasionally turn into panics, to make sure that certain rules take hold and are enforced" (Goode and Ben-Yehuda 2009: 67).

There are different accounts of the origins of the concept of moral panic, but Stanley Cohen's *Folk Devils and Moral Panic* is considered to be the first fully developed definition of the term. According to Cohen (1972: 1), a moral panic begins when

> a condition, episode, person or group of persons emerges to become defined as a threat to societal values and interests; its nature is presented in a stylized and stereo-typical fashion by the mass media; the moral barricades are manned by editors, bishops, politicians and other right-thinking people; socially accredited experts pronounce their diagnoses and solutions; ways of coping are evolved or (more often) resorted to; the condition then disappears, submerges or deteriorates and becomes more visible.

In Cohen's formulation, moral panics are discrete episodes with fairly well-developed phases with a beginning, a middle, and an end that sometimes leave fundamental social changes behind. In one of the earliest applications of the concept, Hall and coauthors (1978) aligned Cohen's model of moral panics with a Gramscian notion of hegemony. They argued that the moral panic over mugging (i.e., black youth criminality) in Britain during the early 1970s was a panic through which the state tapped into anxieties around social order and secured consent to the reconstruction of hegemony through the discourse of "law and order." The panic diverted attention away from the real historical crisis of capitalism during economic recession. Although they related the concept to a larger hegemonic crisis, they upheld Cohen's basic definition:

> When the official reaction to a person, groups of persons or series of events *out of all proportion* to the actual threat offered, when "experts" in the form of police chiefs, the judiciary, politicians and editors *perceive* the threat in all but identical terms, and appear to talk "with one voice" of rates, diagnoses, prognoses and solutions, when the media representations universally stress "sudden and dramatic" increases (in numbers involved or event) and "novelty," above and beyond that which a sober, realistic appraisal could sustain, then we believe it is appropriate to talk about beginnings of a *moral panic*. (Hall et al. 1978: 16)

A number of scholars have criticized different aspects of this model. Waddington (1986), for example, criticizes the concept for not establishing any criteria for comparing the scale of the problem to the scale of the response to it. For Waddington, it is perfectly possible to panic about a genuine problem (cited in Goode and Yehuda 2009: 75). Criticism against proportionality comes also from the opposite camp: the notion of proportionality presumes that reality and the descriptions of that reality are two distinct phenomena and it is possible to judge discourse on reality by reality itself as if we have direct access to reality, bypassing linguistic depictions of it. Hall and coauthors have also been criticized for arguing that moral panics are actually about matters other than the seeming focus (e.g., moral panics about crime masking economic crises), which gives their model the appearance of a top-down conspiracy theory. In another critique, Noble (2012: 218) notes that "there is tendency in uses of moral panic theory to collapse the complex process of symbolization into a singular, dominant, ideological representation of folk devil" and argues that "a moral panic always entails an ensemble of social actors who compete in the definition of the 'problem.'"

Furthermore, Goode and Yehuda (2009: 226) contend that it is often difficult to discern the stages of a moral panic, or assess it by its scope, location, or time span. They also think that a moral panic may represent a limited portion of a much more long-range concern. Thompson (1998) takes it a step further and argues that as the result of the proliferation of moral panics in the 1990s, researchers started to consider moral panics as successive episodes that indicate ongoing large-scale, social, economic, and cultural changes rather than a series of unrelated episodes of public concern.

As this discussion indicates, the walls between the terms "crisis," "moral panic," "controversy," and "hegemonic crisis" are not impervious. Morgan and Poynting (2012: 4), for example, ask if the concept of the moral panic can be used to denote the global stock (i.e., moral turbulence) upon which the individual outbursts of panics draw. They make a case for directing more attention to the connection between discrete moral panics that have an ongoing and cumulative effect of producing global "folk devils" out of Muslims. In their framework, the contemporary globalized moral panic around Islam is not bound by time and space.

Although I use the different terms to denote different scales of crisis in concrete cases, I use "crisis" as a general term that also covers moral panics and heated controversies. From a perspective of poststructuralist hegemony theory, however, there is no sense in engaging in a discussion of the "realness" or proportionality of a crisis. As Moffitt (2015: 197) argues, "The attempt to determine objectively what 'is' or 'is not' a crisis is . . . a relatively fruitless exercise, as the concept relies on notions of normality and stability." These notions themselves are the products of crises performed by various actors rather than being "objective" criteria by which the reality of a crisis can be assessed. For example, the sudden increase in the numbers of refugees between 1984 and 1986 was experienced as a deep crisis because of the moral panic created around it, although a larger number of refugees came to Denmark in 1992 without a huge controversy because of the consensus among the political parties (Østergaard 2007). Thus, my discussion of moral panics will not focus on the proportionality of the perceived threat to the "real" threat, but on how the threat has been produced through rhetorical moves such as the inflation of numbers or the descriptions of the groups and actors involved in the media. I also agree with Noble (2012) that even at the climax of a moral panic there are several actors competing for the definition of the problem as well as the solutions. However, it is my impression that during a moral panic the various actors generally agree that there is a sudden and dramatic development that needs to be addressed.

The Political Landscape and Immigration Discourse Prior to and around 1984

The Danish political system is one of the most open electoral systems in Europe, with a threshold of only 2 percent[9] and a public media system that allocates equal time to all participating parties in an election. Because of the low threshold and relative accessibility of public debate, the Folketing (the Danish parliament) usually consists of many small parties representing a broad spectrum of interests. But the distribution of parties over a broad spectrum also means that Denmark, unlike other Scandinavian countries, has never had a one-party government with majority. Most of the governments since the inception of parliamentary democracy have been coalition governments, often with the small parties from the middle of the political spectrum, and many have been minority governments (meaning that the government did not have a parliamentary majority). Danish governments do not need majority support; they can be in power as long as a majority does not oppose them. As a result, minority governments have to negotiate with small parties or parties from the other side of the aisle over specific issues as well as government programs. The socially liberal, economically conservative Social Liberals have often either been coalition partners with the Social Democrats on the left or the Conservatives and the Liberals on the right.

After the elections in 1981, the Folketing had the Social Democratic Party (*Socialdemokraterne*), the Socialist People's Party (*Socialistisk Folkeparti*), and the Left Socialists (*Venstresocialisterne*) on the left, the Liberal Party (*Venstre*) and the Conservative People's Party on the right (*Kristelig Folkeparti*), and the middle consisted of Center-Democrats (*Centrum-demokraterne*), the Christian People's Party, and the Social Liberals (*Radikale Venstre*). The xenophobic, antitax Progress Party (*Fremskridtspartiet*) was considered to be on the far right of the spectrum. Although the SDP formed a minority government after the elections, Prime Minister Anker Jørgensen resigned after he had problems with the labor unions over his economic program. The neoliberal government that took over in 1982 was a coalition government formed by the Conservatives, Liberals, Center-Democrats, and Social Liberals.

Although xenophobic views were common in Denmark during the 1970s, there was no openly xenophobic party until the late 1970s, when the antitax populist Progress Party,[10] led by Mogens Glistrup, began to express openly racist views. The Progress Party's pamphlet from 1973 did not mention immigration at all. It was only after the mid-1980s that immigration replaced taxation as the main rallying issue for the party (Andersen 2004; Rydgren 2004). Until then, the party's combination of extreme liberal ideology and explicitly racist rhetoric (with biological references) did not entirely speak to the anxieties of workers, who typically voted for Social Democrats. The novelty of the Progress Party was wearing off, and when the Conservatives and Liberals launched a neoliberal program similar to those of Reagan and Thatcher, the electoral support for the Progress Party declined rapidly: from 15.9 percent in 1973 to 8.9 percent in 1981 to 3.6 percent in 1984. But support started to increase again after the party began to emphasize xenophobic views in the mid-1980s. Until the mid-1980s, public debate about welfare state had not been preoccupied with the ethnic homogeneity of the Danish nation, and the issue of immigration was subordinated into the fundamental divide between labor and capital. The "immigrant worker" was just one of the signifiers of the struggle between social classes.

Østergaard (2007) considers 1983 to be a turning point in the immigration discourse and sees the eighteen years between 1983 and 2001 as the period that would shape the immigration debate for the years to come. The year 1983 was a turning point, according to Østergaard, not so much because of the passage of the liberal immigration law that year but because opposition to immigration has become a permanent fixture of the Danish political landscape because of that debate.

The law's central change was that it granted immigrants and refugees legal rights. Until the new law, individual cases of refugees were mainly left to the police and the justice minister. The expulsion of a Mexican refugee in 1977 to Mexico without any legal procedures created a furor and led to demands in the Folketing for an overhaul of the immigration law. The commission that was set up could not reach a consensus and presented two different sets of recommendations. A minority group within the commission recommended extending legal rights to immigrants and refugees. The government and the opposition reached a consensus based on minority recommendations despite objections by the justice minister, Erik Ninn-Hansen, from the Conservative Party. The law passed with a broad consensus in the Folketing between the government and the opposition (the only exception was the Progress Party). During the parliamentary debate prior to the passage of the law, Erik Ninn-Hansen opposed granting extended legal rights to immigrants and refugees. He warned that the Danish welfare system would be a magnet for people from poor countries and this could lead to racial unrest. A more restrictive law, he argued, would help maintain Denmark as a national state in the future. After the immigration law was adopted, with his vote, Ninn-Hansen praised its humanitarian approach but only until 1984. The Progress Party, however, argued that the parliamentary majority was in conflict with the popular will—a populist argument that later became the main ingredient in the populist Right's forceful intervention in the discourse and its main strategy in moving the political center to the right.

The new immigration law of 1983 granted legal rights to refugees[11] and immigrants, including the refugees' right to stay in Denmark while asylum applications were processed and the right to bring immediate family to Denmark once they were granted asylum. The new law also expanded the definition of refugee to include people who did not strictly fit the UN Convention for Refugees but might be in danger if they were sent back to their home country. Unlike "guest workers" of previous decades, who were absorbed into the labor market, refugees were to go through a nine-month integration process with instruction in language and Denmark's social, cultural, and political systems. Once given asylum, they could not be sent back. The jobless were to be integrated into the Danish welfare system at the same level of support as citizens.

The media generally were positive toward the humanitarian intentions of the law both during the debate and after it took effect, except for some of the letters to the editor, and despite Ninn-Hansen's criticism and the Progress Party's protests. The positive atmosphere started to change when the number of refugees began to increase toward the end of 1984: 332 refugees asked for asylum in 1983, whereas the number was 4,312 in 1984, and the number increased to 6,637 in 1985 (Østergaard 2007: 367).[12]

When the first group of refugees started to arrive in the second half of 1984, Ninn-Hansen saw the increase as an opportunity and began campaigning for restrictions to the new immigration law—a campaign that a couple of years later turned into a major moral panic. He connected the sudden increase to the new immigration law, although the number of refugees were increasing all over Europe as the result of the war between Iran and Iraq, Israel's occupation of southern Lebanon in 1982, and the civil war in Sri Lanka.

Center parties, left-wing parties, and humanitarian organizations argued that the numbers were not big enough to panic about and insisted on Denmark's humanitarian responsibilities, but the sentiment that dominated the media by the fall of 1984 was overwhelmingly negative and panicky. It is paradoxical that the creation of the negative atmosphere was not the media's intention: although they published benevolent editorial views across the spectrum, their professional routines led to the extremely negative coverage of the incoming refugees in the news. They responded to the "factual" and "objective" information (e.g., numbers of refugees, apocalyptic projections, and financial costs) fed to them by the police and the Danish Immigration Service (*Udlændingestyrelsen*), both of which were under the Justice Ministry.

The discourse around immigration was, as a result, about Denmark's humanitarian responsibilities, and its capacity to receive and help refugees. The moral character of 1984 discourse differentiated it from earlier debates on guest/foreign workers. It also polarized the political positions: right-wing parties that traditionally defended the free movement of the workforce became increasingly negative toward refugees, whom they considered a burden on the state. Left-wing parties were more generous toward refugees, whom they considered victims of oppression and torture. Within a general agreement about Denmark's moral responsibility toward people in need, however, the Right emphasized Denmark's limited capacity to solve the world's refugee problems and the strain of foreigners on limited resources, whereas the Left argued that Denmark was rich enough to take its share, the numbers of refugees was relatively small, and refugees could be seen making an important cultural contribution.

However, the negative coverage of incoming refugees turned, within a couple of years, into a moral panic that not only prepared the ground for severe restrictions, but created a fertile ground for a hegemonic intervention by far-right forces, an intervention that threw mainstream political parties—particularly the Social Democrats—into a deep crisis. The remainder of this chapter is an analysis of the major moral panic around immigration in 1985 and 1986, which transformed immigration from a labor issue to a cultural issue.

Beginnings of a Moral Panic: 1984

As indicated earlier, scholars point to the mid-1980s as a turning point in immigration discourse. Although scholars generally consider the "dramatic increase" in the numbers of refugees to be the trigger for the politicization of the immigration issue (Andersen 2004; Gaasholt and Togeby 1995; Rydgren 2004; Østergaard 2007), there has been no examination of how immigration became "politicized" in this period.[13] The assumption is that the increase created the intense debate about the issue. In my perspective, whether an issue becomes a public concern depends on the ability of the political actors with access to the media to set the agenda as well as how the issue is perceived in the debate.

My analysis of the media coverage of the refugee "influx" in the period between 1984 and 1986 shows that the Conservative justice minister Erik Ninn-Hansen was a key figure in creating an urgent concern about refugees. His purpose was clearly to force the parliamentary majority—including the two small coalition partners—to introduce restrictions to the new immigration law of 1983, which he considered to be too liberal. Regardless of his intentions, however, his campaign created a major moral panic that gradually convinced the major political actors that the immigration numbers were too big for Denmark to handle and that restrictions had to be introduced.

While close-reading the newspaper clips from the years 1984 and 1986, I recalled the feeling that there was an increasing sense of panic in the coverage of the so-called refugee influx. To test this sense, I read and coded a total of 978 stories from 1984 and 1986, including news, commentaries, interviews, snippets, and letters to the editor. The first thing I noted was that the amount of coverage more than tripled between the two periods: although there were 113 news stories, almost all about refugees, in a four-month period in 1984, the same newspapers published 455 news stories in the same period in 1986. Because I was interested in how the moral panic was created and the sources behind the panic, I created codes for sources in the news and two categories for the news: panic-creating and panic-related news. Panic-creating stories gave rise to a sense of panic in their framing of the event through such titles as "Organized Gangs Help Refugees to Come to Denmark" (*BT*, August 13, 1984), "Refugee Influx without End" (*Jyllands-Posten*, September 24, 1984), or "MP: We Must Dam Up the Mass Invasion of Refugees" (*BT*, August 7, 1984). As other scholars have noted, the news media in this period conveyed a sense of emergency—a chaotic, explosive situation out of control with floods of immigrants (Andreassen 2005; Østergaard 2007).

Panic-related stories, on the other hand, although less apocalyptic in tone, nonetheless dealt with the effects of refugees on Denmark. Taken together with the panic-creating stories, they contributed to the sense that refugees were creating huge problems for authorities, institutions, and society in general. Stories such as "Denmark Will Receive More Refugees" (*Politiken*, August 25, 1984) or "Refugees Erase All Traces behind Them" (*Politiken*, September 18, 1984) do not have an apocalyptic tone but are still concerned about the number of incoming refugees, financial costs, and accommodation problems. The first story informs the readers that the justice minister will ask the parliament for millions of Danish kroner for refugees, whereas the second story is about refugees destroying their identification papers before their arrival.

The coding followed a close reading of the material. I read all the stories at least twice, once when I was trying to determine the codes, once again to code the stories. Out of 113 news stories from fall 1984, 35 reflected a clear sense of uncontrollable influx and chaos and 31 stories indirectly contributed

TABLE 2.1. Panic in News Stories

News stories	1984	1986
None	43	362
Panic-creating	35[a]	44
Panic-related	31	45
No reason for panic	4	4
Total	113	455

[a]Twenty-one stories were solely based on Ninn-Hansen as a source; 20 stories used the police as a primary source.

to that sense by emphasizing the burden that the refugees were putting on Denmark. Together, about 60 percent of all news stories contributed to the sense of panic around refugees, although in only four instances did the main protagonist(s) explicitly argue that there was no reason for panic.

This public discourse of panic about uncontrolled immigration was the result of a convergence of police and bureaucrats within the national administration, particularly Ninn-Hansen, whose purview included the police and the Danish Immigration Service (*Udlændingestyrelsen*). Out of the 113 immigration news stories in 1984, 49 were sourced primarily to Ninn-Hansen or the police (25 and 24 respectively). All but 4 of the 25 Ninn-Hansen stories were panic stories, as were 20 out of 24 mainly sourced to the police. Headlines for stories primarily from these two sources included "46 Iranians in Copenhagen Yesterday" (*Berlingske Tidende*, September 23, 1984), "81 Asians Applied for Asylum in Copenhagen Last Weekend" (*Berlingske Tidende*, September 24, 1984), "Refugees Flow into Denmark" (*Politiken*, September 24, 1984), "New Refugee Influx over the Border" (*Jyllands-Posten*, September 24, 1984), "Refugees Cost the State 60 Million" (*Berlingske Tidende*, October 5, 1984), "Authorities Are Powerless" (*Berlingske Tidende*, October 11, 1984), "Refugee Influx Cost 30 Million" (*Berlingske Tidende*, October 11, 1984), "300 Million More to Refugees" (*Jyllands-Posten*, October 12, 1984), "Refugee Influx Is on Its Path to 6,000" (*Jyllands-Posten*, October 23, 1984), "Refugees into the Country with Dangerous Diseases" (*Jyllands-Posten*, October 27, 1984), and "Refugees Housed with Mentally Retarded" (*Politiken*, November 23, 1984).

The police fed the media with daily numbers of incoming refugees, and Ninn-Hansen provided the framework for interpreting the numbers: in his view, the increase was solely the result of the liberal immigration law of 1983, although the increase was occurring throughout Europe and was not specific to Denmark, something he admitted in his answer to a question from Social Democratic MP Torben Lund (Jensen 2000: 465). Ninn-Hansen's strategy was to create the sense that immigration had become uncontrollable in order to force the Folketing to introduce restrictions on access to seek asylum in Denmark. His goal was to blame the political majority for the chaotic situation, but the chaos itself had to be strategically constructed. To create a sense of chaos, he (and the police) fed the media with daily numbers of incoming refugees (even if the number was miniscule), apocalyptic projections, problems with housing, and the financial burden refugees put on the state.

In October 1984, for instance, Ninn-Hansen projected that six thousand refugees would come to Denmark that year (*Jyllands-Posten*, October 23, 1984). A few weeks later, the number was seventy-five hundred (*Jyllands-Posten*, November 9, 1984). Two months later, in January 1985, he said, "If 30,000 refugees come, we cannot integrate them as we want to" (Østergaard 2007: 368).

He also informed the Folketing that Denmark was unable to manage the numbers of refugees, which at that point (November 1984) had reached 1,322 within the last three months, compared to 332 for the entire year in 1983. He claimed, once again, that the new law was a magnet for refugees, leading to an enormous increase in expenses from a budgeted 60 million DKK ($US10 million) to 401 (about $US65 million) a year. He asked the Folketing if it had intended to create a law that made it impossible for Danish authorities to act on the "flow" and added that if that were the case, then the Folketing had to pay for the huge amount of funds that receiving refugees would require (*Politiken*, October 11, 1984).

Apart from omitting the fact that the increase was not specific to Denmark and therefore not related to the new law in his almost daily briefings, he fed to the media the numbers of incoming refugees, not those who received asylum (which were much lower than the projections), and based his enormous financial cost projections on an immediate trend in the numbers of incoming refugees. The cost projections expressed in millions of Danish kroner created a sense that a huge amount of resources was being channeled to the refugees while Danes were being denied benefits. The fact was that most of the funds actually were allocated to the Danish authorities: the police, social workers, and institutions that dealt with refugees rather than refugees themselves, but this distinction was deliberately lost in the way the question of burden was presented.

My goal here is not to engage in an assessment of whether the numbers really constituted a threat but to underline the rhetorical use of the numbers to create a sense of uncontrollable immigration. One of the main arguments from the opposition for resisting Ninn-Hansen's push for a change in immigration law was that Denmark needed time to assess the impact of the new law. The numbers in themselves did not signify panic or burden: three years earlier, Austria had received fifty thousand Polish refugees without much public controversy.[14] Sweden, with almost the same population as Denmark, was receiving five to seven thousand refugees a year. Numbers, too, are rhetorical resources, signified by an articulating force, used to achieve a goal.

Constructing Refugees as a Threat to Social Cohesion

The involvement of the police led news stories to focus on the criminal aspects of asylum-seeking process, which not only contributed to the sense of chaos but also to the representation of refugees as a threat to social cohesion. In this period (1984), there was not a single news story about the human right abuses in refugees' home countries; news coverage was dominated by themes such as incoming numbers, accommodation problems, economic and social burdens, misuse of the asylum system, and criminal aspects of the escape from the home country. I discussed some of them in the previous section, for example, how numbers were inflated through projections based on short-term trends. Four of the themes that increased the sense of threat are worth mentioning because they originated solely from Ninn-Hansen or the police: (1) the representation of refugees as a huge economic burden for ordinary Danes; (2) the criminalization of refugees' escape; (3) the representation of refugees as carriers of infectious diseases; (4) the labeling of refugees as "convenience refugees" by the police, politicians, and the Danish Immigration Service.

Refugees as a Burden for Ordinary Danes

Above I pointed to two aspects of the burden theme. The first was the erasure of the distinction between incoming refugees and those who are granted asylum, which inflated the financial costs; the second was the impression that the money was used by the refugees when in fact it was allocated to Danish authorities and institutions. This was also reflected in the letters to the editor—there were only twenty-two in four months—which called for a tightening of the immigration law and made arguments about Danes paying the costs for the refugees. The other side of the "burden aspect" was that refugees were often called "refugees of convenience" by both the police and politicians from the right.

Criminalization of Refugees' Escape

The second theme that was prominent in this period was the misuse of the asylum system by refugees—a theme that became even more prominent in the next two years. "Misuse" can be a misleading term here: I coded as "misuse stories" those stories that described the actions of refugees as misuse although the reported actions did not legally or morally misuse the asylum system. Most of the stories that were coded as misuse were actually about fake passports, bribery of officials in escape routes, payment to middlemen to escape home countries, or helping other refugees to enter Denmark—all of which are often the only way refugees can escape from their countries—as the following few titles illustrate: "Organized Gangs Help Refugees to Denmark" (*BT*, August 17, 1984), "DDR [the former East Germany] Make a Good Profit on Iran Refugees" (*Jyllands-Posten*, October 27, 1984), "Helped His Fellow Countrymen to Illegally Enter" (*Politiken*, October 27, 1984), "Illegal Immigration Is Exposed" (*Berlingske Tidende*, October 29, 1984), and "Organized Asylum Swindle" (*Politiken*, January 11, 1984). In the four-month period in 1984, there were seven stories with this theme, and five of them had the police as the primary source, whereas two stories had the reporter as source.

I will discuss one of these stories to illustrate how refugees' escape from home countries is criminalized through discursive techniques such as vague descriptions of refugees' actions. The story, entitled "Illegal Immigration Is Exposed" (*Berlingske Tidende*, October 29, 1984), is about the arrest of an Iranian refugee who had hidden the passports of four other Iranian refugees. Upon arrival, they declared that they did not have passports. The whole enterprise of being a refugee is "illegal" in the sense that many refugees cannot obtain legal documents and passports from regimes that prosecute them in the first place. Any entry without passports or fake passports would, therefore, in principle, be illegal. Refugees from Iran often escaped with passports made in other people's names, and they did not wish to expose the identity of the real passport holders or how the passports were produced. In many cases, these passports were reused to help other refugees follow the same escape routes. The criminal act here was more related to the act of lying about the passports than "illegal immigration." The story had two sources: a judge and a police inspector. None of the sources explicitly described the act as illegal immigration. The refugee was arrested for breaking the law. The reporter merely referred to the law, whereas the actions of the police leading up to the arrest were described in vivid detail. The police source was quoted to the effect that the investigation would be continued and there would be more arrests—a relatively neutral description of the investigation. At this point of the text, there is a sudden change in the use of the subject that corresponds to a change in the transitivity of the verb in English: "More documents are waiting to be translated, and they are expected to show that there are clues for an organization that gets refugees from Iran and Iraq to Scandinavia for large sums of money." The vagueness of the sentence allowed the journalist to make sweeping generalizations without explicitly attributing the generalizations to the police, although it is clear that there is no other way that the reporter could obtain the information (that documents are being translated and they will show the existence of an organization). The police clearly did not—yet—have evidence that they were dealing with "an illegal organization that helps getting foreigners to Denmark," as it was explained by the reporter. The defendant's explanations are rendered irrelevant—as is the case with most criminal cases—and he is only cited as claiming innocence, which was denied by the judge and therefore by the reporter. Then, without any evidence, the Iranian refugee is linked to an organization that is described as a Mafia-like organization that does things for money. Iranian and Iraqi refugees are collapsed into the same category of "illegal immigrants"—two refugee groups who come from countries at war with each other. The combination of vivid details and vague formulations create an aura of authenticity in which sweeping generalizations that describe "illegal immigration" gain truth-value. Thus, "illegal immigration" became the frame in which the event was understood. And the notion of "illegal immigration" contributed to the general image of "uncontrollable immigration."

This story, similar to many others, illustrates how the police have been active in putting a negative spotlight on incoming refugees. The police not only provided the media with numbers but made the very act of seeking asylum suspicious by criminalizing refugees' attempts to escape from inhuman conditions. The focus on the escape not only criminalized but also moved attention from the reasons for seeking refuge, such as torture, persecution, and war, to the negative consequences of the asylum system on the host society.

The focus slowly built the impression that refugees were people seeking better economic conditions, thereby intensifying the anxieties among Danes over the claim that the newcomers were draining the welfare funds designed for needy Danes who had built up the welfare system through their taxes. In particular, stories that emphasized the huge amounts of money that refugees had to pay for false passports and visas helped create the image that these were not needy people but "dream chasers." These stories also described the unrealistic expectation of refugees of receiving social help and getting a free education, although refugees were not quoted for this kind of expectation. Headlines such as "Escape to the Land of Happiness" (*Jyllands-Posten*, October 23, 1984) highlighted this image. The police were not always discreet about their views of refugees; they did not put a negative spotlight on refugees only by criminalizing their escape but in some cases by describing them explicitly as "refugees of convenience who will become a great problem for Denmark in a couple of years" ("Refugee Influx to Denmark," *Politiken*, November 26, 1984). Reporters rarely questioned police officers' expertise to describe refugees as "convenience refugees" or as "a great problem for Denmark." The description of refugees as "convenience refugees" increasingly connected anxieties about the erosion of the welfare system to the question of ethnic access to the welfare system. This feeling of an unfair claim on welfare goods helped, in the long term, to cement the idea that ethnic solidarity (i.e., homogeneous Danish culture) is a precondition for the welfare system; it displaced the original conception of the welfare system as the result of a decades-long struggle by the working class. "Working class" includes immigrants; "Danes" does not.

Representation of Refugees as Carriers of Infectious Diseases

In late October 1984, there was a sudden panic around a typhoid case among Iranian refugees. The police officers did not want to interrogate Iranian refugees unless they were quarantined first. The police officers' demand and anxieties were covered extensively by the media. One interesting observation is that almost all stories about the typhoid case included quotes from medical experts who found that the risk for being infected was minimal. No police officer was diagnosed with the disease, and the medical experts also pointed to the fact that Denmark had several typhoid cases a year and that the Iranian refugee might well have been infected during his stay in Denmark. But the views of the medial experts were not included in the headlines that emphasized the police perspective: "Typhoid Alarm: Refugee Hospitalized and Quarantined" (*BT*, October 26, 1984), "Refugees Enter the Country with Dangerous Diseases" (*Jyllands-Posten*, October 27, 1984), "Police Officers Scared of Contagion from Refugees" (*Politiken*, October 29, 1984), "Typhoid Professor: Examine All Immigrants" (*BT*, October 27, 1984), "Police Officers Scared of Contagion from Sick Refugees" (*Aktuelt*, October 29, 1984). Some stories even portrayed the disease as a threat to the health of the nation in general (e.g., *BT*, October 26, 1984).

Refugees of Convenience

To counter the consensual humanitarian approach, Ninn-Hansen and the institutions under his purview made a distinction between real refugees and refugees of convenience. *Berlingske Tidende*, on September 30, 1984, quoted an officer from the Danish Immigration Service who stated that there were a number of people among the incoming refugees who traveled for comfort (*bekvemmelighed*). *Jyllands-Posten*'s editorial on September 26, 1984, argued that the authorities should make sure that people who come in are really in danger rather than escaping poor living conditions. Any criticism of this distinction was countered with testimony from police officers or Ninn-Hansen. A criminal inspector, for example, described in vivid details that a number of refugees voluntarily had left Denmark with reasons such as "it is too cold here" or "cigarettes are too expensive" (*Berlingske Tidende,* January 12, 1985). They were, according to the inspector, refugees of convenience. Ninn-Hansen supported this view a week after in the same paper: "It is time to tell them that they can't just come to Denmark to study."

This rhetorical strategy of turning refugees into tourists who scan countries for more convenient living conditions would prove to be effective when the first restrictions to the immigration law were introduced in May 1985.

The Media

The media's response to the controversy was as expected: they relied on the justice minister and the police as sources to describe and interpret the situation in the news. Out of a total of 113 news stories in the four-month period in 1984, 25 (22.1 percent) were about numbers, most of them daily or weekly statistics of incoming refugees. Seventeen stories (15 percent) described problems with finding accommodation for refugees, and thirty stories (16.5 percent) were about the political debate on immigration laws and these stories also often contained numbers. Although the police made up almost half of the sources on numbers (44 percent), Ninn-Hansen dominated the debate: he was the primary source in 46.7 percent of the news stories about the political debate. Another dynamic that rendered these sources powerful in their interpretation of events was the conspicuous silence of mainstream political party figures, with only occasional appeals for empathy and tolerance. They did not explicitly challenge the logic that connected the increase in the number of refugees to the immigration law and gave limited emphasis to humanitarian principles, as opposed to the question of burdens on Denmark. It may be that the consensual character of humanitarianism did not seem to necessitate stronger response. Nonetheless, the silence left Ninn-Hansen as the principal actor and the main authority for interpreting immigration.

The emphasis on the numbers and the sense of chaos and doom should be understood in a media environment in which there was only one TV channel (not included in my statistics), which dominated the airwaves, and hundreds of local newspapers, which not only reproduced the numbers but also "concretized" the problems in local contexts by "live" descriptions of the tense reception of the refugees in local communities.

News stories in all newspapers adopted not only Ninn-Hansen's definition of the situation as uncontrollable but also his language. In this period, 45 percent of all news items used, without any reservation, the term "influx of refugees," a phrase that had become so common by August 1984 that journalists had to add adjectives to describe the "severity" of any further increase, such as when a *BT* reporter wrote: "The refugee influx has exploded" ("Organized Gangs Help Refugees to Come to Denmark," *BT*, August 13, 1984). The line between sourced quotes and text written by the reporter was often blurred, rendering specific and local renditions and evaluations of the situation as generalized facts. This is particularly true for the right-wing *Jyllands-Posten*, as when its "Refugee Influx Is Allowed to Continue" headlined a story on the parliament's rejection of Ninn-Hansen's proposal for restrictions to the law. *Berlingske Tidende* quoted Ninn-Hansen saying that "the parliament passed a refugee law that stripped the authorities of their ability to react regardless of how many refugees come in," and the reporter continued by remarking, without quotation marks, that "Social Democrats support [keeping] the refugee law as it is despite the multiplication of refugee numbers ("Authorities Are Powerless," August 11, 1984). All newspapers resorted to this kind of reporting. In *Politiken*, for instance, "Iranians Are Free to Enter to Denmark" (September 11, 1984) headlined a story based on an interview with a police inspector who criticized the justice minister's statement about easing the screening process for Iranian refugees. The story cited the inspector's direct criticism of the plan, but other information, clearly from him, was written in objective, fact-like language without attribution: "Iranians do not have to go beyond giving a very short statement to ask for asylum, *which is a temporary Danish citizenship*" (emphasis added).

News reports tacitly adopted Ninn-Hansen's connection between the sudden rise in numbers and the liberal immigration law. Whereas counterarguments were presented in four stories with clear references to the source (Danish Refugee Council), in nineteen news items, Ninn-Hansen's opinion was reported as if it were established fact. Yet Danish Refugee Council press releases and commentaries argued that the numbers could not be explained solely by the new immigration law because all other European countries had experienced significant increases. Only *Politiken*'s editorial supported this explicitly. The news coverage, inherently episodic and fragmented, included stories that simultaneously pointed to the laxity of Danish laws as cause and noted that other countries were experiencing similar or higher increases in refugee numbers. Some stories attributed Denmark's "influx" to the strict policies of Sweden and Germany. Yet because of the journalistic routine of event-centered news coverage (each reporter writes a single episode from the perspectives of available sources), the stories on other European countries experiencing the same increase were not linked to the increase in Denmark and did not have an impact on the commonly used explanatory framework linking the numbers to Danish immigration laws.

The Discrepancy between Editorials and News Coverage

Print media in 1984 did show a notable discrepancy between editorials and news coverage. Four of five newspapers featured at least one editorial in this period, all but one defending the immigration law of 1983 with reference to Denmark's humanitarian responsibilities to share the burden of the global refugee problem. Even the right-wing *Jyllands-Posten*'s editorial ("Refugees and Us, the Rich," September 27, 1984) argued that "once we have made sure that Denmark receives the persecuted [rather than economically needy], all provincial pettiness should be set aside. Denmark is a part of the world, and we can only benefit from knowing other people." An earlier editorial in the same paper ("Refugees and Freedom," August 15, 1984) suggested that Denmark was able to receive many more than the thousands of refugees projected by the justice minister. The liberal *Politiken* agreed that regardless of the causes of the increase, Denmark was beginning to fulfill its humanitarian responsibility and receiving its fair share of the refugees (September 26, 1984). The daily tabloid *BT* explicitly criticized Erik Ninn-Hansen in an editorial, "Ideals That Disappeared" (October 8, 1984), for "blowing wind into a smoldering fire" of xenophobia with his emphasis on immigrants as an economic burden. The conservative *Berlingske Tidende* was the only newspaper openly sympathetic to Ninn-Hansen's position, asking how vast tolerance was to be in the "honeypot country" (October 14, 1984). The editorial line in most papers was the opposite of the impression one would get by reading the news coverage alone.

Features stories also tended to reflect a humanitarian approach to refugees, relying less upon authorities and political figures than on interviews with refugees' and journalists' firsthand reports from refugee camps and escape routes, or writing about oppressive regimes (mainly Iran) and refugee living conditions in Denmark. In seven out of a total of twelve feature stories in 1984, refugees were described as victims of torture and oppression, as opposed to the news stories that focused on the arrival and accommodation of refugees, which created a sense of chaos and panic.

The news/editorial discrepancy was confined to 1984; two years later, more newspapers editorially aligned themselves with Ninn-Hansen and the news coverage. A careful conclusion is that in 1984 the editorials reflected the political consensus on the immigration law of 1983, whereas the news reflected a typical journalistic orientation toward conflict and reliance on conventional sources (mainly authorities) to describe the problem.

Although coding stories as "positive" or "negative" is beset with problems,[15] the percentage of negative news stories in 1984 was much higher than any other period included in this project. Even when only manifest negativity[16] is counted, 34.5 percent of all news stories were negative, versus 17.7 percent positive stories. "Neutral" stories made up one-third of the total (35.4 percent).[17]

Letters to the editor[18] of this period reflected the negative impression implicated in news coverage: 81.8 percent of all letters to the editor in the fall of 1984 were negative (again, higher proportionally than in later periods). The negative tone of readers' letters was also reflected in opinion polls taken during the same period: 46 percent of respondents found a proposed increase of quota refugees from five hundred to one thousand unacceptable ("Every Other Voter Says No to an Increase in the Number of Quota Refugees" *Jyllands-Posten*, September 27, 1984).[19]

These numbers may be taken as an indication that it was the news agenda that was reflected in the public agenda. According to agenda-setting research, "The agenda-setting influence of the press results in large measure from the repetition of the major issues in the news day after day. The public learns about the issues on the press agenda with little effort on their part, and considering the incidental nature of this learning, issues move rather quickly from the press agenda to the public agenda" (McCombs 2005: 159). The media's focus on problems linked to the arrival of refugees (as pushed onto the agenda by the sources that the media traditionally deem authoritative and reliable) created a widely negative sentiment in the news, as opposed to positive commentaries or statements by politicians and the intellectual elite. It is interesting that the positive commentaries, although overwhelming in volume, did not echo among newspaper readers and poll respondents as much as the negative tone of news coverage. Messages sent by Ninn-Hansen and anti-immigration forces appealed, as intended, to existing anxieties among Danes about the erosion of the welfare system and job security, which were linked to vague but broad feelings of threat and insecurity in an increasingly globalized world.

It is not possible to understand why the media was one of the main agents of the creation of a panic around immigration all the while their editorial lines emphasized the humanitarian responsibilities of Denmark without considering the conventions of news journalism. The increase in the number of refugees and the debate were covered by the media through the normal journalistic routines.

Daniel Hallin (1989: 89) describes the conventions of American objective journalism as the use of official sources, a focus on the president, absence of interpretation or analysis, and a focus on immediate events—action rather than ideas. Being objective, for American journalists, means being "balanced" between the two sides, and there is a watertight distinction between news and views in the mind of journalists. Despite the fundamental differences between American and Danish political systems, all of these "virtues"—save the focus on the president—are also valid for Danish journalism (Esmark and Kjær 1999). Although the Danish political system is not a two-party system, when it comes to single issues, the public space is usually divided between two sides, and this makes Hallin's remarks on objectivity relevant for Denmark.

According to Hall and coauthors (1978: 55–69), news is shaped by a specific conception of society as a consensus based on a "central value system," and crime marks one of the major boundaries of that consensus. However, not all news is shaped by consensus. Here Hallin's (1989) distinction between journalistic spheres of consensus, of legitimate controversy, and of deviance is useful (116–18). In Hallin's model (which can be visualized as concentric circles), the middle circle is the "sphere of legitimate controversy," which is the locus of journalistic objectivity. It is in this region that debates and contests between the legitimate parties are reported and treated with the virtues of objectivity and balance. The outer circle is "the Sphere of Deviance, the realm of those political actors and views which journalists and the political mainstream of the society reject as unworthy of being heard" (117). The innermost circle is what Hallin calls the "sphere of consensus." This is the region where journalists do not feel compelled to be objective or disinterested. On the contrary, the journalist's role is to advocate or celebrate what are conceived of as common values. In this region, objectivity and fairness once again fade away, and journalists play the role of exposing, condemning, and excluding those who challenge social consensus. The limits of acceptable political conflict end here: human-interest stories or war coverage (not the political debate on war) usually fall in this consensual space vacated of potential controversies. Crime stories as well usually reflect the sphere of consensus. The criminal is usually silent because journalists rely heavily on official sources that monopolize legitimate violence, such as courts and the police, whose perspectives infuse reporting. In most European societies, the police are taken to be a disinterested institution without a special stake in politics and a legitimate source to describe events disruptive of the social order. Information from them, particularly when provided as a neutral description of empirically graspable reality, is rarely questioned. Insofar as criminals are heard, they may defend themselves against allegations, but in general they are not allowed to question the nature of the crime or legitimacy of the authorities' definition of the problem. Journalists do not feel compelled to open up alternative definitions of an incident.[20] The police's definition becomes the default definition of the problem. The police's criminalization of refugees' escape from their home country helped make sure that these stories would be treated in the sphere of consensus.

It is the distinction between news and views combined with the notion of objectivity that led to the media's reliance on Ninn-Hansen and the police in the coverage of incoming refugees. While the editorials reflected the political consensus (views), the news reflected the official sources' definition of the problem and was treated in the sphere of consensus because of the legitimacy of the sources. This became the tacit definition in the absence of a more pronounced political debate that would have been covered "objectively" in the sphere of legitimate controversy.

Culture and Immigration in 1984

Culture was not a salient aspect of public discourse on immigration in 1984. The humanitarian perspective was completely dominant in my sample, representing 82.5 percent of all stories, as against 1.1 percent written from a cultural perspective.[21] About 81 percent of news stories and almost 95 percent of commentaries took a humanitarian perspective, whereas almost no stories with an explicit cultural perspective were found that year. Fewer than 1 percent of stories in 1984 and 1986 named immigrants as Muslims.

However, culture was not entirely absent as a discursive resource. It was part of the larger discursive repertoire and would be used for and against immigrants. In July 1984, for example, Svend Heiselberg, an MP for the Liberal Party, was quoted: "We must dam up the mass invasion of Iranian refugees. I am concerned about a situation where 25–30,000 Iranians settle down in Denmark and make an Islamic rebellion" ("MP: 'We Must Dam Up the Mass Invasion of Refugees,'" *BT*, August 7, 1984). The defenders of refugees countered these arguments by pointing out that the Iranian refugees escaped from an Islamic regime. Overall there were almost no cultural explanations of behavior in this period.

The single feature story with a cultural focus in the 1984 sample was positive toward refugees.[22] Built on interviews with a cultural sociologist and a social worker working with refugees ("Would You Like to Walk with Me . . . !" *Berlingske Tidende*, October 7, 1984), the feature focused on cultural difference to promote tolerance. The social worker explained that refugees believed that the individual is responsible for looking after himself and did not understand the Danish system, which was built on the principle of solidarity and the sharing of burdens—an argument that later would become the staple of the right-wing rhetoric for excluding Muslims from the welfare system.

As always, the social and individual contexts of utterance are critical to meaning. The social worker was actually responding to a consultant who had criticized her for taking too much time with individual refugees: the kind of humanitarian work she was doing could not be rationalized or maximized for efficiency. The interview was part of a platform to defend her work at a time of threatened job security: it was the time of the neoliberal mantra that an overhaul of work processes was necessary in order to maximize output and reduce the number of staff to become "competitive" in a globalizing world. Changing deeply embedded cultural beliefs among refugees would take time, she seemed to propose, if refugees were to be successfully integrated into Danish society.

The cultural frame is a rhetorical tool through which the social worker can justify her job by identifying herself as a bridge-builder between cultures in a larger mission of integrating refugees into a tolerant Danish society. As in any use of culture, it is not the positivity or negativity of the story that is most important but how it relates to the general field of discursivity: whether immigrants and immigration are seen primarily as situated in a field of cultural difference and, if so, what valence is attached to the presumed cultural difference.

The cultural content was also hinged to gender by the social worker. Integration is the moral responsibility of Denmark, her argument went, and a good example of integration was when refugee women, having learned Danish and become engaged in society, become emancipated because they can see that housework is shared between couples, that Danish men are not macho. Such rhetoric elaborates an overall argument for Denmark's moral responsibility and the value of cultural integration, a project in which established treatment systems require social workers as bridge-builders and academics who study immigrants' cultures to provide knowledge and expertise about how to build bridges. It is not surprising that the second interviewee in the same article, a cultural sociologist, condemned Danish racism that required "immigrants to be just like us" because he promoted tolerance toward cultural difference, which was transforming Denmark from an ethnically homogenous society into a multicultural society.

Another 1984 feature story was about immigrant children not getting enough help from the state ("Immigrants Are Treated Worse Than Refugees," *Berlingske Tidende*, November 14, 1984). The main point was that immigrant women did not know how to provide a healthy diet for their children. The social worker's strategy here was again based on describing the importance of her work in integrating immigrants into Danish living.

Although this kind of discourse culturalized immigrants and offered essentialized versions of culture, cultural difference was not articulated in mutually exclusive, antagonistic categories of Danes and immigrants. Danishness and Danes were associated with humanitarian commitments, and these descriptions served the rhetorical function of presenting Danes as a culturally hospitable and kind people who cared about the sufferings of other people. A *Berlingske Tidende* editorial, for example—published a couple weeks after a poll showed that half of Danes did not want to help refugees—described Danes as "by nature friendly and socially understanding people with a desire to help people in need" (October 14, 1984). Such descriptions of Danish culture were rhetorical devices enlisted in service of promoting a humanitarian approach rather than straightforward descriptions of an essence of Danishness. Many comments against the growing xenophobia among Danes used these types of descriptions of Danish culture, calling xenophobic utterances "Un-Danish" (*Politiken*, editorial, November 1, 1987). Racism, according these comments, was not a part of Danish culture, which essentially was tolerant. Rather, the problem was lack of information about foreigners (e.g., Bent Østergaard, *Berlingske Tidende*, November 11, 1984). Racism, nationalism, tolerance, and a host of other attributes are all parts of the discursive repertoire available for social action in any given society. Their mere existence or use does not characterize a society as racist, nationalist, or tolerant. The interesting point is not whether these attributes correspond to any given essence but how cultural arguments come to be mobilized to do one or another kind of social work. As I will demonstrate in the next chapter, the descriptions of Danish society as tolerant and humanitarian had the reverse effect: they provided ammunition to the populist Right's claim that the establishment suppressed the real concern of Danish people by denouncing them as expressions of racism.

Intensification of the Moral Panic around Refugees

As Hall and coauthors (1978: 16) argued, a moral panic is "when the media representations universally stress 'sudden and dramatic' increases (in numbers involved or event) and 'novelty,' above and beyond that which a sober, realistic appraisal could sustain," and a moral panic usually results in stricter laws against the group that constitutes the threat (Cohen 1972). However, as Noble (2012: 218) also points out, "A moral panic always entails an ensemble of social actors who compete in the definition of the 'problem.'" My argument has been that although the few editorials and feature stories generally insisted on a humanitarian approach, the news coverage was marked by a characterization of the situation as out of control for the reasons discussed above.

By the end of 1984, the debate on immigration had become so intense that in her annual New Year speech on the last day of 1984, Queen Margrethe felt obliged to scold Danes for being too negative about and unwelcoming to immigrants. She asked Danes to show solidarity with foreigners and help them adjust to Danish society. Despite an overwhelmingly positive reception of her speech by the media, the speech itself initiated a new round of debate.

The official descriptions of the situation as chaotic and out of control soon bore fruit when the panic atmosphere in the news convinced all parties (except the Progress Party) to introduce the first restrictions to the immigration law despite the rhetoric on Denmark's humanitarian responsibilities. The consistent distinction between "real refugees" and "convenience refugees" was instrumental in the shaping of the law. Uffe Ellemann-Jensen, the foreign minister from the Liberal Party, for example, emphasized Denmark's moral responsibility but simultaneously argued for a new law that clearly distinguished between the "real refugees" and the "not real" (*Berlingske Tidende*, January 15, 1984). While tightening the immigration law, the parties strongly condemned the Progress Party's explicit racism (Jensen 2000).

The first modification was made on the last day of May 1985 with the introduction of the so-called manifestly unfounded procedure. This amendment allowed a small committee of three members to view applications quickly and deny asylum without the application being sent through normal review process; moreover, those who were denied entry would not have access to an appeal process (Andreassen 2005; Jensen 2000; Østergaard 2007).

The relatively strict modifications of the law did not stop the debate from intensifying over the next year, although the picture became more complex. News coverage overall became more positive, stories featured more arguments for a humanitarian approach, and there was a corresponding increase in positive letters to the editor, which indicates that the "progressive" forces were becoming more and more concerned about the direction the debate was taking and engaging in writing commentaries and letters to the editor.

On the other hand, there were attacks on refugees by Danish youth during the summer of 1985. Although condemned across the political spectrum (except for the Progress Party), the attacks provided ammunition for arguments that "people's concern" was growing. Furthermore, the number of refugees knocking on the door did not drop; and Ninn-Hansen, his allies in the police, and others, including the other Conservative and Liberal Party MPs (the main coalition partners), began to press for more restrictions. To that end, they started to feed the media more than the daily reports of numbers. To signal the degree to which the situation had become uncontrollable and chaotic, the Danish Immigration Service set up a tent camp for a group of refugees in September 1986 even though several other institutions had offered accommodation for refugees (Østergaard 2007: 368). Despite the fact that the camp was never used to house refugees, it provided dramatic pictures of freezing refugees; military vehicles driving around; Red Cross leaders speaking of chaos, rain, and mud; and right-wing politicians who warned about mass migrations.

Although the picture had become more complex, the feeling of panic had reached a climax by the fall of 1986. The idea that the "influx of refugees" had to be reduced or stopped had almost become common sense, and there were only a few dissenting voices to this commonsense solution, but the calls for closing off the borders changed direction and became grounded in humanitarian arguments. As in 1984, the main sources for stories coded as "panic-creating stories" were politicians from the two government parties (including Ninn-Hansen), the police, and other government agencies. The Danish Red Cross, somewhat involved as a source of 1984 panic stories, however, became an important voice for the humanitarian argument of closing off the borders, advanced through persistent descriptions of refugee conditions as out of control. The leader of the Red Cross, Eigil Pedersen, described the situation as chaotic and called the government's proposal for temporary border closing "timely" and necessary. According to Pedersen, the existing open border laws were "beautiful but naive" (*Jyllands-Posten*, September 10, 1986), and the journalist's description of the "open border laws" reflected a new elite consensus that the refugee situation was out of control and that something had to be done. Municipal authorities tasked with helping the Red Cross find empty buildings to house refugees had also become a source for stories about accommodation problems.

Another development was the polarization of the media. Three national right-wing papers, *Berlingske Tidende*, *Jyllands-Posten*, and *BT*, became critical of the 1983 refugee laws, closing the gap between their news coverage and editorial postures. These papers did not desert the humanitarian perspective but turned it around to call for restrictions. A *Jyllands-Posten* editorial on September 16, 1986, entitled "Refugee Halt Is Urgent," began with the Association for Danish Refugee Friends' criticism of the government for "a degrading treatment of refugees that equals psychological torture," then used it as an argument for closing off the borders "in order to provide the refugees already in the country with better and more humane conditions." *Berlingske Tidende*'s line was similar: like government spokespersons, it cited a "mass migration" and asked for new restrictions (September 10, 1986). The call was based on two arguments: (1) neighboring countries such as Sweden and Germany had not followed Denmark's example and liberalized their immigration laws, which rendered Denmark more attractive for refugees; and (2) a restriction was in the interest of the refugees who had already managed to come to Denmark. If situation got out of control, it would lead to confrontations between refugees and Danes, *Berlingske* argued. The very scope of immigration made it difficult to treat refugees humanely.

These were the exact arguments of Ninn-Hansen, who called for a one-year halt to immigration (*Ekstra Bladet*, September 8, 1986). Ninn-Hansen argued that a moratorium would give the authorities time to find better accommodations and process accumulated asylum applications. The same arguments were advanced by Social Democrats to oppose Ninn-Hansen's moratorium proposal. Social Democratic spokesperson Ole Espersen cited a need for restrictions, not border closure, arguing that "as the situation has developed, we cannot just watch passively. [If we do that, we will end up] . . . introducing a panic-like measure for a complete stop" (*Jyllands-Posten*, October 11, 1986). Restrictions, in other words, would prevent extreme action on the very same problem: too many refugees. The formulation "as the situation has developed" indicated a tacit accept of the definition of the situation as uncontrollable. Thus, elite political disagreement was about the extent of the measures to be taken rather than the definition of the problem, although both sides now used humanitarian arguments. As will be seen below, this consensual basis was not to be found among ordinary newspaper readers who wrote letters to the editor.

It is easy to see how in the period between 1984 and 1986 the unavoidability of reducing numbers had been made into common sense through the repetition of panic stories. By the fall of 1986, the focus on the numbers of incoming refugees remained intense, and apocalyptic prognoses continued.

Ninn-Hansen declared on September 9, 1986, that if the trend continued, Denmark would be receiving 25,000 refugees a year (*Jyllands-Posten*, September 10, 1986), even though 10,318 refugees entered Denmark in all of 1984 and 1985, and not all of them were granted asylum (*Ekstra Bladet*, September 8, 1986).

The numbers argument was reinforced by stories about the impossibilities of accommodating refugees, the net impression being that the scope of the refugee "flow" was much larger than Denmark could manage. From September through November 1986, 70 stories about these challenges appeared in national newspapers. Almost half the sources for these stories were mayors and the Red Cross.

The sheer volume of the news stories reflects the intensity of focus in this period. Compared to the 30 news stories in September 1984 and 113 stories for August through November that year, in 1986, 236 news stories appeared in September, with a total of 568 for September through November. Story headlines still indicated "uncontrollable flow": "Ninn Wants to Close Off the Borders" (*Ekstra Bladet*, September 3, 1986), "Fear of Losing Control with Refugees" (*Jyllands-Posten*, September 4, 1986), "Refugee Export Is Proven" (*Jyllands-Posten*, September 5, 1986), "Red Cross Threatens with Leaving Refugee Chaos" (*Jyllands-Posten*, September 6, 1986), "Brakes on the Influx of Refugees" (*Berlingske Tidende*, September 10, 1986), "Police: Refugee Numbers Explode" (*Berlingske Tidende*, September 10, 1986), "[Police] Guarding the Border" (*Politiken*, September 12, 1986), "Few Refugees Are Rejected at the Border" (*Jyllands-Posten*, September 18, 1986), "The Government Wants to Close Refugees' Airport Route" (*Jyllands-Posten*, September 20, 1986), "Red Cross: Refugee Situation the Worst Ever" (*BT*, September 22, 1986), "Refugee Influx Breaks All Records" (*Jyllands-Posten*, September 23, 1986), and "Record Influx of Refugees in September" (*Berlingske Tidende*, September 29, 1986).

These stories were from national newspapers.[23] The local papers, of course, relied on local sources and local police officers, who not only provided numbers but also a particular perspective, often characterizing refugees as fakes and criminal elements. A story from *Fyens Stiftstidende* (September 6, 1986), for instance, was headlined: "The Magic Word Is 'Asylum' [*asyl* in Danish]: The Four Letters Are Better Than All Passes and Papers." It presented the perspective of an anonymous police officer who explained that many Lebanese and Palestinian refugees had already applied for or received asylum in Germany but came to Denmark to have "milk and honey" (i.e., the luxurious life). He said:

> If a person can just pronounce the word "asylum," we are whipped to put the whole system at work. . . . Several times I had the experience that refugees who could not explain what they wanted would come back and say the word "asylum. . . ." Politicians will not talk about this, and the police chiefs must not—or dare not. But the ordinary police officers . . . do sometimes ask if there is not something completely wrong with the Danish refugee laws.

Refugees or their perspectives, on the other hand, were hardly ever heard: in national press, I counted only 11 out of 903 stories in which the protagonist was a refugee or immigrant. When they were quoted, they were allowed to tell about their own experiences, but their story was usually framed by the perspectives of the local or national sources.

Such local stories about "convenience refugees" used eyewitness accounts to give concrete details describing what happened at the border—without saying much about refugees' actual reasons for entry into Denmark. In general, these stories offered no concrete detail that supported the idea that they had applied for or achieved asylum in Germany, or that they came to Denmark for better economic conditions. In the story above, the reporter saw passports showing the refugees had been in Germany prior to their arrival, nothing more. The story relied on the ethos of the police officer, built through rhetorical moves that placed him at the center of the events and enabled him to draw conclusions.

This distinction between real and convenience refugees was consistently made by police and government agencies, implying that many refugees did not need protection (Jensen 2000). The distinction was used by the government to promote further restrictions while sustaining a humanitarian rhetoric. Ninn-Hansen argued, for instance, that young Iranians were to be prevented from entering just because they were denied access to the university in Tehran (*Berlingske Tidende*, January 16, 1985).

This common sense that refugees had to be stopped from entering Denmark was clearly reflected in almost all stories in the right-wing media. However, if one side of the 1986 story is the negative press on refugees, the other side is the polarization among newspapers. Although there was less separation between editorials and news in the right-wing *Berlingske Tidende* and *Jyllands-Posten*, the situation was more complex for the liberal *Politiken* and the tabloids *BT* and *Ekstra Bladet*. Among the big three daily national newspapers (*Politiken*, *Jyllands-Posten*, and *Berlingske Tidende*), panic stories make the polarization clear. The number of panic stories in

1984 in the three newspapers were almost identical. In 1986, there is a clear difference (table 2.2).

TABLE 2.2. Changes in the Number of Panic Stories

Newspaper	1984	1986
Politiken	10	6
Berlingske T.	11	19
Jyllands-Posten	13	27
Ekstra Bladet	1	1
BT	4	4

These numbers indicate that the press had become more active in promoting its own agendas and perspectives. Right-wing papers *Berlingske Tidende* and *Jyllands-Posten* used the panic stories more deliberately. *Politiken*, on the other hand, offered stories to balance the negative information about refugees. Deportation stories, often about the tragic consequences of restrictive laws and practices and therefore more open to "positive" perspectives, are a good index of this. It is not surprising that *Politiken* had an overwhelmingly larger share of these stories, most of them coded "positive," whereas the few *Berlingske Tidende* and *Jyllands-Posten* stories were mostly negative (table 2.3).

TABLE 2.3. Positive Stories

Newspaper	Total	Positive
Politiken	29	25
Berlingske T.	6	2
Jyllands-Posten	12	4
Ekstra Bladet	4	4
BT	15	11

Although *BT*'s editorial line was closer to that of *Berlingske Tidende* and *Jyllands-Posten*, its deportation stories were more positive regarding refugees. In this aspect, *BT* was similar to *Ekstra Bladet*, whose editorial line was the most critical of the government of all newspapers in the sample. *Ekstra Bladet*, long positioning itself as the voice of "the little man" against the elite, in the mid-1980s chose to be the voice of refugees, including them within the definition of "the little man." This choice, and the sensationalist character of the paper, produced news stories that took a clear stand for refugees. The subtitle of the story "Ninn Wants to Close Off the Borders"

(*Ekstra Bladet*, September 3, 1986) reads, for instance, "Doors Closing for Refugees even Though We Have Space Enough," criticizing Ninn-Hansen's call for closing the border. The story listed the locations of empty buildings to which the state and municipal authorities had access and implied that Ninn-Hansen and immigration authorities lied about not being able to house the refugees. It also criticized the government's attempt to represent refugees as "convenience refugees" seeking better conditions by pointing out that a refugee had to live on 2,300 DKK (less than US$400) a month.

The intensification of concern about immigration is also apparent in letters to the editor. From September to November 1986, there were 213 letters to the editor, compared to 22 letters in the four-month sample from 1984. Again, there is a move toward the positive: 81.8 percent of writers were negative and only 13.1 percent positive toward refugees in 1984; 31.3 percent wrote positively in 1986, against 59.8 percent negatively. The same trend appeared in opinion polls showing that Danes' attitudes toward immigrants had become more positive in 1985. Bent Østergaard, a frequent commentator on immigration, gave credit to the influence of the humanitarian position when he attributed the attitude change to those media and political elites who spoke with one voice against "petite racism" ("Danish Refugee Policy," *Berlingske Tidende*, September 12, 1986).

Letters to the Editor: Distance between the Elite and the "People"

Two important themes emerged in letters to the editor in 1986: refugees as an economic burden and the insensitivity of the political elite to people's concerns. These themes came up in various concrete arguments that appear incoherent at an analytical level but, in their local contexts, function to support the main argument. Arguments and ideas are not related to one another through a universal logic but, once introduced into discourse, take on a life of their own, connected through an articulatory logic within the heterogeneity of the social, where the constant battle for hegemony enlists the same flexible elements of discourse for different, sometimes contradictory, ends.

For example, one letter might argue that refugees are an economic burden in a society that cannot even provide housing to its own people, such as Danish squatters (referred to as BZ youth), although in the context of another letter squatters (BZs) would be described as a threat to the cohesiveness of Danish society. Some letters called for a stop to refugee immigration by repeating Ninn-Hansen's argument about failure to provide humanitarian conditions, whereas others would accuse the government of discriminating against Danes in favor of refugees: "While we can be proud of our refugee policy, can we also be proud of the way we treat our elderly, [who] have through their work and taxes contributed to society and now when they need help, we fail them?" ("Racists?" *Kristeligt Dagblad*, September 11, 1986). Arguments about the burden of providing for refugees were often supported with facts from the media, such as how much refugees cost the Danish state. The burden theme gained additional power when linked to the distinction between real and convenience refugees presented in the press. Letters describing refugees as an economic burden often also identified them as "convenience refugees" who came to Denmark to share wealth that they had not built. Several readers preferred, they wrote, to support real refugees in Afghanistan or Africa instead of those who could afford to come to Europe. The idea that unlimited resources were channeled to refugees while people who had contributed to the nation's wealth suffered became a powerful discursive moment for voicing opposition to the political establishment in an environment of profound anxiety about the reductions to welfare benefits, a wage freeze, and job insecurity.

These attempts to qualify the priority of Danes indicate readers' orientations toward a public political discourse that repeatedly emphasized Denmark's moral responsibilities and humanitarian principles, as if the humanitarian perspective was a substantial part of Danish character. Rather than directly challenging the moral responsibility perspective, letter writers often mobilized a rhetoric that positioned refugees as people without a need for the humanitarian protection they received in preference to native Danes. Although such us/them (wealth creators / wealth stealers) distinctions in 1986 sometimes moved toward a signifying structure of Danes versus alien immigrants, the distinction was uneven and not fundamentally culturalized. Race, religion, and culture appeared in letters as rhetorical resources rather than central categories that characterized the ontological structure of society. Iranian refugees could be described as Muslims with fanatic ideas and as secular people fleeing Islamic fundamentalism. In only 14 of 214 letters to the editor in 1986 was culture the main explanatory frame. A year later, the number was slightly higher, 29 out of 215 but still insignificant compared to 2001's total of 53 out of 149. Nonetheless, this discursive constellation of aliens, Danes, and welfare had begun to open up space for a rearticulation of social identities with reference to culture rather than class and to make imaginable a link between the Danish state's welfare system and ethnic access.

It is not surprising, therefore, that letters to the editor included explicit critiques of the political elite who channeled resources to refugees while being deaf to the voice of ordinary people. The criticism was mostly directed at the centrist parties, the Social Democrats, the intelligentsia, and the Danish Refugee Council, although it was frequently generalized to all politicians and intellectuals under the umbrella of "upper Denmark." For instance, letters in *Aktuelt*—the only party-affiliated newspaper in Denmark published by the labor unions—from workers, employed or unemployed,[24] did not agree with the paper's obeisance to the Social Democrats' humanitarian refugee policy. One response to the queen scolding Danes for intolerance to foreigners called her "a right-wing-oriented, high-class lady who patronized people. I am an old working-class woman, and I see a lot of young Danes who wander around without job, education, housing, or even a hope for a future. Are they not a kind of refugee?" (January 6, 1985). Another letter opined: "You hear that an Iranian refugee cost 100,000 kroner, that is, more than the double the cost of a retiree whom nobody cares about, whose teeth fall out of one's mouth. The authorities are about to make us racists in Schlüter's [Conservative prime minister] Denmark" (January 8, 1985).

Such readers, however, also expressed dislike for right-wing parties and positions that, coupled with the distance between *Aktuelt*'s editorial line and readers' sentiments, indexes a developing crisis of representation for working people who felt that they were no longer represented within the political system as they had once been by the Social Democratic Party. The letters expressed anxiety and anger in a fragmented and episodic way, drawing on various arguments, but fell short of articulating a social vision that might fill the representational void and restore order. In other words, there was a need for a radical vision that could articulate these concerns into a new social formation with a promise to restore order. That vision came from the populist Far Right, which disarticulated the traditional link between the "people" and the "workers." This dislocation destabilized the Social Democratic hegemony. If social identities are constructed in an antagonistic manner, the identity of what would come to be called the "Danish people" as a cultural unity was here given resources for such an antagonistic articulation through a political target: the cosmopolitan political and cultural elites[25] that opened the path to the destruction of the nation by letting Muslims overflow Denmark.

Moral panics can be useful for introducing more coercion into the equilibrium (e.g., more restrictive laws), but like other social phenomena, they cannot be controlled. Ninn-Hansen's deliberate strategy of creating a sense of chaos and despair by focusing on the numbers and the unsurmountable financial costs of refugees and by targeting the political majority had much greater implications for the political system than "merely" tightening the immigration law; his strategy helped create public animosity against the elites indifferent to ordinary, working Danish people's concerns and created a sense that people's interests were not represented by the political system. The discursive environment was fertile for an intervention by far-right forces. They successfully articulated the distance between the political/cultural establishment and the "people" as a political antagonism.

Populist Intervention

The populist Right's intervention came in the form of two similar newspaper ads in *Jyllands-Posten*, on September 21 and 28, 1984, paid for by a priest, Søren Krarup, who was also a columnist in the paper. Both ads, similar in content, called for boycotting a refugee donation campaign organized by the Danish Refugee Council. He asked people to turn the donation campaign into a referendum on the Danish refugee policy—a referendum that the politicians were denying "us," the Danish people.

What seemed to be as just another racist outburst by a right-wing extremist who was on the fringes of political discourse came at a such a fragile moment that it turned the moral panic around the refugees into a major crisis for the entire political, intellectual, and cultural establishment. His intervention had both an immediate and long-term impact on the political discourse.

However, Krarup never became the leader of a populist far-right party. Rather, his intervention created a moment that within a decade led to the formation of the Danish People's Party—one of the biggest and most influential populist far-right parties in Europe. Before I move on to analyzing the rhetorical strategies that turned Krarup's intervention into a transformative moment, I want to discuss what it means to represent the popular will and clarify how I use terms such as "Far Right" and "populism."

The first question to ask in this context is this: Can a single person have such an impact on political discourse that he sets a hegemonic transformation in motion? This question is related to another question about the nature of representation: Do "leaders" lead or represent the groups of people (crowds, mobs, constituencies, social classes, or the "people") and their "interests?" In democratic theory, leaders are conceived as representatives of various interests, and in a larger context, of the popular will. In Marxist theory, leaders represent social classes even if the classes are not aware of their own interests, which are determined by their place within the relations of production. Both theories conceive the groups (e.g., classes) and their "interests" as objectively measurable entities that exist prior to representation.

Krarup's own answer to this question may give some clues about this relationship. He wrote a book about the events around his boycott campaign in a diary format that was published a year after the controversy:

> We have a feeling that we are about to write a modest history of Denmark and mutter among ourselves about it. There is no reason to be too excited about it, but the Danish popular manifestation will not be without consequences. The present disastrous refugee law cannot survive the storm, something that the politicians are about to understand. We also receive news from Christiansborg [the parliament building]. Politicians pay attention to the commotion with anxiety. "Will they form a party?" they ask in the corridors of Christiansborg. We have a feeling that if we wanted, we could win several seats in the parliament. The same feeling probably haunts the politicians—not only the nonsocialists but also Social Democrats whose constituents we mostly hear from. . . . I included my phone number and address in the ad and now the storm has formed. We do not have time for anything else than talking on the phone. . . . And it is . . . downright liberated people we are speaking with. Some even cry on the phone. (Quoted in Engelbreth Larsen 2001: 13; my translation)

In this excerpt, Krarup makes a distinction between "we" as the small group of people who organized the boycott campaign and the manifestation of Danish "popular will." The distinction allows him to present himself as the leader and founder of a popular movement, but simultaneously describes the popular will as something already there, prior to his leadership, just silenced (hence the term he came to use later: "the silent majority," which has a rich history in populist discourse, e.g., George Wallace and Richard Nixon from the US, or Enoch Powell from the UK).

But as we have seen in the analysis of the letters to the editor, although many readers expressed concern about the refugees, there was no consensus about the nature of those concerns and the definition of the "political elite." Many readers simultaneously worried about the economic burden the refugees were imposing on Danes and expressed concern about Denmark's humanitarian responsibilities. The concern for the nation's future was not a prominent theme. The letters also blamed different parties for the chaotic situation. In other words, there was no single "popular will" readily accessible prior to the boycott campaign; the diverse, and at times contradictory, expressions of concern and anxiety were articulated into a coherent "popular will" by Krarup and company in the ads and the debate that followed. The "popular will" came into existence in the process of representation that retroactively articulated the interests of the "people" and the "leader" who claimed to represent those interests. As Laclau (2005: 99) argues, "The popular subject position does not simply *express* a unity of demands constituted outside and before itself, but is the decisive moment in establishing that unity."

This is a crucial point if we want to understand the hegemonic transformation that has taken place in Denmark (and elsewhere). In classical accounts of hegemony, classes—as defined by their role in economy—enter into an alliance and form a "historical bloc" with other classes even if it means modifying their own demands/interests. From a poststructuralist hegemony perspective, a hegemonic formation (i.e., historical bloc) does not consist of predefined classes; the identity of these "classes" is transformed in the process of the hegemonic displacement. In other words, it is not that the "working class" entered into new alliances; the identity of the "working class" has been transformed in the process that has reconfigured the ontological structure of society from class to culture as the basis for social division. In this sense, it is not that cultural cleavage dimension has come to the forefront while the basic ontology of the social has remained intact (as many scholars of the populist Right seem to assume).

Populism and the Far Right

What is remarkable in Krarup's own account is his description of people's emotional reaction to the boycott campaign as one of being liberated. As Mudde (2004: 546), one of the prominent scholars of populism, argues, "Populists [claim to] speak in the name of the 'oppressed people,' and they want to emancipate them by making them aware of their oppression." Another populist notion clear in his account is the dichotomy between the "people" and the politicians who are out of sync with the people's demands. Although there is no agreement on what populism is, most scholars agree that populism is based on a dichotomy between some notion of people pure and uncorrupt, and some elites that are alien, corrupt, or debased. Taggart (2000) sees the dichotomy being between the "heartland" and the margins, whereas Mudde (2004: 543) and Mudde and Kaltwasser (2013) define populism as an ideology that separates groups into two homogeneous and antagonistic camps, "the pure people" versus "the corrupt elite," and argues that politics should be an expression of the collective will of the people. Nonpopulist movements or leaders also talk about "people," but the main characteristic of populism is the antagonistic relationship (i.e., "us" versus "them") between the "people" and its "other."

Although scholars agree on the centrality of dichotomous division in social space, they have different conceptualizations of populism. Some scholars consider populism to be an ideology (i.e., a bundle of loosely interrelated ideas), whereas others see it as a political strategy focusing on forms of mobilization and organization, and still others see it as a political style—mode of articulation—that divides the political space into two antagonistic camps while the specific content (i.e., the identities) of those camps "varies in accordance with the different ways this antagonistic relationship is defined" (Panizza 2005: 4). The ambiguity of the term "populism" is partly related to the third definition—the variations of populism across geographies, historical periods, and political spectrum (left and right)—as well as the fact that it is an analytical attribution (or just a negative label), not a term that most political actors would use about themselves. What complicates the use of the term further is the fact that in modern politics every political speech appeals to the people or claims to speak for the people, which makes it difficult to distinguish populist from nonpopulist discourse. Moreover, as many scholars have noted, many mainstream parties in Europe have adopted populist rhetoric, which, in my case, indicates the hegemony of the populist vision.

There is a consensus that in Western Europe most of the populist parties belong to the right wing of the traditional political spectrum; they all have anti-Muslim immigration at the center of their focus and they generally participate in the electoral process; except for some small extremist groups that operate outside the parliamentary system. There are also disagreements about whether they should be considered as part of the democratic system or as a threat against democracy.

I use the term "populist Far Right" because the populist right-wing parties and movements typically place themselves to the right of the mainstream Right in terms of their nationalist, nativist, and racist views. Their members are often recruited from extremist right-wing groups even if they put a damper on extremist rhetoric. The Left is always at the top of their enemy list. But as with "populism," populist right-wing parties do not use the ideological template of a left-right division, which is in line with their own understanding of the simplified division between the homogeneous "people" and its antagonistic "other," which, they argue, transcends politics as such (Lowndes 2005: 146). If we accept that there is no ultimate meaning to the notion of people, and that its meaning and homogeneity is determined by its antagonistic relationship with the external other, then the characterization of the threat retroactively determines the political character of the people. Because Islam and Muslim immigrants are the "real" political target of the most populist parties in Europe, in their mobilization against Islam and

Muslim immigration the far-right populist forces have increasingly become defenders of not only the welfare state (albeit only for the ethnic majority) but also gender equality, gay rights, animal rights, and secularism, which has the effect of transforming their own political identity. This also complicates where to place them on the traditional left-right continuum. Despite these complications, there is almost no disagreement among scholars that they belong to the right wing of the political spectrum.

The proposition that "the divide between the people and its 'other' defines the political nature of populism" and "it is through antagonism that political identities are constituted" (Panizza 2005: 28) does not sufficiently address the question of who the antagonistic other is: there is a general agreement on the centrality of Muslim immigration as the political target in populist discourse (Meret 2011),[26] and it is easily articulated with antiglobalization and anti–European Union sentiments. But there is also an agreement that populist parties and movements dichotomize the political space between the "people" as underdogs and the corrupt political elites, as was the case with Krarup's ads (as I will show in the next chapter): he clearly targeted the political establishment even though the real threat was Muslim immigration. Although there is a general tendency in the literature to identify the antagonistic relationship as between the "people" and the "elite," this relationship needs to be qualified. The real culprit for the European populist Right is usually Islam; it is the presence of Muslim immigrants that prevents the people from achieving plenitude. The corrupt cosmopolitan political elites are treasonous collaborators with the enemy. They may be the antagonistic political targets, but the real antagonism is between the "people," which equals the nation as a harmonious cohesive force, and Muslims, who threaten the harmony and unity of the nation. The politicians are evil insofar as they do not prevent the Muslim invasion from happening or, at worst, because they facilitate it. This is why the populist right-wing parties can justify joining governing coalitions: to make sure that the evil is prevented from happening and restore order and reinstate the system to its original unity.

It is within this framework that I will analyze Krarup's political intervention at the peak of a true moral panic about immigration. As Laclau (2014: 176) argues, "A true political intervention is never merely oppositional; it is rather one that displaces the terms of the debate, that rearticulates the situation in a new configuration." I will now demonstrate how Krarup's intervention displaced the terms of the debate and rearticulated the situation in a new configuration.

CHAPTER 3

Rhetoric of the Hegemonic Intervention

Populist practices emerge out of the failure of the existing political institutions to restore social order during the times of crises. The failure, however, is not objectively given; populists intervene in political discourse by claiming that the system has failed in handling a crisis and that there is a radical alternative: ditching the extant political parties. Populists use a language of politics in which politics as usual is no longer possible. And they offer a new form of representation based on a new mode of identification that displaces the social borders that previously structured society; their political appeal seeks to redefine political frontiers (Panizza 2005).

The crisis of representation, which according to Laclau (2005: 137) is at the root of any populist, anti-institutional outburst, was clearly in embryonic form in the demands of the letter writers discussed in the last chapter. People's concerns were often expressed in terms of access to welfare at a time when the coalition government of the Conservatives and Liberals was trying to dismantle the social welfare system and the mainstream Left (i.e., the Social Democrats) had joined the Right in the idea that the "rationalization" of the economy was the solution (Mondon 2013; Betz and Meret 2013). Popular resentments about refugee policy and the political system were often articulated around the allocation of resources and access to welfare benefits. Many letter writers expressed disgust with politicians who wasted tax money on refugees rather than supporting Danish retirees, the unemployed, youth, or health care—all of which Danes had worked hard for—but many letter writers were nonetheless highly responsive to the humanitarian framework in which the question of refugees had been debated. Thus, it is not a straightforward task to conceptualize the resentment as the expression of a collective will with a shared core demand.

The letter writers' views of the immigration policy had a wide range: some expressed a concern about cultural harmony or the survival of Danish identity, some invoked Danishness as a trait inherently associated with tolerance, and some referred to those people whose taxes enabled the welfare system that politicians were now wasting on refugees. The future of national identity was one among other concerns that did not have a necessary and logical relationship with concerns about not getting a fair deal in the allocation of resources or with resentment about the neoliberal economic policies of the right-wing government. These various concerns were not always articulated as the related parts of the same struggle; on the contrary, they were often flexibly and creatively woven with arguments about the humane treatment of refugees and with diverse solutions of the problems. Anti-institutional resentment was also articulated in various directions: for some, it was the politicians from left and center parties; for Social Democrats, it was the right-wing coalition government; for others, it was the vague class of "politicians." As such, popular discourse was responsive to elite discourse—as conveyed by the preferred sources of the national press—rather than being an expression of an organized movement manifesting the popular will. The letters were certainly too heterogeneous to be an articulation of such a will whether conceptualized as an aggregation of different opinions or as a consensus formed through deliberative process.[1] It had to be articulated into existence by an intervening force that could inscribe the various demands in some kind of radical discourse.

Ninn-Hansen and his collaborators in the police and immigration service may not have intended to create a crisis of representation, but their attempts to create a sense of chaos and despair caused by uncontrollable immigration in order to force the political majority in the Folketing to intervene and tighten the immigration law had created an increasingly severe moral panic and destabilized an already fragile political environment by the fall 1986. The intervention, however, came from a far-right pastor, Søren Krarup, who was on the fringes of political discourse and outside the parliamentary system. Krarup targeted not only immigration laws but the entire political and cultural establishment, which he cast as cosmopolitan traitors "acting like a foreign occupation army" with no respect for the Danish people's concerns. He claimed that the political system no longer represented the popular will. His intervention displaced the terms of the debate and transformed the debate around refugees from being a question of economic burden or Denmark's humanitarian responsibilities into that of cultural threat. And it moved the focus of the debate from the refugees to the political establishment, and therefore the political representation.

The moral panic around refugees and Krarup's intervention occurred in an environment where the Social Democrats, having largely accepted the inevitability of a neoliberal agenda, had moved toward the center and were no long in a position to articulate dissatisfactions into a popular movement against neoliberalism. They were trapped between humanistic principles and the expressions of the ethnocentric welfarism of their constituency, and they were closely affiliated with the immigration laws that had become related to dissatisfactions with the systematic erosion of the welfare society. The radical Left was trapped between defending the principles of humanism and international solidarity and giving in to tangled strains of envy and indignation among working people. The Left was not an alternative but increasingly seemed to be part of the very system that had created the problems. If there was an opening to articulate the popular will and channel protests around a tangible social division, there was no political entity on the left to undertake the task.

As I indicated in the previous chapter, the impact of Krarup's intervention was both immediate and long lasting. In this chapter, I will be analyzing the rhetorical strategies that catapulted him into prominence and enabled him to define the terms on which immigration was discussed (i.e., his immediate impact) and the hegemonic articulation of the popular will around the signifier, the Danish people as defined by their opposition to Muslims and their enablers within the nation: the cultural and political elite—an articulation that reached a relatively stable and normalized status (i.e., the long-term impact).

September 21, 1986: A Rhetorical Intervention

The populist-style intervention came from a well-known right-wing columnist. On September 21 and September 29, 1986, Krarup placed advertisements in the right-wing newspaper *Jyllands-Posten* (where he was a regular columnist), calling upon Danes to boycott Refugee 86, the donation campaign organized by the Danish Refugee Council (DRC), and to effectively turn the campaign into a referendum on Denmark's immigration policy.[2]

The ad that ran on September 21, 1986, was a head-on confrontation with the DRC and Danish refugee policy. He accused the DRC of ruining the fatherland; of running the country like a dictatorial shadow government by imposing its laws in the Folketing; of terrorizing public debate; and of draining the treasury. He claimed that the DRC wanted to silence the Danish people's voice and stop them from expressing their concerns about the uncontrolled and unconstrained immigration of Muslims, which would destroy the nation and turn it into a Lebanon torn by wars between minority groups. He compared the DRC to an occupation force in a foreign country that had taken a position against the Danes, who were rightly concerned about the future of their country. In the footnotes to the ad, he explained that he chose to insert the article as a paid ad (rather than in his regular column) to have greater striking power. He hoped that people would turn Refugee 86 into a referendum on the refugee policy by contributing to another ad that he intended to run the following Sunday.

The next ad was similar in its essence: it claimed that the door to Denmark was wide open and the political and cultural elites that let the door stay open were destroying the nation. This time his target was not only the DRC but the entire political and cultural establishment. He also addressed some of the responses to the first ad, including charges of racism. He turned the accusation upside down and used the charges of racism as an indication that the DRC did not respect the people. He once more called for a boycott of the aid collection to turn it into a popular protest.

In the footnotes to the second ad, Krarup thanked people for the support and approval he received, which he said confirmed his assumption that the people felt terrorized by the refugee policy's powerful advocates. He also announced the formation of a committee against refugee laws and named the members (a small group consisting of his family members, friends, and affiliates).

The effects of the ads were immediate. The ads and the following fulmination immediately catapulted him into the center of the debate on refugees and consequently opened the channels of discourse to him. The media coverage was extensive. The ads were covered in all newspapers; having sensed a huge controversy, reporters began to collect reactions to the ad campaign from all quarters.

The day the ad was published, an avalanche of complaints flowed into various institutions: the Association for Danish Refugee Friends as well as pastors and individuals complained to the church minister and to the bishop as the head of the church. The next day, Krarup was reported to the police for racism by a pastor.

The media's coverage of the ads and reactions to them was so intense that although only a few people had seen the ads, the entire population knew Krarup's arguments within a couple of days after the first ad ran. He received an incredible amount of attention and space to promote his arguments, even if mostly in a negative light. Although *Ekstra Bladet* headlined "Now Krarup Runs Amuck" and called him "the right-wing extremist priest" (September

23, 1986), *DR TV*, the only TV channel at that time, invited him to a prime-time debate with the chairman of the DRC three days after the first ad; the debate was covered by the entire media the following day.

The crucial ideological element in Krarup's intervention, I argue, was articulating feelings of envy and indignation against refugees around the empty cultural signifier "the Danish people." "The people" were defined by their concerns about the future of their being as a nation, and this articulation changed the direction of the debate on immigration from economic burden to national identity and its future survival.

As powerful as the change of rhetorical direction were the new links Krarup forged among diverse and often contradictory arguments, concerns, and demands as instances of a popular will. What bound all these fragmented arguments, concerns, and demands into a unity was the articulation of a singular popular will. The particular arguments, concerns, or demands did not matter: they were all expressions of the concerns that "the people" had about the future of their nation, concerns that were being ignored by the treasonous political and cultural elite. The empty signifier "Danish people" forged a link between all of the concerns and demands. The antagonism between the Danish people and their adversaries (i.e., the political/intellectual elite and the alien intruders) operated as the key that made the disintegration of the nation—and the inevitability of national recovery—intelligible. This articulation promised a solution to the major problems of "society" by overcoming the chaos and reinstating order. For many working-class people, it was no longer a question of getting rid of the right-wing government and its neoliberal policies but reinstating the unity of the Danish nation, which would prevent the wasting of resources on Muslim "aliens" who did not belong. The intervention itself was the decisive moment in establishing that unity. This is the significance of his intervention, which explains his impact on the direction of "history."

Søren Krarup was born in December 1937. His father, also a pastor, had been involved in the resistance during the Nazi occupation of Denmark. Krarup described his father's involvement in the resistance against the German occupation as formative for him and compared his father's involvement to his own 1986 campaign, which he described as the new resistance movement against a political and intellectual elite who had become "a foreign occupation power" (Engelbreth Larsen 2001).

His father's influence also came from his position as an important figure in a religious movement represented by the journal *Tidehverv* (*Epoch*), which argued against humanism in religion. Under the influence of his father, Krarup studied theology and became a Lutheran pastor and the coeditor of *Tidehverv* in 1965. For *Tidehverv*, the main enemy is humanism and all forms of idealism that take issue with injustice. According to the journal, the idea of human rights is a substitute religion alien to the basic Christian spirit of the Danish nation. Injustice, according to Krarup, is God's reality, which cannot be changed through political or social action. Justice will be taken care of by God. The Christian commandment "Love thy neighbor" is impossible and against human nature. Christianity is not a sentimental religion, but humanism makes it look so (Engelbreth Larsen 2001: 15). Because evangelism comes first as the defining element of Danish culture, the task of state power and the democratic system is to protect it. If there is a conflict between state power and evangelism, one should stand against power. Krarup has always been critical of both what he called the degeneration of national feeling and the power of political parties because it has grown at the expense of the people. Treasonous immigration and European Union policies, he maintained, were the result of the political parties' dominion.

By the time his ads were published, he had already written eighteen books following his first, *Harald Nielsen og Hans Tid* (*Harald Nielsen and His Time*, 1960), including *Begrebet Anstændighed* (*The Concept of Decency*, 1985) and *I Virkeligheden* (*In Reality*, 1986). The year after the ads, he published *Det Tavse Flertal* (*The Silent Majority*, 1987), which elaborated one of the central terms of his populist intervention. His last book is a celebration of his life achievement: *Systemskiftet* (*The System Change*, 2006). He has written regular columns (for the right-wing *Jyllands-Posten* and the tabloid *Ekstra Bladet*) and countless commentaries in Danish newspapers. Krarup had been a sharp voice, notorious for pointed and provocative language. He was called a "discussion butcher" with whom it was spiritual "hara-kiri" to engage (*Berlingske Tidende*, September 27, 1986). In his books, columns, and commentaries, Krarup castigated the welfare system, women's movements (the "lady cause," as he put it),[3] democratism (*sic*!), the European Common Market, and European integration, and promoted the right to chastise children, which he called self-defense. He raged against permissiveness and in this regard considered his mortal enemies to be political parties, human rights ideologists, psychologists, pedagogues, experts, and social workers (often mentioned as a general category of "managers"). Krarup was routinely placed on the extreme right of the political spectrum by his opponents (*Politiken*, September 25, 1986; *Berlingske Tidende*, September 27, 1986), and his appeal was seen as generally limited to religious audiences and right-wing intellectuals. As can be seen, his populist style was informed by his ideological background.

Right Time, "Wrong Target," and Appropriate Rhetoric: Gaining Access to Discourse

If similar ideas, even if in a fragmented and episodic manner, were already expressed and "the popular will" was invoked in discourse prior to his ad campaign, why did these particular ads gain ground at this juncture? In other words, what catapulted him to prominence?

Part of the answer is the extent of the moral panic that was created around refugees. Krarup's timing was, therefore, crucial. His challenge came at a time when there was an unvoiced consensus among politicians and in the media that the refugee situation was out of control and opposition parties were signaling their willingness to enforce measures to stop the continuing "flow" of refugees despite the radical measures introduced in 1985.

Part of the answer was his choice of target. Krarup had been arguing against the immigration laws in his *Jyllands-Posten* columns and was already known for his uncompromising language against opponents. But his columns were one voice in a sea of voices. It was his choice of medium (newspaper ads that asked for donations) and the target of the boycott that made him immediately notorious in 1986. He shockingly demonized what had been a harmless, humanitarian donation campaign sponsored by the DRC. The timing, the medium, and the choice of target gave him a visibility that he had not had through his writings. In short, what catapulted him into such prominence in public debate was the combination of the moral panic and his rhetorical skills to cut through at the right time, at the right place, with the right "speech."

Berlingske Tidende's portrait of Krarup (September 27, 1986) described the situation immediately before his newspaper ads as one in which Danes "were routinely about to delve into their wallets to buy some good conscience from the Refugee 86 collectors. Until the infamous ad, the greatest concern was if the collector would ring the doorbell in the middle of a Marilyn Monroe movie on TV." Suddenly, there was this man who claimed that the DRC was running the country as a shadow government/terrorist organization, an occupying force targeting the Danish people, that it was about to turn Denmark into Lebanon, that the Danes were in danger of annihilation as a people, and that it was altogether the fault of the politicians who let—or helped—it happen.

Rhetorical Strategies

Krarup's strategy was simple but effective: creating the greatest possible controversy, which gave him full access, even if negatively, to the debate on immigration. His call for a boycott of Refugee 86 was an effective tool for his showdown with the immigration laws and a head-on collision with the political and cultural elite, which he called "upper Denmark." He was the voice of the "silent majority."[4] And as expected, the establishment reacted furiously.

Krarup's ads pursued four interrelated rhetorical strategies:[5] (1) choosing the right time; (2) creating a new controversy as a way of opening up the discourse for himself as a central protagonist; (3) constructing a silent majority ("the people") through his claims about censorship and casting himself in the role of an organic intellectual[6] who speaks on their behalf, represents their concerns, and tells the truth; and (4) in the opening made by the discursive destabilization, gaining broad acquiescence to his premises as the basis for future discussions through the role he assigned himself as the "spokesperson" of the Danish people. Krarup articulated three main claims that became the tacit premises for the following debate: the future of the nation was the primary worry of the Danish "people"; alien Muslim immigrants posed a real threat to the Danish nation; and there was a gap between "the people" and their political representatives, who promoted the alien Muslims' interests. All of these claims were based on a single premise: the existence of a clearly identifiable popular will through the signifier "the Danish people." Once this basic premise and the three main claims were accepted, the path to articulating a counterhegemonic social formation was wide open.

Timing

As I argued in chapter 2, Krarup's timing was crucial: he intervened at the peak of a moral panic that had already destabilized the political discourse. As noted above, populist intervention emerges in a time of crisis during which there is a widespread sentiment that the system has failed. Moreover, that failure is not a given: populist actors often claim that the system has failed and there is a radical alternative. Even before the ads appeared, there was some unease that the popular resentment against refugees might harm the fundraising campaign. The head of the Refugee 86 campaign, Finn Slumstrup, acknowledged that resentment against refugees might have negative effects on the campaign and felt it necessary to make clear that the refugee policy and the fundraising campaign were not related (*Politiken*, September 21, 1986). *Jyllands-Posten*'s story the day before the Krarup's ad expressed the same sentiment: "Refugee Debate May Harm the Collection" (September 20, 1986).

Krarup's intervention came at a fragile moment and used the moral panic around refugees as evidence that the system did not work. His call for boycott moved the focus of the debate from the refugees to political representation of the popular will.

The power of this kind of intervention in discourse lies as much in its timing as its radical vision in answering some of the most pressing questions concerning political representation. Although the media's response to Krarup's boycott campaign was fierce, they continued running daily stories about the "inflow" of refugees. The day after the infamous ad, *Jyllands-Posten* wrote: "The pressure on asylum centers has grown so alarming during the last 24 hours that the Red Cross describes the situation as the worst ever" (September 22, 1986). *Berlingske Tidende* again brought the panic onto the front page: "Record: 1,700 Refugees This Month" (September 23, 1986). According to another story in the same newspaper, the Red Cross had lost fifteen thousand members, who had resigned as a protest against refugees in 1986 (September 22, 1986). A meeting between Ninn-Hansen and the Danish Red Cross was reported with headline "Crisis Meeting: No More Place for Refugees" (*Jyllands-Posten*, September 29, 1986). The government and opposition were negotiating about introducing new restrictions to refugee laws, even though the Social Democrats had reservations about imposing serious restrictions on the right to access to apply for asylum. Krarup was, in other words, the right man at the right time in the right place to use the moral panic, not to just promote restrictions to immigration laws but to articulate the panic and anxieties as expressions of the popular will.

Creating Controversy as a Way of Entering Discourse as a Central Figure

Refugee 86 was the right target if controversy was what Krarup intended. Not only did he rage against an organization that was relatively nonpolitical (its primary function was to help refugees to integrate into society *after* they had achieved refugee status), the organization did not have anything to do with the government's refugee or immigration policies. Moreover, the DRC was constituted by a number of humanitarian organizations and therefore represented the consensual, nonpoliticized nature of the humanitarian viewpoint. The Refugee 86 donation campaign raised funds for refugees abroad, a purely humanitarian effort and was not connected to the refugee policy in Denmark. Targeting Refugee 86 challenged the humanitarian image of Denmark itself. It seemed inevitable that it would create a feeling of animosity against Krarup.

The crucial difference between what Krarup articulated and what the ordinary Dane he purported to represent in his ad might have said or written was the articulation of the main problem. Most letters to the editor had associated refugees with economic problems. Krarup mentioned economic problems only as part of a bigger problem: that the establishment was not listening to the concerns of the Danish people. He boldly redefined the political terrain by directing attention to what he represented as popular resistance to a tyrannical hegemonic political center symbolized by Refugee 86.

The destabilizing effectiveness of this rhetorical strategy was evident immediately. Media coverage was extensive although not favorable to Krarup. He received an incredible amount of attention and space to disseminate his arguments; most newspaper stories published excerpts from the ad and interviewed him, allowing him to elaborate on his views while simultaneously attacking him. The reaction by the media and the intellectual and political elite was fierce and contemptuous: the tabloid *Ekstra Bladet* called him "Black Søren" and "the apostle of hate"; an editorial in the paper described its reactions to Krarup as "vomiting feelings"; *BT*'s headline was "Krarup Is on a Crusade against Refugees." The intellectual daily *Information* titled its editorial in a similar manner "Krarup's Crusade," in which he was described as being possessed by an evil spirit. *Politiken*'s portrait of him had the title "The Dangerous Priest." The mayor of Århus, the second largest city in Denmark, Thorkild Simonsen, described the campaign as "petite racism." Paul Hammerich, a well-known writer, described Krarup's "silent majority" as a "cartoon team." In the following weeks, he was the man mentioned most in the media.[7] Thus, Krarup became the principal participant in a public controversy he created.

Krarup's ads suggested the simple, everyday act of answering the door and saying a polite no could turn into an important political act of protesting the refugee policy and the political establishment. This image terrified and galvanized his opponents, who feared that people would actually do this. The fear of this possibility brought together organizations and individuals from across the political, economic, and social spectrum. The queen declared her support for the campaign, whereas the foreign minister, Liberal Party leader, and member of the governing coalition with the Conservative Party Uffe Elleman-Jensen signed up as a Refugee 86 collector. The Confederation of Labor Unions (LA) and Danish Employers Association (DA) supported

Refugee 86 with full-page ads in seven daily newspapers over three days. The Industry Council and the Association for Municipalities also put counter-ads in newspapers. Many churches (Lutheran, Catholic, Baptist, Methodist) published alternative announcements in which they declared support for the fundraising campaign. Three hundred and fifty well-known writers, artists, and actors condemned Krarup's call for a boycott and offered to perform in support of Refugee 86. Every newspaper urged people to volunteer and to donate. The government donated 7 million kroner. Never in Danish history was there a mobilization of this magnitude for a single cause. Against them stood a lone priest.

In short, the anti-Muslim, nationalist statements by Krarup "were interpreted by majority parties, by the Left, by the press, and by much of the Danish intelligentsia as manifestations of xenophobia and racism, if not pure pathology. The laments of the Right about the 'threat to Danishness' were seen as incoherent articulations by individuals who were uninformed, manipulated, 'racist' or simply 'crazy'" (Sampson 1995: 59).

The attacks and accusations of racism did not scare Krarup; on the contrary, he turned these accusations around and used them in his counter-attack. He specified that he was not against refugees but the DRC—the organization that "terrorized" the Danish people. He sued the mayor of Århus for calling his campaign "petite racism," not because he was sensitive or revengeful but because it was a principal case through which "I would, once for all, like to have the loathsome and terrorist term of abuse 'racism' banished from public debate as a tool to bring to heel and to bully the other side" ("Report from the Battleground," *Jyllands-Posten*, October 4, 1986).

In both ads, a crucial thread is what cannot be said: "The Refugee Council wants to forbid us Danes to speak"; "Thor A. Bak [leader of the DRC], commented on [Mogens Glistrup, leader of the Progress Party], 'Coop him up!'" The suppression of ordinary people's real concerns, whatever they may be, is stated as fact. In the second ad, Krarup emphasized this point by stating that the charge of racism is a way for those in power to ignore and blame ordinary people for having unspeakable concerns for being "unrepresentable." In this way, the attacks and accusations of racism against Krarup had the reverse effect: they not only put him into the role of martyr but also proved his point that anybody who expressed dissent against the political and cultural establishment would be bullied. In other words, racism was a tool the authoritarian elite used to suppress people's expression of dissent. His intervention had also the effect of legitimizing racist utterances. It was not shameful to express those concerns; on the contrary, suppressing the discussion about those concerns was a shameful, dangerous, and treasonous act. This was his rhetorical strategy in polarizing society—galvanizing resentment against immigration policy and channeling it into a general dissent against the political establishment.

The attacks helped Krarup establish himself as the daring spokesperson for "the people" whose views were suppressed, but this was a double move typical in populist rhetoric: Krarup constructed for himself a double identity as a member of that terrorized group of Danish citizens ("a dictatorial Refugee Council that speaks to us as if we are dogs" and "snaps its fingers at our concerns") and a man apart from it, an intellectual with a clear diagnosis and correct responsive action. This double positioning allowed him to echo a sense of injury while distancing himself somewhat from the vernacular discourse of ordinary Danes in order to articulate on their behalf their silenced "thoughts and concerns" in a coherent, action-oriented political position. He therefore appeared rhetorically representing a silent Danish majority, speaking on the same level as (but not to) other elites, those isolated from the realities of ordinary people. He appeared simultaneously as a man both of and above the people, equal to those he targeted—an "organic intellectual."

Constructing a New Cultural Subject, the Danish People, through the Metaphor of Silent Majority

As I have argued, Krarup's intervention came at a fragile political moment, when it was difficult to argue openly against the idea that Krarup was expressing what everybody else was suppressing. His definition of refugees as a threat to the nation did not contradict widespread feelings expressed through attacks on refugees, letters to the editor, or opinion polls that indicated that people felt that refugees were taking resources from Danes. On the contrary, it welded the two.

An interesting analytical observation is that Krarup focused on the silencing of people's concerns and did not engage in an argument about the silent majority and the nature of its concerns but presented these as given and therefore as a basis for further discussion. His avoidance, in fact, had a greater rhetorical effect: any discourse about reality is at the same time an attempt to undermine alternative claims about reality, or in Mercer's words, "The struggle for hegemony at the level of discourse begins with the struggle to render 'unthinkable' the versions of reality put forward by one's opponents" (Mercer 1990: 206). One of the most effective ways of dealing with potential alternatives is to force one's definition of the reality as the basis for further discussion. In this case, not only did his opponents avoid challenging

Krarup about his definition of reality, they also seemed to tacitly accept the claim that people were concerned about the invasion of their country. By tacitly accepting it, they also confirmed that the people's worries were not being considered.

How could they challenge him? The government had already been pressing the debate in the same direction in order to create a moral panic with the result that opinion polls were indicating the unpopularity of the immigration laws. Krarup's intervention, which redirected these sentiments against the entire establishment, caught them by surprise and pushed them into a defensive position.

The controversy that Krarup created was crucial for enabling the constitution of a "popular will" embodied in the Danish people, a category of indeterminate meaning that, as shown in chapter 1, functions as an empty signifier. In order to fix—however temporarily—the meaning of a social formation such as the "Danish people," it is necessary to think about society as two irreducible camps structured around two incompatible sets of values. A radical frontier implies a broken space, a gap in the harmonious continuity of the social. "There is a fullness of the community which is missing. This is decisive: the construction of the 'people' will be the attempt to give a name to that absent fullness" (Laclau 2005: 85). What Laclau describes as "absent fullness" was clearly articulated by Krarup in the first ad: "if an uncontrolled and unconstrained mass migration of Mohammedan and Oriental refugees comes through our borders, then we cannot be here ourselves—in any case not in naturalness and peace. The Danish Refugee Council has tremendously damaged our fatherland."

Krarup used the fierce reaction to the ads by the political and cultural elite as an evidence for this broken space between the popular will and its oppressors represented by the DRC and its collaborators within the political and cultural establishment. The unity of the Danish people could no longer be sustained because of open borders, which allowed culturally alien immigrants to flood Denmark, putting its very existence as a nation in jeopardy.

Krarup actively fanned the antagonism through his rhetoric, invoking "an occupation army in a foreign country" allowing "Mohammedan" refugees to invade Denmark. He conjured up World War II, when "the entire people united in a newly awakened but immemorial love that the Germans were about to take from us" (*Jyllands-Posten*, October 4, 1986), a mythical predecessor resistance movement imagined during the postwar national healing process.[8] The identification helped construct the antagonistic relationship between good and evil, and between the people and the elite who let evil happen. The reference to the resistance movement rendered political differences more than mere differences that can be contained within the differential system of one social formation. The reference alluded to an unbridgeable gap between the Danish people and its political representatives who chose to ally themselves with the Muslim invaders. Krarup did not focus on the invader and said nothing about "them."

The alien invader is a powerful metaphor for constructing an "us" without having to define with any precision what we are. "We" becomes fantasy, an empty space. It signifies our incompatibility with the alien. The metaphor also allows for the emptiness of the opposite camp; we do not need racist designations to know what they are; we do not need to describe them as inferior. On the contrary, their superiority/inferiority is ambiguous because they could annihilate us. What is important is the incompatible nature: "we" and "they." This rhetorical move allowed Krarup to sidestep to some degree the particular epithets that signal racism and xenophobia in the vernacular discourse.

Gaining Acquiescence to His Premises

The fierce reaction to Krarup's attack on Refugee 86 came not only as a response to the derangement of his characterization of the fundraising campaign but from an awareness that his call to action might affect the fundraising goals and that a failure could be interpreted as popular support for his claim that the political system was out of sync with the people it was supposed to represent. His opponents therefore made the success of Refugee 86 the immediate goal. Thus, Krarup's first ad created more than a controversy. It staged a battle. Krarup's opponents did, for tactical reasons, what they were trying to avoid: they accepted Refugee 86 as the battleground over immigration. He was challenged not on his basic claims about people's concerns and their inaudibility but on what appeared to be the weak link in his logic: the false equation between Refugee 86 and Danish refugee policy. This equation had to be challenged.

The core response was simple: Refugee 86 donations would go to refugees abroad, not to refugees entering Denmark. DRC chair Thor A. Bak stated in an interview the day after Krarup's first ad that "it is probably correct that people are not happy about the refugee influx to Denmark, but then they should be much more willing to contribute to refugee help whose task is to help refugees out in the world" (*Berlingske Tidende*, September 22, 1986). Gitte Wedersøe, secretary for Refugee 86, was even clearer: "We do not support people in Denmark. Danes who are fed up with refugees should be even more motivated to support Refugee 86. For the better the conditions are for refugees in their homeland, the fewer will have to come here" (*BT*, September 22, 1986). Mimi Stilling Jacobsen, leader of the Center Democrats, also argued against the linkage between refugee laws and Refugee 86: "Those who are in deep disagreement with Denmark's existing refugee laws . . . can therefore safely contribute" (*Ekstra Bladet*, September 26, 1986). *Berlingske Tidende* assured its readers that money for refugees was not a referendum on Danish immigration laws: "On the contrary, the government with its proposal, which will probably be supported by Social Democrats, . . . has already made it clear that the immigration law is going to be tightened. The collection today will not have any influence on the . . . new law, which is going to limit the number of refugees coming to Denmark" (October 5, 1986). *Ekstra Bladet*'s editorial explained: "It is a good trick to support the collection because those who through voluntary Danish donations achieve a reasonable existence at a faraway place will hardly come to Denmark!" (September 30, 1986).

These positions were, like Krarup's own, elaborated and supported with humanitarian arguments subordinated to the main point. In addition to helping refugees stay elsewhere, contributions were a humanitarian gesture for people entitled to protection and care. Thus, humanitarianism remained intact, but keeping refugees away became a powerful tactical move to stop Krarup from making his call to action a referendum on Denmark's refugee policy and on the political representation of the popular will.

Thus, although Krarup's opponents seemed to have the upper hand in terms of mobilization, they were in fact pushed into a corner. The only viable, short-term strategy for securing support for the collection seemed to depend on the distinction between Refugee 86 and the Danish refugee laws. The sentiment was that because Krarup made Refugee 86 into a referendum on the legitimacy of political representation by claiming an unbridgeable gap between the rulers and the ruled, the collection campaign had become too important to fail. In this sense, it did not matter whether there was a logical connection between Refugee 86 and refugee laws: Krarup made the connection, and if the collection campaign failed, it would be understood as a confirmation of what he had been claiming—the existence of an unbridgeable gap between the Danish people and their political representatives. A failure would deepen the hegemonic crisis, and Krarup's opponents did not seem to have many alternatives that could enable them to come out of this situation with their authority intact. It was as if reaching the fundraising goal could be taken as an implicit affirmation of the existing order, a denial of any crisis of representation.

The government felt squeezed between the people's demand for stopping further immigration of refugees and Denmark's international obligations, and they were also taken aback by Krarup's intervention, which turned the moral panic that their own Ninn-Hansen had created into a hegemonic crisis. The Social Democrats were in even worse shape and were squeezed by their allegiance to the "working class," whose resentment against refugees was about to dissolve the traditional connection between humanitarian and "liberal" values and Social Democratic welfarism. Thus, both the government and the opposition responded by signaling that they were willing to introduce severe restrictions on refugees' access to Denmark.

Krarup's opponents generally did not reflect on how their response was leading them into a dead end. Only one commentary in my data sample reflected on the distinction between Refugee 86 and refugee laws. An editorial in *Politiken* pointed to the defensive nature of the distinction: "It [the distinction] is a fact, but the horrifying afterthought is why is it so important to emphasize this fact? Naturally to avoid hurting the collection. If this is the answer, it is an alarming surrender to racism, an indirect acknowledgment that it [racism] has a firmer grip on [the Danish population] than it is comfortable to admit openly" (*Politiken*, October 3, 1986).

Krarup's opponents went further than granting him Refugee 86 as the battleground for his hegemonic struggle. To win the immediate battle, they conceded and tacitly accepted his claims about the alien/Muslim threat to Danish nation.

A counterad by priests, nuns, and members of the Lutheran, Catholic, Methodist, and Baptist churches was a good example of this tacit acceptance. The ad not only attacked Krarup for being indecent, demagogic, and incorrect, but also called for "contributions so that refugees can have a homestead in *countries and cultures they are familiar with.* Let the fundraising become the expression of our will that human rights are respected all over the world" (*Berlingske Tidende*, September 28, 1986; emphasis added). A popular novelist, Thorkild Hansen, went further: "They are not like us; they come from another world where they have another culture, and maybe another skin color than us, and their numbers increase and increase." Hansen described a new mass migration, noted that mass migrations were always followed by wars and chaos, and concluded, "We do not need to help because we are so good. We can content ourselves with helping because it is in our damn interest" (*Politiken*, October 5, 1986).

The invocation of culture here was interwoven with a humanitarian perspective. The priests did not only say, "Let us help refugees to stay where they culturally belong"; the contribution itself was presented as a humanitarian gesture and refugees as people who were entitled to protection and care wherever they were. In this context, culture as a defining feature of refugees provided a powerful resource against Krarup's call for boycott and in favor of making a humanitarian contribution. But when arguments are organized hierarchically, some propositions are assigned subordinate places in relation to others. In this case, humanitarian arguments were subordinated to the overall cultural premise. In other words, the opponents tacitly accepted Krarup's definition of those concerns as being primarily cultural. This concession had the effect of pushing the debate onto the terrain of culture and ethnicity and turning refugees and immigrants into the cultural category "alien," and they therefore do not belong. In other words, this strategy granted Krarup enormous influence on immigration discourse.

I suggest that agreeing to the battle on the terrain of culture had yet another implication. The argument that it is better to help people where they are was also a tacit acceptance of the proposition that they were "convenience refugees" who traveled to Europe only to escape poor living conditions. Krarup's intervention and the only "viable" reaction to it (as the opponents saw it) forced them to accept many of the propositions that hitherto were considered part of a racist discourse.

Après the Intervention: Culturalization and the Political Mobilization of the Far Right

Refugee 86 appeared to be a huge success, as newspapers and other media covered the collection day and the results extensively. Success was measured by the number of Refugee 86 volunteers and funds collected and pledged. Not just Foreign Minister Uffe Elleman-Jensen, but also mayors of several cities and politicians from both sides of the political spectrum as well as celebrities (e.g., artists, writers, journalists) volunteered as collectors. More and more volunteers registered as October 5 drew close. Danish public television aired a gala evening telethon with people calling in pledges. The press and TV coverage enacted a campaign without political connotations.

The media declared the collected amount a blow to Krarup. According to *Berlingske Tidende*, "Denmark's big silent majority snapped their fingers at Krarup" ("Søren Krarup Blown Down by 50 Million [Kroner]," October 6, 1986). *Jyllands-Posten* itself declared Refugee 86 to be a great success (October 6, 1986). Refugee 86 campaign chef Finn Slumstrup said that the boycott call actually had a positive effect on donations and that "Danes really showed a willingness . . . to go against Søren Krarup" ("Success for

Collection," *Berlingske Tidende*, October 6, 1986). A mixed sense of victory and relief dominated the media: the battle was won, Krarup was defeated.[9]

However, it was also time to take the people's concerns seriously. On October 7, 1986, the day after Refugee 86 was declared a success, the government presented a new proposal that introduced severe restrictions to the legal right to seek asylum in Denmark and closed many avenues through which refugees had previously exercised this right in Denmark. According to the proposal, which passed the Folketing ten days later with broad support from almost all the political parties, refugees without a legitimate passport or a visa could be denied entry and sent back to their country of departure unless the country of departure was a country where they could be prosecuted. It meant also that if the refugee changed planes or even if the plane had landed in another country, refugees would be sent back to that country. Denmark became the first country in Europe to introduce fines on airlines that brought passengers without a legitimate passport or visa, effectively putting asylum decisions into the hands of the airlines' personnel. The other European countries followed suit and copied the so-called Danish paragraph (Østergaard 2007: 370). Further increases in incoming refugees were effectively stopped by the new restrictions, which turned out to be more restrictive than the parties had expected: according to UN Human Rights Council, only 770 refugees entered Denmark between October 1986 and September 1987 ("Nordic Kick to Refugees," *Politiken*, September 17, 1987), whereas the government had expected the restriction would bring down the numbers to around 5,000 ("The Limit Is Reached," *Jyllands-Posten*, October 18, 1987).

Krarup's achievement with the boycott campaign was not the introduction of the new restrictions to the refugee law but his ability to turn the moral panic into a crisis of representation and to galvanize and mobilize far-right forces, which increased their influence on public discourse. His committee against the refugee law became the first in the series of new far-right organizations such as Danish Forum, the National Socialist Movement (DNSB), Stop the Immigration, the Nationals, and the National Party Denmark. The most influential of these organizations was the Danish Association (*Den Danske Forening*), which was founded in 1987 by a far-right circle of intellectuals including Krarup (Karpantschof 2002; Rydgren 2004). The Danish Association was the most articulate organization and became the ideological center of the Far Right in Denmark. Its populist-nationalist ideas became the ideological foundations of the Danish People's Party (DPP), which was founded in 1996 by a breakaway faction of the explicitly racist Progress Party, and Søren Krarup and Jesper Langballe, two of the prominent members of the Danish Association, who were elected as MPs in the

2001 elections. The DPP, one of the biggest and most influential populist right-wing parties in Europe, adopted its master frame from the association: "'Ordinary Danes' are fooled by the 'establishment', and . . . Danish national identity is threatened by immigration and multiculturalization and by the EU [European Union]" (Rydgren 2004: 483). The DPP's success and the making of its populist vision into the new common sense have mainly been attributed to Krarup's influence. *Politiken*'s celebratory portrait on his seventy-fifth birthday in 2012 described him as the educated son of an academician who not only became part of the popular uprising against the elite but *put it into words* ("Danish People's Party's Chief Ideologist Turns 75," *Politiken*, December 2, 2012; emphasis added). Krarup himself described the DPP "as kind of my own child" (*Jyllands-Posten*, October 29, 2000).

Rydgren (2004; 2010) draws a direct ideological line between the Danish Association and the DPP. Central to both the Danish Association and the DPP is the threat to the homogeneity of Danish culture and people by Muslim immigrants who are associated with fanaticism, criminality, oppression of women, and breakdown of the welfare state. Both accuse the political and cultural establishment, especially the Left and social democrats, which Krarup calls "the goodness industry," of being alien to their own people.

The Danish Association parlayed its management of the crisis into a huge influence on public discourse. As I discussed in chapter 2, crises open up the political terrain for interventions by fringe forces, and once they gain access to the discourse, their existence depends on the perpetuation of the crisis. The Association's protest meetings provoked antiracist counteractions and controversies, which attracted massive media coverage of the Association and its messages just as Krarup had attracted attention during his boycott campaign (Karpantschof 2002: 25). Indeed, Krarup and the DPP's leader, Pia Kjærsgaard, were some of the most quoted people on immigration matters and played a key role in making immigration the dominant topic in the media (Rydgren 2010: 63).

In sum, Krarup became one of the key forces that pushed the entire political spectrum to the right through the question of immigration. His significance lies in his radically different vision of Danish society, which not only answered but also transformed some of the most pressing questions around political representation.

Krarup's campaign also managed to turn the moral panic around refugees into a larger hegemonic crisis. Through his construction of himself as the daring spokesperson of the silenced majority, he convinced the establishment that it was time to take people's concerns seriously if the system's legitimacy was to be protected. This, in turn, was premised upon the tacit acceptance of an easily identifiable popular will that was at odds with the political system when it came to immigration. Once this premise was accepted, Denmark reached the point of no return and Muslim immigration began to move to the center of political discourse and was increasingly framed in cultural terms.

Krarup's intervention opened the path for the culturalization of the immigration debate by forcing opponents to challenge him on his premises. Even those who argued against the claim that immigrants posed a cultural threat confirmed the centrality of culture by accepting the battle on the cultural ground. A group of students and a lecturer at the University of Copenhagen published a commentary in *Politiken* immediately after the Refugee 86 event (October 11, 1986) where they challenged the idea that immigration was a threat to Danish culture. The writers commented that "the refugee threat to Danish culture can hardly be taken seriously. This is probably the reason why we Danish ethnographers did not make ourselves conspicuous in what is considered to be a serious public debate on the issue. What we have is not at all a threat but a meeting of difference." According to the writers, it was not Danish culture but Denmark's borders that were threatened. Culture was not a fragile thing that could easily be broken; it was an ever-changing enterprise that constantly combined elements from other cultures; it reflected Denmark's integration in the world. Refugees did not threaten "our culture" but "our self-image." A closer look would reveal a contradiction in the commentary: they admitted that this was a meeting of difference as if difference was a new phenomenon (to fend off the threat argument). Whatever the intentions of the writers, both their admissions and their refutations confirmed the importance of culture in the debate. The debate began to bend around the cultural ontological category.

Benson (2013) tells a similar story about the change in immigration discourse in France in the same period. The media, particularly *Libération* (a French daily), focused mainly on the humanitarian suffering of immigrants (wages, working conditions, and slum housing) during the 1970s; during the 1980s, however, "This focus on immigrant *workers* was quickly displaced by a concern with the 'second generation' and their relationship with French culture. . . . *Libération*'s framing of immigration in cultural terms was also influential, at least in terms of setting up one of the intellectual poles against which other actors were forced to contend" (112; emphasis added). Benson argues that the (positive) cultural framing enabled the far-right National Front's (FN) municipal election victory in Dreux in 1983. After the election victory, FN turned multicultural antiracism on its head on behalf of "the French" and thus "created a new reconfiguration of positions in the field" (113).

The Far-Right Symbiosis

Indeed, Rydgren (2004) argues that Krarup and the far-right forces in Denmark learned from the FN's experiences and used the master frame developed by the FN to succeed. The master frame, according to Rydgren, consists of ethnonationalist xenophobia and antiestablishment populism. However, neither element is unique to the National Front. There are several examples of far-right populism that mixes ethnonationalism and racism—Enoch Powell in Britain, George Wallace in the United States, Pauline Hanson in Australia, Jörg Haider in Austria, and Geert Wilders (Pim Fortuyn before him) in the Netherlands. Although they all draw on similar rhetorical resources to articulate populist far-right views with their construction of "the people" or "the silent majority," Krarup's intervention has many similarities to Enoch Powell's infamous "Rivers of Blood" speech on April 10, 1968, in terms of immediate context, content, style, and effects.

According to Mercer (1990: 5), "In the drama of its form as an exemplary rhetorical performance in political discourse, Powell's speech was a major event in its own right." The immediate context for Powell's speech was similar to Krarup's ads. In 1967, the government in the newly independent former colony Kenya passed a law that gave British passport holders two years in which to choose between British and Kenyan citizenship as a part of its Kenyanization policy, after which non-Kenyans—mostly Asians from the Indian subcontinent—would not have the right to work and live in the country. This presented the British Asians with a dilemma that soon became a dilemma for the British government. By September the same year, 8,443 Asians had already entered Britain. In the beginning, the Labour government chose to be silent, whereas the right-wing Conservatives started to draw attention to potential mass immigration and demanded tighter restrictions. Even though the number of potential Kenyan Asian immigrants was 66,000, the number was blown up to millions in the media. Sir Cyril Osborne of the Conservative Party predicted that if it went on like this, there would be more blacks than whites in seventy years' time. In other words, there was a moral panic brewing around immigration. In February 1968, the bipartisan consensus collapsed. The Conservative shadow cabinet issued a public declaration demanding restrictions. The Labour government did more: it introduced a bill that limited the right of entry to "British passport holders who had substantial connections with the UK by virtue of birth, or their father's or grandfather's birth, in the UK" (Hiro 1992: 214).

However, Labour's proposal also extended the rights of existing immigrants by strengthening antidiscrimination legislation. This set the stage for

Powell's speech. The resentment against immigration laws created a gap between the working class and its political representatives in the Labour Party, and a crisis of authority emerged. It was under these conditions that Powell delivered his "Rivers of Blood" speech. His speech was designed and staged to gain maximum media coverage. He succeeded in forcing both the Conservatives and Labour to conform to the "public opinion" he engineered. When the Conservative government later passed restrictions that, according Hiro (1992: 252), were unnecessary (the number of immigrants to Britain could be reduced within already existing laws), the reason for them as stated by Prime Minister Edward Heath was to still "the fears of our people."

In his speech, Powell took up the projected immigration from Kenya and amplified the demand for restrictions on Kenyan Asians' entry to Britain. But there were no major distinctions between what he and the other conservative politicians said. The distinctiveness of his speeches was his rhetorical vision: he spoke as the representative of the people (the silent majority) against the entire political elite, who held a monopoly on channels of communication. Like Krarup, he spoke of the betrayal by the political elite, of the prospect of racial confrontations ahead, and of the demise of the British nation.

The speech had immediate impact. Chanting "the only white man in there," thousands of dockers marched to Parliament in protest of Heath's decision to sack Powell from his position in the shadow cabinet (Schwarz 1996). For the first time, people freely discussed immigration everywhere: in buses, pubs, and work canteens. And the shift in public opinion made it easy to pass the Race Relations Bill, which imposed severe restrictions on immigration. The long-term effects of Powell's intervention are long recognized in Britain: working class's detachment from the Labour Party and support for Thatcher's two-decade-long neoliberal government, which has been followed by the successive Labour governments that adopted her neoliberal policies (Hall 1988; Smith 1994). His articulation of white British concerns and racist resentments against the establishment was articulated by Thatcher in her neoliberal project of dismantling of the welfare system. Popular support for Thatcher's project is generally explained by the fact that she succeeded in mobilizing resistance to the bureaucratic character of the hegemonic consensus. Thus, the antagonism was constructed between two poles: "the 'people,' which includes all those who defend the traditional values and freedom of enterprise [which connoted the defense of inequalities of sex and race]; and their adversaries: the state and all the subversives (feminists, blacks, young people and permissives of every type)" (Laclau and Mouffe 2001: 170).

The Long-Term Effects of Krarup's Intervention

Although Krarup seemed to lose, to use Gramsci's terms, the "war of maneuver," he won the "war of position."[10] A "war of position" can be, in this context, understood as a strategy of building up a broad bloc of social forces (i.e., a historical bloc), unified by a common conception of the world. The purpose of a war of position is to shape the social horizon, which in my terminology means changing how the ontological structure of society is imagined. His ability to turn Muslim immigration into a question of a lethal threat to the cohesive force of society achieved just that. It does not mean that culture or religion was not part of earlier discourse, but they were not the defining elements of social division. The cultural antagonism brought cultural arguments into focus (even if they were used to argue against the antagonistic nature of the difference), whereas other arguments were pushed to the background (but never erased). Once social division is envisioned in cultural terms, public discourse focuses on cultural arguments. Major social questions become oriented toward the dividing line, which in turn reorganizes the argumentative web along the dividing line into the two sides of the division.

As I discussed in chapter 2, there is a general agreement that a fundamental shift took place in immigration discourse in which the focus moved to the immigrants' problematic culture. Madsen (2000: 87) noted a remarkable jump in polls of Danes' views on "whether immigrants constitute a threat to our national character": 23 percent declared agreement with the statement in 1985. That figure jumped to about 40 percent after 1987. He noted also that the media coverage in 1987 was extremely concerned with "the Muslim threat." Madsen could not explain the change because he had not done a detailed analysis of media coverage. The extensive media analysis in this study, however, allows me to suggest what was going on. As discussed in chapter 2 (see table 2.1), newspaper stories written from a cultural perspective constituted 1.1 percent of all stories in 1984 and 1.7 percent in 1986. There was a significant jump to 13.1 percent in 1987. The jump in the percentages of cultural frames in letters to the editor was not as significant over the four-year period: 9.1 percent in 1984, 3.7 percent in 1986, and 12.6 percent in 1987, which indicates that the cultural arguments were already in their embryo in the concerns of letter writers.

Although there were many types of stories in 1984 that described immigrants as a threat, there were no significant fluctuations. In 1984, 4.8 percent of all stories described an immigrant/refugee threat. That fell to 2.4 percent and 2.2 percent in 1986 and 1987, respectively. More significant is the change in describing refugees as victims. In 1984, 19.6 percent of stories described refugees as victims of oppression and torture; that fell to 12.2 percent in 1986 and 7.5 percent in 1987. At the same time, refugees were less likely to be described as economic and social burdens in 1986 (5 percent) and 1987 (6 percent) than in 1984, when 16.9 percent of all stories described them as burdens (see table 3.1). Although not definitive, these numbers may indicate an increasing tendency toward culturalized discourse.

TABLE 3.1. Description of Refugees in the Press

Description	1984	1986	1987	2001
Victims of oppression and torture	19.6%	12.2%	7.5%	3.9%
Economic and social burden	16.9%	5.0%	6.0%	3.6%

These numbers suggest that the media and the political and cultural establishment had moved in the direction of readers' letters rather than the other way around. Even so, the number of readers who thought of the refugees in cultural terms was not overwhelming, and the arguments made in letters to the editor tended to be fragmented. What was overwhelming in the letters was the negative tone toward refugees. In 1984, 81.8 percent of all letters had negative overtones and only 13.6 percent were positive. In 1986, the negative letters decreased to 59.8 percent and positive letters increased to 31.3 percent, only to become more negative again in 1987: 67.9 percent versus 26 percent positive (table 3.2).

TABLE 3.2. Tone in Letters to the Editor

Tone	1984	1986	1987	2001
Positive	13.6%	31.3%	26.0%	27.5%
Negative	81.8%	59.8%	67.9%	61.1%

The relative increase in positive tone in 1986 has to do with the strong response to Krarup in support of Refugee 86. That mobilization, however, did not translate into a popular front against Krarup and his small circle of friends because the tactical oppositional response tacitly conceded the unpopularity of existing refugee laws.

The Focus Moves from Refugees (Victims) to Immigrants (Cultural Aliens)

When the immediate battle was over, the political establishment had two contradictory responses to the scare: a long period of silence and a political consensus on not politicizing immigration—a consensus that was broken by Social Democrats right before the elections in September 1987 and local politicians' pandering to the voters by taking up anti-immigration rhetoric. Two important moments in the following months and through 1987 were significant in not only keeping the focus on immigration but also further affecting the shift onto the ground of culture. The first is the period before and through the September 1987 parliamentary elections, when Social Democratic mayors began voicing their concerns about immigration with spectacular statements about immigrants and their culture. The second was a deliberate attempt by Ninn-Hansen to create a new moral panic around immigration with the intention of winning further restrictions in immigration laws.

The period after the restrictions in October 1986 on refugee laws and the controversy around Krarup's boycott of Refugee 86 was characterized by a long period of silence about immigration policies among mainstream political forces until the next summer. This silence can partly be explained by a wait-and-see attitude among political parties after the changes to immigration law. Krarup's intervention had certainly made the political mainstream wary about appearing to go against the people's wishes but, at the same time, also wary of appearing racist if they indicated they were in agreement with him.

It is not surprising that Krarup's intervention had the most destabilizing implications for the Social Democrats, who were seen as most responsible for the liberal immigration law, and a huge gap between the working class and the Social Democratic Party's humanitarian consensus was created. Krarup, who gained almost unlimited access to the mainstream media, appealed primarily to the working class, the Social Democratic constituency who complained about their resources being wasted on foreigners and about not being heard by the political establishment.[11] The Social Democratic leadership's response to the situation in late 1986 and in 1987 was to pull back quietly from engagement with the Far Right's vision until, as will be seen, local politicians within the party gave in.

The silence among mainstream politicians did not mean silence in the immigration debate. On the contrary, the void was filled by now-mobilized far-right actors. The Danish Association and other small far-right groups initiated a persistent campaign against immigration with stories about immigrants' abuse of Danish hospitality, about criminality, and about cultural problems, especially religious difference. With refugee laws already tightened, the next target was refugees' right to bring their spouses to Denmark. As a UN Human Rights Council official, Søren Jessen-Petersen, remarked, "Silence or statements by politicians that can be interpreted as direct consent [to xenophobic statements] run the risk of legitimizing attitudes toward foreigners, attitudes that a democracy neither wants nor can survive" ("Nordic Kick to Refugees," *Politiken*, September 17, 1987). One frequent commentator, Jacques Blum, a sociologist of culture, argued that racism was advancing thanks to the silence by the established parties, who feared looking either too "refugee friendly" or prejudiced ("Racism Sneaks In," *Politiken*, September 27, 1987). By 1987, polls showed a significant increase in support for the Progress Party, whose new leader, Pia Kjærsgaard, had shifted the party's focus from taxes to immigration (Rydgren 2004: 3).

A new wave of anti-immigrant sentiment surfaced in 1986. Many working-class people lived in cities where housing projects accommodated refugees and other immigrants. Social Democratic mayors of some of these towns soon began complaining about bearing the refugee burden, as opposed to municipalities (mainly in richer, conservative areas) that bore no such responsibility, having fewer or no housing projects. Mayor Per Madsen of Ishøj—a working-class suburb of Copenhagen with many immigrants—started a new controversy in August 1987 with a sharp criticism of Muslim immigrants' failure to adapt to Danish society, using the slogan "When in Rome, do as Romans do" (Jensen 2001: 75). He accused Turkish immigrants of misusing the welfare system, but the greatest problem, he emphasized, was cultural: Turkish youth still preferred to marry women in Turkey and therefore increase the number of subsequent immigrants. The rising population was, in this sense, described as a cultural problem translated into an economic burden. Madsen concretized his cultural views later in the Danish Association's member journal, *The Dane* (*Danskeren*): "Muslims live at a Middle Ages stage with their disrespect for women and women's culture, which is unheard of in this country. They trade with women as if they were cattle stock, and women are beaten and mistreated" (Engelbreth Larsen 2001: 180). Only a decade later, Karen Jespersen, who would become the face of the Social Democrats on immigration questions, would say that politicians "should have listened to Per Madsen" (*BT*, October 22, 1999). The debate on refugees turned into a debate on immigration in general and thereby into a question of immigration's cultural impact.

The snowball that Krarup had started was rolling. Although the SDP leadership in general distanced itself from Madsen's statements, newspapers that had been critical of Krarup's rhetoric gave Madsen sympathetic consideration. *Vestkysten*, a local daily, wrote, for instance, that while it was important to denounce Pia Kjærsgaard for "her incredible pandering to cheap, irresponsible views," one had to "discuss seriously the problem that the Ishøj mayor raised. . . . It is a given that if immigrants . . . *with a completely different cultural background* constitute 14 percent of a municipality's population, it must create problems" (emphasis added). The editorial concluded that immigrants had to stay home if "they felt dirtied by any contact with Danish culture, Danish norms, and Danish tradition. . . . It is okay to tell them this. Hospitality, too, has limits" (Jensen 2000: 481). Madsen's statements also received support from *Ekstra Bladet*, which had less than a year earlier called Krarup "the apostle of hate" ("Ishøj split: Mohammed or Madsen [typical Danish surname]," August 11, 1987). According to the editorial, Denmark should receive a good number of refugees who were threatened by torture or execution, but "we cannot take the steam off the Turkish unemployment lines without it having profound political, economic and cultural consequences." When Torkil Sørensen of the DRC remarked the sharp change in the editorial line of the paper, the editors responded with a reference to "the limited capacity of people's hospitality" ("On the Other Hand," October 24, 1987). The media's acquiescence to Krarup's main claims—that "the people" worried about the threat immigrants posed Danish cultural unity—was evident. Turning the gaze from refugees to immigrants already living in Denmark was also moving the focus from Denmark's humanitarian responsibilities to the problems that immigrants with alien cultures created for society.

Whether Mayor Madsen entered the debate to use increasingly legitimized popular hostility to force the government to allocate more resources to his municipality or to win back Social Democratic voters, or a combination of both, Krarup's cultural framing of immigration and links to antagonism between the political elite and the Danish people provided an opening and the resources for using cultural arguments in local contexts. Other local politicians from the party soon joined the fray. On September 5, 1987, immediately before the general election, *Det fri Aktuelt* published a front-page article headlined "Social Democrats Bury Critical Report." According to the article, the party leadership had delayed the publication of a report prepared by the party's committee on refugees and immigration. The committee, chaired by local politician Vibeke Storm Rasmussen, not only reproduced Krarup's attack on the DRC and the Danish Red Cross for acting without public oversight but also criticized immigrants for having "attitudes, practices and phenomena that are unacceptable for Social Democrats." The committee recommended making stricter demands that immigrants adopt to Danish society and that the laws further restrict their right to bring their spouses from their country of origin. The recommendations for restricting access to family reunification were therefore supported with arguments that emphasized the incompatibility of immigrants' culture(s).

It is difficult to see much difference between the views of local Social Democrats and those of Krarup except that the Social Democratic arguments were not packaged in strong nationalist rhetoric. Local politicians' statements signified a shift in focus to culture as the main problem. They delivered what Krarup lacked: firsthand accounts of cultural problems. Turks, for instance, kept marrying Turks, even in their second generation of residence. Thus, the focus was neatly enlarged to include immigrants who had long been living in Denmark. The alien threat was already present in Denmark; the frontier was no longer located at the border around Denmark but within it.

In short, by the fall of 1987, immigration discourse was already permeated by arguments about immigrants' culture. Krarup already seemed to be winning the "war of position" even if he had been declared the loser of the battle over Refugee 86. The controversy around Refugee 86 had turned him into one of the principal actors in the debate on immigration and enabled him to define the premises for the debate;[12] his definition of the problem as "uncontrolled alien immigration" was gaining ground and forcing the debate about immigration onto the ground of culture. As I will show later, it became progressively typical to speak of immigrants as a cultural category opposed to a purportedly homogenous Danish culture. The content of those cultures became progressively determined through repetitive crisis and moral panics around immigrants' "cultural practices," which were deemed a threat to Danish culture.

Although local Social Democrats joined the far-right groups and raised their voices against immigration with cultural arguments, there was an unspoken consensus among mainstream political parties, including the Social Democratic leadership, about not taking up immigration as a theme during the election campaign out of fear of voter punishment. It came, therefore, as a shock when the leader of the Social Democratic Party, Anker Jørgensen, proclaimed the day before the election that "Denmark is a small country and must not be overrun by foreigners. Too many refugees will damage Denmark economically and culturally. . . . We have to maintain our value basis" (*Jyllands-Posten*, September 6, 1987).

The governing parties expressed their frustrations about Anker Jørgensen's statements. Conservative prime minister Poul Schlüter accused the Social Democratic leader of breaching the consensus about not campaigning on immigration (*Berlingske Tidende*, September 13, 1987). Uffe Elleman-Jensen, leader of the right-wing Liberal Party, also criticized the Social Democrats for "scoring points by playing on the insecurity that has been created by developments in the last years," but he also added that

> we have to be careful not to destroy the popular support for the Danish refugee policy . . . we have to be very careful that our social security systems are not used in a way that can offend—and concretely it may be necessary to change the rules around the access refugees have to bring their families and relatives. (*Jyllands-Posten*, October 7, 1987)

The political consensus about not making immigration into a political issue collapsed.

The 1987 elections took place under these conditions. Parties with strong anti-immigrant parties made gains: the Progress Party and a self-proclaimed left-wing party, Shared Path,[13] which ran an explicit anti-immigrant election campaign. Shared Path representatives pushed the Socialist Left (VS), an ardent supporter of liberal immigration laws, out of the Folketing.[14] Although the Progress Party attracted a number of protest votes, it was not enough to change the political landscape. Anker Jørgensen's last-minute statements had secured many Social Democratic workers' votes that might have gone to the Progress Party. The Liberal and Conservative coalition parties were the big losers in terms of voter support, though they managed to keep power with the support of center parties.

The fact that Social Democrats prevented bigger voter flight by last-minute statements against immigration convinced mainstream parties that people wanted more restrictions. The leader of the Conservative Party's parliamentary group expressed it this way: "We wanted to create a balance in this case, but people obviously still think that the law is too liberal" (*Jyllands-Posten*, September 13, 1987). Because the key support for this interpretation was the success of anti-immigrant parties in the elections, Krarup's articulation of the concerns of the Danish people became the basis for a new heated debate around family reunification laws.

A New Round of Crisis around Immigrants

The first important moment was, therefore, the elections in which the political consensus broke down and local Social Democrats entered the political discourse with anti-immigrant statements. The second important discursive moment of 1987 came when conditions were ripe for Ninn-Hansen to begin a new campaign to further curb immigration. Jørgensen's statements before the elections broke the last remnants of the temporary political consensus, local Social Democratic politicians were complaining about immigrants and asking for further restrictions, and there seemed to be a general renewed anti-immigrant sentiment.

This time, Ninn-Hansen had both expected and unexpected allies across the political spectrum for creating a new crisis around immigration. The opening salvo came from Per Madsen, who published manipulated statistics about Turkish immigrants' family reunification rates. According to statistics based on twenty-three immigrants who lived in Ishøj, one Turkish immigrant, who had come to Denmark in 1970, had increased into a family of 23 in 1987. Including birth in the country, 23 became 371 in the same period. The problem, according to the mayor, was that immigrants did not adapt to Danish culture. Asking for restrictions to family reunion rights, the mayor sent the results to the justice minister, who immediately declared that he would intervene with lightning speed to put brakes on mass immigration ("Lightning Intervention against Mass Immigration," *Jyllands-Posten*, October 27, 1987). Based on the report, Ishøj's deputy mayor, Leif Grundsøe, concluded that by the year 2000 there would be half a million Turkish immigrants in Denmark.

The statistics were covered extensively in the media. Most national newspapers sampled for this study did not comment on the statistics in their editorials but covered the debate around the Ishøj statistics among politicians, pundits, and academics. Local papers took the numbers for granted and reported that "Denmark's very liberal rules for family reunion have led to a tremendous growth of the number of immigrants" (*Lolland-Falsters Folketidende*, October 29, 1987). There was also recognition that this was a part of a deliberate attempt to benefit from general anti-immigration sentiment. *Politiken*, for instance, called these gambits "tricks" to avoid the promise that Denmark would continue to receive five thousand refugees a year—a promise Ninn-Hansen made during the parliamentary debate in the fall of 1986, when refugee laws were being tightened. *Politiken* pointed out that the numbers of family members that refugees were said to bring to Denmark were inflated by collapsing the categories of refugees and immigrants and called Madsen's calculations "statistical manipulations meant to appeal to the beast within people, which is beyond any standards of decency." If the numbers were correct, there would have been ninety-six thousand Turkish immigrants in Denmark instead of twenty-two thousand at this point (editorial, November 1, 1987).

The national Christian daily, *Kristeligt Dagblad*, called the inclusion of immigrants in the family reunion debate "scare propaganda without foundation in reality," although it did not challenge the Ishøj statistics. Rather, it blamed the cultural characteristic of immigrants for the increase in the immigrant population: "the traditional, ethnic moral rules of marriage of the Turkish immigrants that inflated the numbers" (editorial, October 21, 1987). The DRC and academics also challenged the numbers. However, they had been so discredited during and after Krarup's intervention that they lost their authority as experts or objective sources and were now regarded as interested parties. For example, the DRC's calculations, which showed that one hundred refugees had brought only sixteen family members to Denmark was not covered as part of the news but merely published as a letter to the editor in *BT* (November 5, 1987). When the numbers and projections were denounced by Statistics Denmark, the official statistical institute of Denmark (*Politiken*, "Numbers of Turks Were Completely Wrong," November 4, 1987), there was little other press coverage. *Politiken*'s article also revealed, between the lines, that it was indeed Ninn-Hansen who had commissioned Madsen's statistical report, selecting a sociologist of culture, Eyvind Vesselbo, known for anti-immigrant views, who later became a Liberal Party politician. Criticism and corrections received little coverage and did not stop Ninn-Hansen's use of the report in his project to restrict family reunification rights. The report provided firsthand testimony to the local problems related to immigration.

Ishøj's report was a deliberate strategic intervention to create a new crisis that would enable the government to propose further restrictions on immigration, but the controversy the report generated did more than produce ammunition for the government. It further ensconced immigrants' culture, in this instance the form of marriage practices, on the discursive map as the most significant aspect of the issue. Debate was now spinning around culture as the benchmark for assessing arguments. In 1987, humanitarian comments were pushed into a defensive position. A letter in *Jyllands-Posten*, for instance, responded to Krarup's call for a defense of Danish culture, and argued that the real threat was not Islam but rather the American culture that permeated Danish culture (October 15, 1987). Another letter in the same paper found that "the claim that Danes risk becoming a minority and that around the year 2000 10 percent of the population will be immigrants is wildly exaggerated" (September 23, 1987). These readers clearly felt that they had to respond to the increasingly negative claims about immigrants, and they did so not by rejecting the premise that the issue was a cultural threat to the Danish people and nation but by downplaying the numbers and the threat Muslim immigrants might pose, as if to concede that they could be a threat if their numbers increased.

Engaging in a discussion of Madsen's numbers meant generally engaging in cultural arguments about marriage and family norms. A feature story in *Politiken* about the Ishøj report ("Immigrants' Many Children Is a Myth," November 1, 1987) interviewed Christian Horst, a sociologist of culture known for his antiracist views. He accused municipal authorities of grossly manipulating the numbers to make it appear that Turkish immigrant families had an average of six children, whereas only 11 percent of the Turkish population had four or more children. Horst also explained that immigrant birthrates slowly decreased the longer they lived in the new host country, and this was true for Turkish birthrates. The implication was that Denmark did not have to be nervous about the numbers of immigrants or their culture as the latter came to resemble Danish culture after a few years. Horst also criticized municipal authorities for collapsing different family categories into a single category and using the manipulated results to call for restrictions to family reunion rules.

Regardless of his intentions, Horst's argument—typical of the antiracist argument of the period—was responsive to the cultural framework used to explain social phenomena. The focus shift to family reunification laws as the new battleground centered the debate on immigrants' culture. Once immigrants' "cultural practices" came into the focus, both anti-immigrant and pro-immigrant (i.e., multiculturalist) arguments became oriented toward culture both as the object of discourse (cultural traditions) and as an explanatory framework (immigrants' cultural mind-set).

Schierup (1993) traces the origins of the culturalization of immigration debate to the "culturalist" focus of academic research, which, he argues, has provided the foundation for both the notion of the "clash of cultures" and the multiculturalist notion of the "meeting of cultures."

Scholars have generally been critical of essentialist notions of culture, but criticism in many critical works is limited to refraining from attributing ingrained cultural characteristics to ethnic, religious, or racial groups. A nonessentialist approach usually emphasizes the ever-changing, hybrid, and cosmopolitan character of culture and cultural identity by a web of influences from other cultures. Thus, the disagreement between essentialist and nonessentialist approaches is about the degree to which culture determines individual lives and the pace of its change. Yet culture is maintained as the basis for understanding putative social identities and, as such, it opens up a field of inquiry for researchers—essentialists and nonessentialists alike. To study an entity one has to know what that entity is. That is, the first step when studying culture is to delimit, describe, and construct the culture or the cultural identity to be studied, which starts with labeling/naming. Here, both approaches are similar in their categorization of social groups in cultural terms: they both identify and therefore objectify cultures regardless of how the culture is described—whether as something influenced by other "cultures" or not. One of the "multiculturalist" arguments often used in the debate was that Danes and Danish institutions did not know enough about immigrants' cultural background to be tolerant and better able to deal with them.

However, studying and mapping out immigrants' practices implies engineering proper behavior according to "our norms." But because immigrants, like anyone else, behave in different ways in the same situations as well as in similar ways in different situations, culture has to be constructed by the researchers who are given grants to study and produce knowledge about immigrants and their culture. Thus, academic "expertise" and "insider information" (provided by "native informants") started to become a standard for sourcing stories and participating in public discourse on immigration, leading to the process of institutionalizing the cultural focus.

Once Islam and Muslim immigrants came into focus, the need for knowledge about them to explain things to Danes gave rise to new kinds of experts. One of them, frequently featured in the columns of Danish newspapers, was Hussein Shahadeh, who told Danes that "the Koran is the Muslims' holy book; a guideline in everyday obligations, and even the basis for the worldly laws. . . . Islam has a particularly firm hold on the ordinary Muslim and determines his entire everyday life in a much more detailed manner than religion does from a Western point of view" ("Muslims in Exile," *Jyllands-Posten*, November 12, 1987).[15]

Not only do effective hegemonic articulations produce their own kinds of experts, credible sources, and designers of polls, who reflect the ascendant ontological understandings, but they also gradually render irrelevant experts who may bring a different perspective to social phenomena, therefore gradually transforming the nature of the social phenomena themselves. In this sense, the far-right hegemonic project initiated by Krarup's ads became a centripetal force redirecting and orienting arguments toward its own definitions, which, in the Bakhtinian sense, had quickly become the already uttered, the already known, the common opinion. Those on the far right were joined by their antagonists in elaborating an ontology of the social based on cultural differences. As I demonstrated in chapter 1, the tacit ontological categories centralize language by imposing ontological limits to it: it is through these limits that the antagonists are able to make arguments on the same "object." In other words, mutual understanding appears to be possible only if we speak of the same objects and phenomena. In the period after Krarup's intervention, the immigrant as a cultural category became a central object that fixed the meaning of concepts that were disarticulated from their class-based contexts. The term "integration," for example, was increasingly used in the sense of integrating into Danish culture rather than into the institutionalized "Danish society" (e.g., labor unions, employment or unemployment institutions, the health-care system).

Whether others argued for or against the reality of an unbridgeable frontier between Muslims and the Danish people, Krarup's intervention brought the cultural divide into the center of social imagination—the divide that worked as a centripetal force that reoriented arguments along its own axis. The power of the Far Right's vision to bend public discourse toward its definitions was most evident in the radical reorientation of the DRC's comments, which used to describe the oppression and prosecution from which refugees escaped prior to Refugee 86. By the fall of 1987, they too had shifted focus in response to the changing discursive environment in which culture and religion were emphasized as the locus of the problem. Public relations officer Torkil Sørensen argued, for example, that Iranian refugees escaped from Khomeini's regime and therefore would not be interested in the "Khomeinization" (i.e., Islamization) of Denmark. He also noted that the DRC in principle did not allocate housing to refugees in areas with many immigrants, to prevent concentrations enabling immigrants to maintain their culture ("Escaped from Khomeini," *Berlingske Tidende*, September 13, 1987).

The centripetal force of the new cultural ontology of the social could also be seen in explicitly antiracist positions. According to a news story that appeared in *Berlingske Tidende*, the teacher's union wanted to participate more actively in the immigration debate to stop "immigrants and refugees from being made into scapegoats for all social problems" (November 13, 1987). For the union, this meant that teachers had a responsibility to teach immigrant children to respect Danish culture and to school them on "what is allowed in our country and how to navigate in the Danish system." That is, to stop racism one must change the objects that necessitate it: the immigrants themselves. If immigrants learn to respect Danish culture—however vague it appears—Danes' resentment toward them may decrease. This has been a main strategy in arguments against racism: that immigrants will change and begin behaving just like Danes. A *Politiken* commentator exploring earlier immigrations to Denmark explained that even though immigrants kept their culture for a while, their cultural characteristics were erased over time. He concluded that "integration takes time" and urged Danes to be patient and tolerant despite the fact that "apparently when there are problems in places such as Ishøj, it can have adverse consequences for both parts [Danes and immigrants]—and the [Danes'] goodwill" ("Tolerance Is Not Dead in Denmark, Well?" November 11, 1987). This argument has been repeated numerous times over the last two decades of immigration debate.

While those considered to be in the antiracist camp were reorienting their argumentative strategy toward the cultural framework, characterizations of immigrants considered to be extreme and the property of the Progress Party were becoming legitimate views in newspaper columns. Once Krarup was taken as a legitimate interlocutor and, in fact, as representing one pole of the debate, more extreme rhetoric became acceptable. A commentator in *Jyllands-Posten*, for instance, could not accept that "Islamic foreign workers refuse to take orders from their female supervisors" ("Poul Meyer's Hodgepodge," September 21, 1987), although this had never been an issue in earlier decades of immigration from Muslim countries. According to another commentator in the same paper, "A Muslim neither can nor wants to adapt to Danish conditions (with the exception of using the welfare office). For a Muslim, religion is the law, and therefore he cannot be integrated into Danish society" ("Professor Is on the Wrong Path," September 21, 1987). These kinds of statements, which would have been seen as racist only a couple years previously, were now articulated as justifiable concerns for the future of the cohesion in Danish society.

It is possible that, as a result, readers' letters began to make more coherent references to and linkages among economic burden, the representational gap, Danish culture, and national threat. For instance, a letter to the editor in *Berlingske Tidende* commented that immigration policy should be adjusted to the people, not people to immigration policy, and continued: "Ethnic [*folkelige*] unity has been the foundation for the wealth, peace, and stability in Danish society" ("Arrogant Attitude," September 13, 1987).

In news and feature stories, both sides of a controversy invoked cultural arguments to advance their agendas. One Social Democratic municipality wanted to close down a special kindergarten where immigrant children were placed while their mothers received Danish language instruction. According to the deputy mayor, "We bring together immigrant children and they do not learn Danish. We want them to come out among Danish children to learn Danish and get integrated in ordinary kindergartens." Kindergarten teachers protested but did not challenge the assumption about what integration meant: "This is not Little Turkey or Pakistan. We function according to Danish norms and traditions" ("Immigrant children Have to Learn Danish," *Politiken*, September 13, 1987). The Left Socialist (VS) council representative also opposed the closing, for "the result will be that women have to stay at home and not learn Danish." No one actually bothered to define what Danish norms and traditions were and how kindergartens functioned according to them. Danish norms and traditions, in this sense, function as empty signifiers pointing to the cultural divide. The statements indicate what the teachers believed would constitute the strongest argument against the mayor's desire to close down the project.

The "already known," the common opinion that the arguments were oriented toward, was, in this sense, the assumption that something called "Danish culture" was the benchmark for successful integration. Disagreement concerned whether the project helped or hindered the integration of immigrants, although both sides agreed that Danish culture was to be protected as an absolute yardstick of social conduct. The statements by the Left Socialists' representative in the municipal council has strong feminist undertones defending immigrant women, but her argument, oriented toward the cultural dichotomy, because of its location within the argumentative web, was tainted by the Orientalist view of "Muslim culture" often associated with keeping women at home. Madsen used the same argument to support restricting family reunions. In the Danish discursive context, Orientalist views could be enlisted as rhetorical resources to defend any project deemed good for immigrants or to criticize any project deemed bad for them or Danish culture. By the late 1987, culture had taken a central role in explaining any phenomena in relation to immigrants, who were slowly being recast from being immigrant *workers* to *Muslim* immigrants, collapsing the ethnonational categories that had so far designated the immigrant groups under a single ontological category: Muslims.

Thus, arguments and descriptions of social reality that were recognized in the mid-1980s as far-right or racist articulations became commonplace among all politicians, including leading Social Democrats, within ten years. Some of the people who used sharpest language against Krarup in the fall of 1986 aligned themselves with him just a few years later. By 1990, Krarup was a columnist in *Ekstra Bladet*, which he had designated as "the royal voice of goodness industry" and which in turn had called him an "Apostle of Hate." And in 1993, Thorkild Simonsen, who in 1986 had called Krarup's campaign "petite racism," had come to realize that "if one wants to live in Denmark, one should live under the Danish conditions. We have Turkish families who . . . have no desire to become part of Danish society. The time is ripe to say things as they are. There are immigrants who exploit our liberal laws" (Engelbreth Larsen 2001: 167). In 1997, he was appointed interior minister by the Social Democrats to carry out severe restrictions on immigration. SDP leader and prime minister Poul Nyrup Rasmussen declared in 1997 that it was unacceptable for Muslim immigrants to have breaks to pray at workplaces even though the practice had never been problematized by Danish employers or coworkers. Karen Jespersen said it clearly: "To live in Denmark, you have to be Danish" (*Berlingske Tidende*, July 14, 1997). When the Liberal Party won the 2001 elections and formed the government with the support of the DPP, the leader of the Liberal Party, Anders Fogh Rasmussen, used the same language of "system change" against "arbiters of taste," "opinion tyranny," and the "elite" as Krarup (Lykkeberg 2008: 53).

Clearly, ethnicity, culture, race, and immigration have long been a part of public discourse in Denmark and Europe, but the meaning of these concepts is not fixed: they are, to repeat the much-appropriated idea, subject to ongoing struggles over meaning—struggles that color these abstract concepts with particular signification in political discourse. The main argument in the next chapter is that these concepts have now coalesced to construct a new kind of hegemonic antagonism between the Danish "people" and "Muslim immigrants." A "diagnostic and prognostic" frame presuming that

> social problems largely should be interpreted in ethnic terms and/or as being the result of moral lassitude (and not in terms of social class and economic marginalisation); and that they should be resolved by implementing stricter immigration policies and more law and order . . . has become hegemonic in the political as well as mass media discourse. (Rydgren 2004: 491)

CHAPTER 4

Culture, Ethnicity, and New Hegemony

In her annual New Year speech on December 31, 1985, Queen Margrethe scolded Danes for their negative attitudes toward immigrants, calling their utterances "dumb-smart." In a humanitarian tone she criticized the hostile immigration debate and asked Danes to be tolerant and help new guests to adjust to Danish society. Since then, the immigration debate has become increasingly hostile; yet in an interview in June 2002, the queen only had praise for the debate and said, "It is not so dumb to talk about it" (*Politiken*, June 30, 2002). In an official biography published in 2005, the queen "confessed" that she had been "crazily naive" because she had come to realize that Islam constitutes a great challenge for Danes, who had not met the challenge because "we were tolerant and lazy." She found that there was "something frightening about such a totality, which also is a feature of Islam" and argued that "a counterbalance has to be found, and one has to, at times, run the risk of having unflattering labels placed on you. For there are some things for which one should display no tolerance. And when we are tolerant, we must know whether it is because of convenience or conviction" (*Telegraph*, April 15, 2005).

I concluded the last chapter with the observation that by late 1987, culture had already taken a key role in explaining phenomena related to immigrants, recasting them as Muslim immigrants rather than immigrant workers. The main argument in this chapter is that by 2001, culture had become the key not only to immigration but to the social imaginary in general through the signifier "Muslim immigrant"—a change of focus that displaced social struggle from class to culture. In this process, the figure of Muslim immigrant has become indispensable; it structures the social imaginary in fundamental ways in both political and everyday discourse. It has become difficult to think about the future of the welfare state or the future of your child without the culturalized category of immigrants being central to that thinking. In this chapter, I will first demonstrate the centrality of culture to immigration discourse, then discuss how immigration shapes the ontology of the social, that is, how the figure of the Muslim immigrant structures the social horizon (imagining the past, present, and future) followed by a discussion of the centrality of culture and immigration in political and everyday discourse.

The transformation was the result of a hegemonic intervention that rearticulated uncertainties about the welfare system as the result of immigration rather than the neoliberal policy of shrinking the state's role in the economy. The Conservative/Liberal governments in the 1980s were trying to dismantle the welfare system incrementally, and that role was taken over by the Social Democrats in the 1990s under the guise of the "third way" (Betz and Meret 2013). The move toward the neoliberal position on economic policy, including privatization, capping unemployment, and social aid payments, was in process in the 1990s, and the consensus on such policies made it difficult for voters to see significant differences between the mainstream parties in terms of economic policy. That blurring enabled issues such as immigration—and its role in eroding social rights—to become important in distinguishing the parties' appeals to voters.

As the Social Democrats gave in to the "no alternative dogma" that "the tight fiscal constraints faced by governments are the only realistic possibility in a world where global markets would not permit any deviation from the neo-liberal orthodoxy" (Laclau and Mouffe 2001: xvi), "working class" voters started to move to the anti-immigrant Progress Party and, subsequently, to the populist Danish People's Party, which adopted a "nativist conception of welfare state" and criticized the Social Democrats for having "repudiated their role as protectors of welfare values and principles in the name of libertarian stances—on immigration, for instance—undermining the welfare state present and future" (Betz and Meret 2013: 118). The populist Right argued that political and cultural elites' multicultural agenda was "a Trojan horse of globalization since it must invariably lead to the destruction of national communities and identities. . . . This line of reasoning could effectively appeal to those workers feeling that levels of welfare were threatened by an increasingly globalized world, where growing immigration is among the consequences" (Betz and Meret 2013: 118). The Social Democrats responded to this voter flight by adopting an anti-immigration rhetoric increasingly focusing on "their culture," "their religion," "their criminality," and "their misuse of the welfare system." Between 1993 and 2001, the successive governments led by the Social Democrats tightened the immigration laws thirty-six times ("Ali and the 36 Restrictions," *Politiken*, July 8, 2001). In the same period, the Social Democratic prime minister replaced the minister for internal affairs—the minister responsible for immigration-related issues in that period—three times, each time with a political figure whose rhetoric on immigrants was harsher than the previous one; but none of these "measures" helped them recapture voter support that they had lost to the DPP and the Right.

This displacement of the traditional structures of identification (i.e., social classes or the corresponding division between left and right) occurred through a gradual but relatively rapid shift from humanitarian and compassion-based approaches (to the question of asylum and refugees) to culture-based approaches (to the question of immigration in general). The questions asked in the first phase, "How can we help them?" or "Can we afford it?" were gradually replaced with "Can we sustain our national identity?" "Can the welfare system survive immigration?" "Do immigrants challenge our 'common' achievements?" (i.e., gender equality, tolerance for gays, and freedom of speech). In the 1990s, answers to such questions, from political actors, media pundits, and ordinary citizens, became increasingly negative or skeptical. These questions forced even those who were critical of the racist tone of the debate to think of the central social and political questions in relation to immigration. As Gullestad (2002: 45) explains, the notion of equality, for example, has increasingly become connected to an "imagined [cultural] sameness" that "underpins a growing ethnification of national identity" (see also McIntosh 2015).The assumption in the new discursive environment is that the welfare state and other "common" achievements are grounded in solidarity and trust, which, in turn, have been built upon shared cultural values. As I have argued, these achievements, which were the result of decades of "internal" struggles, came to be imagined as common in the face of an external force that threatened the validity of these "values."

Hegemony is not a given state of affairs once it is achieved: social life is too heterogeneous to be neatly articulated in antagonistic categories. Every articulation leaves out surplus meaning that threatens the stability of the hegemonic articulation. In other words, hegemony has to be continuously fought for; the antagonisms have to be continuously reproduced. The reproduction of an antagonistic relationship requires an ongoing focus on the antagonistic force. Frequent controversies and crises (e.g., moral panics) around the antagonizing force do just that: crises are strategic moments of discourse that keep the focus on immigration and reproduce immigrants as a threat to the cohesion of society. Crises help turn single acts of deviance (e.g., murder, rape, or other crimes of violence) into symptoms of a larger cultural pattern. Thus, a murder becomes more than a murder: it becomes an example of the general threat immigrants pose to "our values," which underpin social peace and cohesion. An "honor killing" becomes, for example, a threat to "our core value of gender equality." The threat not only converts "gender equality" from an aspiration into an already established "common value" but also culturalizes it. This is achieved in a circular manner: murder is equated with the immigrants' culture because it is committed by an immigrant; the immigrant as a cultural-ontological category turns murder into an instance of "immigrant culture"; and "immigrant culture" in turn is used to explain murder as a cultural act as if the uniqueness of the murder is given a priori. The tautological reasoning also contributes to the construction of antagonism: murder as "immigrant criminality" draws the boundaries of society and simultaneously keeps immigrants outside those boundaries as if boundaries were already there.

I want to discuss how the culturalization of an issue tautologically produces the antagonistic categories. In November 1996, the doorman of a dance club was killed by a Palestinian teenager who had been denied entry. This murder was discussed exclusively as a matter of culture—as if murder would be natural in Muslim cultures. *Ekstra Bladet* chose to interview an ordinary Dane, who said, "I cannot tolerate their violence. Vikings do not carry guns and knives. It is not part of our culture" (November 25, 1996). The absurdity of such a statement—that murder is a natural part of "the" Muslim culture and Vikings did not carry guns and knives—gets lost once a murder is explained culturally. Murder understood as a cultural act reproduces the Muslim immigrant while simultaneously the Muslim immigrant (i.e., Islam) explains murder as a cultural act. The normalized absurdity of cultural explanations becomes more clear when two identical acts are compared. About a week after the murder by the Palestinian teenager, another murder in a dance club was committed by a Dane who fired into the crowd, also because he was denied entry. This time, no reference was made to his cultural background or ethnicity. He was a "madman," and it was an individual act of deviance (Diken 1998: 60).

Incessant crises and controversies around issues such as immigrant criminality, immigrants' misuse of the social system, honor killings, forced marriages, immigrants' birthrates, headscarves, and gang rapes—all of which are explained with reference to immigrants' cultural and religious norms—help cement the boundaries of society in the social imaginary and keep alive the sense that immigrants pose a threat to "our" common interests. In other words, the sustained focus via perpetual crises around immigrants draws attention to cultural differences as the defining moments of social division and ontologizes the Muslim immigrant vis-à-vis the nation.

Crises around Muslims, 1987–2001

The period between 1987 and 2001 was characterized by a series of crises around Muslim immigrants provoked by various actors[1] or deliberate media campaigns that pushed the progressive parties, movements, and organizations into a defensive position where they were continuously forced to respond to criticism for being too tolerant and for letting society fall into decay through their "misplaced" multiculturalist ideals.

The year 1991 began, for example, with a campaign by the Progress Party against plans to build a mosque in Copenhagen. The Progress Party portrayed Islam as a threat to Danish society. Although other parties did not join the fray, they defended the plans merely on the grounds that the state had already entered into an agreement to rent the lot without challenging the premise that Islam was a threat (Jacobsen 2009: 24). The 1990s were the decade during which phenomena such as "honor killings" and "forced marriages" were introduced and took up a significant portion of the coverage, especially in the second half of the 1990s (Andreassen 2005: 163). Crime, violence, gang rapes, private religious schools, ritual (Muslim) slaughter traditions, child brides, ghettos, and immigrants' misuse of the welfare system were the topics that dominated the media's coverage of immigrants (Andreassen 2005; Gaasholt and Togeby 1995; Madsen 2000).

Toward the end of the decade, the tabloid *Ekstra Bladet* ran a two-and-a-half-month campaign in a series called "The Foreigners." One of the stories, about a Somalian refugee named Ali, created a controversy that quickly developed into a moral panic. The story, headlined "Receives 631,724 Kr. in Social Welfare" (June 23, 1997) (about US$104,000 as of January 2015), painted a picture of Ali "as a foreigner who was exploiting the Danish welfare system and posed a threat to Danish majority values and interest" (Hervik 2011: 60). The article was accompanied by a color image of a smiling Ali and his family next to a black-and-white image of a Danish woman and her mother who were not smiling because, according to the story, they were not receiving the help they needed. The story, as expected, was a manipulation of the numbers: it added up the payments to his ex-wife and his children, as if it was a single amount paid to Ali (62).

As customary for this kind of campaign journalism, once the story was published, the paper asked for comments from politicians, experts, and ordinary people. Karen Jespersen, the Social Democratic minister for social affairs opined that the family clearly belonged to Africa, not to Denmark, whereas Anders Fogh Rasmussen, the vice chair of the right-wing Liberal Party—who became prime minister following the 2001 elections—was outraged that "non-Danish citizens have access to precisely the same welfare benefits as Danish citizens, who one may assume contribute to the system of taxation" (Hervik 2011: 61). Politicians and experts from all quarters weighed in, blowing up the case; Ali became the symptom of Muslim immigrants who misused the welfare system, whereas Danes who had built up the system were left behind. An editorial in *Ekstra Bladet* called for lower welfare payments for the newly arrived immigrants, and the controversy ended with the new Integration Act of 1999, which introduced a lower "integration payment."

This was the newspaper that only a decade earlier had criticized Krarup for being racist and called him "the Black Priest." The tabloid's traditionally populist motto—on the side of the ordinary man on the street against the system that oppressed him—had turned the "ordinary man" into the "ordinary Dane," as opposed to a system that protected undeserving Muslims.

The Social Democrats hoped that the Integration Act of 1999 and the replacement of Thorkild Simonsen (who was already a hardliner) with Karen Jespersen—whose rhetoric against Muslims was indistinguishable from that of the DPP—as the minister of internal affairs would end criticism that the party was too soft on immigration. But as the 2001 elections showed, it only contributed to the success of the DPP and accelerated the hegemonic imaginary based on the antagonism between "ordinary Danes" and Muslim immigrants.

Centrality of Culture in Immigration Discourse

By 2001, many people inside and outside Denmark testified to the preoccupation with Danish national identity, immigrants, and their culture. Sasha Polakow-Suransky (2002), for instance, wrote that

> it came as a surprise to nearly everyone when this icon of northern European welfare-state progressivism, and the erstwhile poster child of liberal immigration policy, descended into an inflammatory election campaign last November [2001]. The issues of immigration and

> refugees took center stage, despite Denmark's record-low unemployment and the fact that less than 8 percent of its population is of foreign origin.

Likewise, Stephen Smith (2002), cofounder of the UK-based Beth Shalom Holocaust Centre, reported that

> what we are witnessing in Denmark is nothing less than the return of rightwing extremism to respectability—not through the acceptance of a controversial Haider [at the time the leader of the Far Right in Austria] or Le Pen [the leader of the far-right FN in France], but through the quiet adoption of their stance by mainstream political parties. . . . Denmark's government is now taking steps which will turn one of the world's most liberal countries into a bastion of introverted nationalism.

Many scholars note that Muslims have become the ultimate "other" since 2001 and attribute this development to the events of September 11, 2001, or the Danish parliamentary elections the same year (Hervik 2004; Jensen 2008; Mudde and Kaltwasser 2013; Meret 2011). However, by 2001, immigration had already become the most important issue (Andersen 2004; Bjørklund and Andersen 2002; Rydgren 2004), and culture and religion had already become central to immigration discourse (Madsen 2000; Gaasholt and Togeby 1995; Horsti 2008; Togeby 2003). The election campaign of 2001, in which immigration and Muslim immigrants became the most important election issue, was the culmination of what had already been taking place: the right-wing Liberal-Conservative coalition government came to power with an election campaign that almost solely focused on immigration, and the main figures behind the 1986 campaign against the Refugee Council, Søren Krarup and his cousin Jesper Langballe, were elected as members of the Folketing for the DPP. Furthermore, the coalition government was formed with the parliamentary support of the DPP, which became the key to keeping the government in power, which in turn gave the party enormous influence on the political decisions, especially immigration policy. As Polakow-Suransky (2002) observed, by 2001, "Nowhere [was] the contrast between the old political discourse and the new more dramatic than in Denmark."

My data confirm these observations. There is a substantial body of work that shows that a clear dichotomy of "us" and "them" was established in the immigration debate in the 1990s (Gaasholt and Togeby 1995; Hervik 1999,

2002, 2011; Hussain, Yılmaz, and O'Connor 1997; Meret 2011; Meret and Siim 2013), and the data of this study show that these categories had become highly culturalized by 2000.

As I explained in chapter 2, the coding comes out of a close reading of the newspaper clips. I coded 2,152 newspaper articles from 1984, 1986, 1987, and 2001 in terms of their perspectives: humanitarian, cultural, economic/social burden, or rights. My codes for humanitarian and cultural perspectives were constructed after a qualitative analysis of some stories typical of the genre, and the coding process itself was a semiqualitative analysis of each story (I determined their perspective qualitatively rather than defining some words as indicators of a particular perspective and counting them). "Humanitarian perspective" indicates stories where the issue of immigration is discussed (by the author or by the agents in the story) in terms of helping people in need. Unless it is explicitly discussed through other perspectives, stories about problems with providing housing for refugees or the process of receiving them are coded as stories with a humanitarian perspective. "Cultural perspective" indicates either that the issue is explained by the immigrants' background or in relation to what it does to Danish culture/identity. Neither perspective is inscribed with a particular tone: a story or commentary coded for humanitarian perspective may argue that Denmark cannot afford to help all of the refugees in the world (a typical argument in letters to the editor in 1984); a story coded for cultural perspective may argue that immigrants' culture is not a threat to Danishness (a typical argument in 1987).

One of the most striking findings was the complete dominance of the humanitarian perspective in 1984 (82.5 percent of all stories vs. 1.1 percent cultural perspective) and the dominance of the cultural perspective in 2001 (32.2 percent cultural vs. 26.6 percent humanitarian; see table 4.1). Considering that the sample included all kinds of stories, from sports activities to short reports of crime or violence (which could not be coded as cultural), one-third of the sample is an impressive proportion.

In news stories in particular, the humanitarian perspective decreased from 81.4 percent in 1984 to 34.0 percent in 2001, whereas the cultural per-

TABLE 4.1. Perspective in All Stories

Perspectives/all	1984	1986	1987	2001
Humanitarian	82.5%	87.3%	47.2%	26.6%
Cultural	1.1%	1.7%	13.1%	32.2%
Mixed	0.5%	1.0%	4.9%	8.5%
Not clear	9.5%	4.7%	22.6%	17.6%
Other	6.4%	5.3%	12.2%	5.1%

spective increased from 0 percent in 1984 to 21.5 percent in 2001 (see table 4.2). Commentaries also presented a striking picture (see table 4.3). While 94.7 percent of 1984 commentaries were humanitarian, only 16.0 percent were in 2001. No commentaries from 1984 were coded as cultural, but 50.6 percent were in 2001. In addition, a review of how immigrants were defined (or named) over time reveals that fewer than 1 percent of stories in 1984 and 1986 named immigrants as Muslims. In 2001, 19.2 percent did so.

The higher percentage of the cultural perspective in the commentaries than in the news in 2001 is indicative of the methodological constraints of content analysis. Content analysis focuses solely on manifest content. If the numbers in news stories do not seem to reflect the obsession with immigrants' (i.e., Muslim) culture in 2001, it is because many news stories in 2001 were about problems with finding decent housing for refugees, most of which I coded as having a humanitarian perspective in order to have consistent coding across time. This is where we see the limitations of content analysis: the stories may be coded in a particular way to be consistent, but how they are actually understood depends on the discursive environment in which they are embedded, but that is not manifest in the story itself. For example, a debate on housing in 1984 may have been motivated by the problems of finding decent housing for refugees, whereas the same debate may be motivated by the desire to disperse refugees to prevent the formation of Muslim "ghettos." But this background will not necessarily be reflected in the news stories. I coded many stories as "not clear" (15 percent in 1984; 17.2 percent in 2001). All of the "unclear" stories from 1984 were initially coded

TABLE 4.2. Perspective in News Stories

Perspectives/news	1984	1986	1987	2001
Humanitarian	81.4%	86.8%	57.4%	34.0%
Cultural	0%	0.9%	7.4%	21.5%
Mixed	0%	0%	2.8%	5.7%
Not clear	15.0%	6.2%	20.4%	17.2%
Other	3.6%	6.1%	12.0%	21.6%

TABLE 4.3. Perspective in Commentaries

Perspectives/comments	1984	1986	1987	2001
Humanitarian	94.7%	90.9%	44.8%	16.0%
Cultural	0%	4.5%	29.3%	50.6%
Mixed	0%	4.5%	3.4%	11.1%
Not clear	0%	0%	15.5%	12.3%
Other	5.3%	0.1%	7.0%	10.0%

as humanitarian (because there were almost no other perspectives available at that time), but I recoded them after finding similar stories in 2001 that could, despite the similarities, be interpreted as being written from a cultural perspective if the context was included in my considerations.

To make this point clear, I want to discuss the same type of stories from different periods. The first story is from *Jyllands-Posten* (October 22, 1986), "Convicted for Murder Attempt," which is about an Iranian refugee who had stabbed his wife. The reporter explains that the incident probably had to do with the divorce proceedings between the couple, implying that the attack was motivated by jealousy. There is no word of culture, tradition, or religion to explain his conduct; the story is treated the same way as a story about Danes.

A decade later, by the mid-1990s, it had become common on both sides of the political spectrum to talk about cultural differences in connection with violence or a murder committed by an immigrant. On September 1, 1996, for example, a teenager from an immigrant family beat a young Dane to death after pulling him out of a taxi in Aarhus. The homicide led to a protest demonstration against violence led by Minister for Social Affairs Karen Jespersen (Social Democrat) with the participation of Danes and immigrants. When interviewed by TV2 News, Jespersen said "They have to learn to get on with the Danish culture and learn to behave like Danes. They are going to live here, but the problem is that there is a long distance between them and us" (*TV2 News*, September 15, 1996). It is ironic that, two weeks later, an immigrant youth was pulled out of a taxi and beaten into coma by three young Danes without any prior argument ("19-Year-Old Gets His Face Smashed," *BT*, September 18, 1996). I read the newspaper clips from the rest of the month and did not see much coverage of this attack; the police admitted that the attack was racially motived, yet there were no protest demonstrations against racist violence or any condemnations of racism by any officials. Nor was there any mention of culture as the background for the attack. Around the same date, the newspapers were full of stories about a law proposal by the Social Democratic minister of internal affairs that would make it easier to deport immigrants convicted of drug crimes.

By the beginning of the new millennium, culture had become the pivotal category for explaining any kind of phenomenon related to immigrants, even in cases that normally would defy cultural explanations, as illustrated by the following example: According to a statistics, immigrant women had a higher abortion rate than Danes (*Jyllands-Posten*, June 17, 2001). If we assume that most religious traditions do not condone abortion, the statistics could be read as an indication that culture or religion falls short of explaining immigrants' behavior. Yet culture had become so indispensable to understanding immigrants that the reporter chose to interview a Danish social worker as an expert on immigrants' cultural background, who explained that "Muslim women do not demand that their men use protection"—an explanation that turned abortion into an example of the unequal gender relations in "Muslim culture." In short, it was almost impossible to not use "culture" as the defining characteristic of the category of immigrant by 2001.

As these examples illustrate, the numbers alone cannot illustrate the degree to which immigration discourse had been culturalized in fewer than two decades; it is difficult to capture in numbers the fundamentally different discursive environments in which seemingly similar stories are "encoded/decoded" by the media and audiences (Hall 1980). Some of the stories in the later periods may "only" recount what happened and consequently are not coded as "cultural" because they do not have an explicitly manifest cultural perspective, but these "factual" stories would still be understood within the social horizon, whose contours are shaped by the new cultural ontology of the social.

Researchers often try to understand changes in discourse in terms of changes in opinions or attitudes as expressed through opinion polls (Andersen 2002; Blum 1986; Gaasholt and Togeby 1995; Körmendi 1986; Madsen 2000; Togeby 1997, 2003). The changing nature of the categories, however, is also an often unacknowledged problem in public opinion polls. Despite the fact that both scholarly and vernacular observations repeatedly point to the immense preoccupation with national and cultural identity in discourse, public opinion polls about immigrants nevertheless show a remarkable stability (Togeby 2004). The problem with trying to understand change in terms of public opinion is the assumption that people express the same opinion about the same object (e.g., immigrants) each time they are asked over time. The transformation of the meaning of "immigrants" as a category is rarely acknowledged: The category of immigrants people expressed opinions about in the early 1980s was fundamentally different from the immigrants they were asked about in the early 2000s: the first was essentially a labor category associated with the "class struggle," whereas the latter is associated with "cultural struggle." It does not mean that the difference in the ontological character of "immigrant" necessarily corresponds to an increase in negative opinions about immigrants. Immigrant as a labor category can still have a "negative" association depending on the debate in the polling period: if immigrants are primarily discussed in terms of being cheap labor force that will undermine working-class solidarity, opinions expressed about immigrants may be negative, whereas immigrants as Muslims can awake sympathy if they are portrayed as victims of oppression in their home countries or of racism.

There is also another sense in which opinion measurement is problematic. What exactly constitutes a "positive" or "negative" evaluation? My sample from five daily newspapers shows that the number of news stories about immigrants coded as positive increased from 17.7 percent in 1984 to 40.4 percent in 1986 and 48.1 percent in 1987 even though the category of immigrants was increasingly culturalized in the same period, where I recorded a corresponding decrease in negative stories. The "discrepancy" was due to the changing nature of the same topics. When the focus in news coverage in 1984 was on incoming refugees, and the right-wing government attempted to introduce restrictions to immigration, I coded stories that promoted restrictions as "negative" and resistance against restrictions as "positive." Once the laws were tightened in 1986, both the parliamentary opposition and the government defended the already restrictive laws, but their rhetoric became "positive" because the government and the parliamentary opposition mobilized humanitarian arguments against the Far Right's push for further restrictions. In other words, what was negative in previous phase of coding was now coded positive because the new status quo was now being defended against the demands for further restrictions. As a result of this change in rhetoric, opinion polls recorded a positive change in attitudes in the same period (Körmendi 1986; Blum 1986; Gaasholt and Togeby 1995).

The same observation can be made about surveys around 2000. An analysis of the Eurobarometer 2000 survey concluded that Danish attitudes toward immigrants became increasingly positive in the period between 1997 and 2000 (Thalhammer et al. 2001). The authors explain the positive tendency with decreasing unemployment rates (which might have reduced Danes' concerns about immigration). The analysis raises more questions than it answers: How (and why) was the Social Democratic / Radical Party coalition ousted in 2001 by the Liberal/Conservative coalition despite the positive attitudes toward immigrants and Denmark's record low unemployment rates?

The answer may be more in the preoccupation with the question of immigration and cultural identity than in just the numbers. Regardless of the negativity or positivity of stories or opinions, immigrants as a labor category do not have the same sociopolitical significance as immigrants as a cultural/religious category, and numbers cannot account for this qualitative change in terms of its significance: immigrant workers can still be considered to be a part of working-class solidarity, but immigrants who are interpellated via religion are situated in a new network of discursive associations that relegates them outside the national collectivity that is now considered the basis for solidarity. It is in this context that the numbers in tables 4.1, 4.2, and 4.3 should be read: by 2001, the cultural perspective was so pervasive that even stories with a humanitarian perspective would be understood in relation to a culturalized ontological structure of society. Cultural identity problems, unsuccessful integration, religion, blood revenge, traditions, and honor were all conceptual resources used to understand the immigrants' behavior. And it was the intense focus on Muslim immigrants and their "culture" during the election campaign in the fall of 2001 that culminated in the change of power to the right and the DPP's unprecedented election victory. As Ulf Hedetoft (2003), the director of Academy for Migration Studies in Denmark, testified, "The issue of immigration . . . dominated the general election campaign. The general tone of the debate was acrimonious, bordering on vengeful; immigration was projected as the most imminent and serious threat to the history, culture, identity and homogeneity of 'little Denmark.'" Thus, 2001 became the turning point in the sense that the hegemonic transformation that had been taking place since the mid-1980s finally crystallized in a political outcome: a new government that immediately initiated institutional changes, a process Krarup described as "system change 2001," which, he wrote, was the culmination of what had started in the mid-1980s ("Krarup: Denmark Has Become a Pioneering Country in Europe," *Politiken*, November 10, 2009).

Centrality of Immigration and Cultural Identity to Social Imaginary

That Muslims have come to signify immigration and that immigration has become one of the most important issues is common knowledge among scholars of immigration and the Far Right. I argue that immigration is not only one of the most important issues with a "priming effect" on how people vote (Iyengar, Peters, and Kinder 1982), but that immigration is central to the hegemonic structure of society within which fundamental social and political questions are thought and discussed. As Garbi Schmidt explains, "We speak a great deal of immigration in Denmark. We speak of what immigration does to Danishness, to our welfare state, to so-called Danish values. We debate Islam, cohesion, ghettoization, radicalization. Some even speak of Danes as a tribe and as historically homogenous" (qtd. in Brink 2014).

As Laclau and Mouffe (2001: xv) argue, "The establishment of a new hegemony . . . requires the creation of new political frontiers." What is different from how Gramsci envisioned hegemonic change, however, is that the new political frontiers are not, as I discussed in earlier chapters, drawn between already existing social groups; the creation of new political frontiers also produces its own ontological categories even if the names of those ontological categories remain the same (i.e., the immigrant of the 1970s is not the immigrant of the new millennium; the category has been transformed in the hegemonic transformation process). In this sense, "society" is a hegemonic construct that can only be represented by its limits, which prevent it from being harmonious and coherent. During the decades following World War II, with the hegemony of the Social Democratic vision, it was the capitalist class that prevented the working class and its allies from achieving equality and prosperity, and all other emancipatory projects were configured within a vision of class society characterized by its external limits: capitalism that was "tamed" through social democratic reforms intended to achieve a better distribution of resources. The social democratic political program articulated the indignation over inequality as a matter of class struggle, which had a mobilizing function.

This is where the hegemonic displacement has taken place: the culturalized immigration debate has moved to the center of political discourse and has restructured the notion of who "we" and "them" are. The fundamental social antagonism is now imagined to be between "us" (the "Danish people") and "them" (the Muslim immigrants): "confronted" with the "alien" element, a sense of "belonging together" prior to the arrival of the alien force must be created, and this sense is produced through an emphasis on the "core common values." However, neither the existence nor the nature of these values is given a priori; they are produced by reference to the antagonizing force whose presence prevents "us" from functioning in harmony through the "core" values that are imagined to characterize "us." In other words, it is the "nature" of the alien element that determines who "we" are. This antagonizing force is now considered to be "the Muslim immigrant," and subsequently the "core values" are characterized as those that "the Muslim immigrants" challenge, such as democracy, gender equality, freedom of speech, and the separation of politics and religion. The presence of Muslim immigrants prevents us from having the cohesive force built on mutual trust necessary for social and political solidarity, which in turn is the precondition for sustaining the welfare society. Thus, it is the welfare state that is threatened by the presence of Muslim immigrants. It is in this context that debates such as the so-called meatball wars fit. "Democracy," as Lykkeberg (2008: 254–60) argues, "is [now] identified with 'core values' that secure the political collectivity. . . . One debate book after another by researchers, editors, and journalists insists that welfare democracy implies a 'value community,' a religion, or even ethnic homogeneity in order to function" (my translation).

This is not to say that everybody agrees with the particulars of this hegemonic vision. Hegemony is not entirely a question of a particular set of policy proposals becoming commonly accepted. Indeed, a recent survey shows that half of the population in Denmark is ashamed of the way immigration is debated (Baumann and Schefte 2014). Rather, a hegemonic political project operates as a social imaginary that establishes a single horizon of intelligibility; the imaginary constrains what is "thinkable" or feasible within the ontological boundaries of society. As Smith (1994: 36–37) explains, "A hegemonic project does not . . . require [the political subjects'] . . . unequivocal support for its specific demands. It pursues, instead, a far more subtle goal, namely the naturalization of its specific vision of the social order as the social order itself" and renders alternative representations unintelligible. In the new social imaginary, the figure of the Muslim immigrant has become indispensable to thinking about the past, present, and future of society.

I will start with the past. One of the basic arguments of the populist Far Right is that there is a gap in the harmonious continuity of society caused by the presence of Muslim immigrants and that society can be restored to its original unity if certain steps are taken to keep the nation culturally homogeneous.

The clearest articulation of the gap is a controversial book published by the DPP in 2001. The cover of the book, *Denmark's Future: Your Country—Your Choice . . .*, pictures a crowd with a fierce-looking Muslim immigrant with a gun in the foreground, who was photographed at a demonstration in the main square of Copenhagen. The book is organized in two main parts: the first is about immigration and what it means for Denmark; the second is about DPP policies addressing Denmark's future. The first part contains a section with a brief history of immigration, a section called "The Impossible Combination of Islam and Democracy," a section with statistics on immigration and immigrants' criminality (e.g., murder, violence, and rape), and a section that compares Denmark's problems with immigration with those of Germany (to connect the problems to immigrants' religion and culture). The first part of the book draws a picture of Denmark drowning in problems brought by Muslim immigrants, which is in stark contrast to the second part, "Denmark's Future," which draws a picture of an idyllic country that Denmark will again become when and if the DPP's immigration policies are implemented.

The visual organization of the book is striking. The first part is filled with photographs of immigrants in everyday situations that could be found in any mainstream newspaper, but the sheer number of the photos with dark-skinned immigrants in every corner of Denmark and in every aspect of everyday life, and the combination of pictures and the text, create an image of Denmark being invaded by these alien intruders. For example, the caption of a picture of some Somalian teenagers at a suburban train station punching their tickets reads: "Stabbing, assault on train staff, vandalism, and trouble have been driven out of suburban stations on the Køge line" (p. 71). Most women in the pictures wear headscarves. This image is in stark contrast to the visual organization of the second part, which begins with the section titled "Denmark's Future" and an uncaptioned, full-page picture of the Danish landscape with meadows and blue skies. This is not an arbitrary choice of picture; landscape paintings were an important part of the Danish nation-making process (Hvenegård-Lassen 1996). The rest of the chapter is full of idyllic pictures of Danish landscapes, peaceful blond Danes in everyday activities, and children with blond hair. Pictures of the Danish flag—the most important signifier of the Danish nation and omnipresent not only in formal but also in everyday situations like birthday parties—are scattered throughout the second part. In short, the cultural antagonism between the Danish nation and the Muslim aliens is represented by these two sections: one describes the grim realities of Denmark; the other describes the desire for a cohesive Danish nation characterized by cultural/ethnic sameness.

The second part of the book portrays a future that implicitly refers back to the past: a future Denmark that can be restored to its original state with cultural unity before the arrival of Muslim immigrants by implementing the DPP's immigration policy. The implicit premise for the argument is that there was an original culturally (i.e., ethnically and racially) cohesive Denmark before Muslim immigration. It is this past cultural unity (based on sameness) that is now broken but can be restored.

Reimagining the Past

If this vision of past unity/sameness were confined to the populist Far Right, I would not call it hegemonic. What makes the far-right vision hegemonic is the commonsense status of the assumption in both vernacular and academic discourse that the past was characterized by ethnic and cultural homogeneity and that welfare democracy requires social cohesion based on a "value community" (Lykkeberg 2008). The various viewpoints coalesce around the issue of how to deal with the new situation in which the cultural homogeneity is presumed to be broken.

For instance, Gaasholt and Togeby (1995) argue that anti-immigrant forces "have won the struggle both for access to the media and for the way the issue is presented in the media" (163). Nevertheless, they begin their book with the much-repeated view that "the Scandinavian countries have long had some of the most uniform—or homogenous—populations in the world. . . . It is hardly wrong to describe postwar Scandinavian countries as relatively free of ethnic dividing lines" (9). "Denmark is transformed from being an ethnically homogeneous society to a country with a big dominant majority and a plurality of small ethnic minorities. . . . [O]ne has to make an effort not to see immigrants as a burden for Danish society" (27; my translation).

Ümit Necef (2000: 134) likewise argues that the question of immigration changed from being an economic and labor issue to a cultural one in the mid-1970s, but he identifies immigration as a problem that challenges two fundamental constructs of the modern democratic, and wealthy countries in the West: the nation-state and the welfare state (31).

This is the common way of talking about the shift in the immigration debate: the sheer numbers of immigrants from "other cultures" challenge the homogeneity of Danish society, which is the basis of the welfare system.

The first problem with this view is the positive distinction between reality and discourse. Social reality is treated as a preexisting entity prior to articulation and discourse as its symbolic reflection. In such a distinction, reality (i.e., a social category) is privileged over the symbolic realm; the actions of the ontological category (e.g., Muslim immigrants) come first and determine the symbolic realm (i.e., discourse on immigration). The discursive shift, however, is not about well-defined new groups entering the scene and changing the way we conduct our social and political business; it is about the production of new groups even if the names remain the same. Once the articulation of the new frontiers becomes hegemonic, the social practices they structure can appear so natural that members of a society can fail to see that the ontological structure is the result of political processes.

Phillips and Jørgensen (2002) explain it with the example of childhood. Modern Western societies view the treatment and understanding of children as a group with distinctive characteristics as a matter of common sense. However, just a few hundred years ago, children were regarded as "small adults" and were treated accordingly. The category of children is now treated as if it has always existed and constitutes an ontological entity on which a wide spectrum of research is conducted.

The second problem with this common wisdom is the temporal space from which it speaks. Although it presents itself as a universal wisdom, it speaks of the past through a contemporary perspective. When researchers (and others) discuss today's immigration as a challenge to Denmark's ethnic homogeneity, they look to the past from today's hegemonic perspective. In other words, the narrative of the past reflects the focus on cultural difference as the main signifier of social antagonisms in contemporary Denmark rather than being a neutral descriptive statement about how the country was in the past. It is not that immigration and debate on immigration is new: Denmark has received immigrants throughout history (e.g., Jews, Swedes, Germans, Poles, and Hungarians), but it is assumed that these immigrants were "successfully" assimilated without great problems because they were culturally similar, as opposed to the culturally alien Muslim immigrants.

It is not my purpose here to completely discard the idea that there may be a relationship between demographic changes and immigration discourse. Rather, I want to question the deterministic assumptions behind these historical narratives: our understanding of this relationship is shaped through political struggles, not dictated by "objective" criteria such as numbers or "cultural sameness/difference."

First, Lucassen (2005) and Lucassen, Feldman, and Oltmer (2006) show us that in the period 1850–1940 intra-European immigrants (especially Italians, Irish, and Poles) were perceived as culturally and "racially" different in some host countries, and they were detested mostly because they were Catholics. In other words, the perception that intra-European immigrants were similar to the populations of the host countries is a projection of contemporary perceptions into a past that is retrospectively reproduced as ethnically more homogeneous—a state of cohesiveness to which society can be restored.

Second, cultural difference/sameness was not always the criterion by which the immigrant groups were treated. Niels Finn Christiansen explains, for example, that Danish "workmen" did not have nationalist orientations in the first half of the nineteenth century (cited in Jensen 2000: 60). Only after confrontations between Denmark and Germany in 1848 and Denmark's defeat by Germany in 1864 did Danish "workmen" begin demanding that Germans not be allowed to work in Denmark. There were several newspaper stories in 1865 and 1866 about groups of Danes attacking German workers. Jensen notes that in both cases there were no characterizations or descriptions of the German workers in the media. The incidents were treated as an instance of Danish internal political controversies rather than as problems caused by the Germans and their background (Jensen 2000).

Swedish immigrants, however, were described as "stupid," "lazy," "loose," and "unreliable" by the progressive, urban *Politiken* (which at the time had an arrogant attitude toward peasants and immigrants), and their presence created the potential for confrontations with Danish workers because Swedish workers were seen as wage suppressors by the emerging Danish working class. In this context, the coverage by the working-class press is interesting. The Social Democratic Party's official newspaper, *Social-Demokraten*, described the problems with Swedish immigration in terms of wage suppression and strikebreaking, but the internationalist orientation of the party also meant that its strategy was to co-opt the Swedes into the working-class struggle for socialism. Social Democrats were relatively subdued in their criticism of Swedish immigrant workers as long as they agreed to be organized in labor unions. On the other hand, right-wing political parties, although generally favoring "mobility of the workforce," were simultaneously restrictive about granting residency permits and citizenship, which would have allowed immigrants to use public resources and curb foreign workers' desire to break strikes.

As noted above, this was a period when the working-class movement was trying to establish itself with a distinct internationalist notion of socialism. Immigration entered the discourse as—to use Laclau's language—a "heterogeneous element," and the struggle was about articulating this new element into existing social formations. The working-class movement articulated the immigrants as yet another group of workers to be included in the popular struggle, whereas, for the capitalists, they were just another resource for production similar to other types of resources and goods. Positive and negative descriptions of immigrants seem to be used flexibly to fit the rhetorical demands of these struggles. In short, in the late nineteenth century, when political discourse was dominated by class struggles and when society constituted itself around these antagonisms, "immigrant," it seems, was articulated within the framework of class struggles rather than ethnicity and culture.

In the 1960s and 1970s, immigration occurred in a social context in which working-class organizations, stripped of internationalism, were well established as modern trade unions, but their demands were incorporated in the hegemonic system characterized by a social democratic consensus. Danish society was articulated in terms of the welfare state; working-class demands were advanced through negotiations rather than confrontations, and wage increases were linked to increased productivity. The dividing line in the debate on immigration was similar to earlier debates: on the one hand, between labor unions and their political organizations, who were traditionally skeptical about the imported workforce on the one hand and employers, and, on the other hand, right-wing political parties who traditionally were open to the controlled importation of foreign labor. The labor unions were inclined to accept foreign workers if they were employed according to existing labor agreements and regulations, including automatic membership in labor unions. When culture and religion entered the debate, these aspects of immigration were mostly configured within the general framework of the class struggle. According to Jensen (2000), there was a consensus among political parties and the news media concerning the importance of decent treatment of foreign workers (who were called "immigrants" toward the end of the decade).

As discussed in previous chapters, it was only after mid-1980s that culture came into focus as the defining feature of immigrants' presence. Rod Benson (2000: 224) describes a similar situation in France:

> The rise of a negative cultural framing of immigration in France is difficult to "see" in the sense that it has become so widely accepted today as the essence of a distinctive French model of immigration and integration. Many journalists, activists and even academics have come to accept a distinctive approach to cultural difference as not only the French reality but the French "way." They thus deny or can no longer even remember that a cultural framing of immigration was only one among many ways that immigration was understood in France during the 1960s and 1970s and that its taken-for-granted status of the 1980s had in fact to be won in the political and media arenas.

When researchers and politicians discuss immigration as a challenge to Denmark's ethnic/cultural homogeneity, they look at the past from today's hegemonic perspective, where homogeneity or the lack thereof is the main criterion for assessing the impact of immigration. In this view, Muslim immigration becomes the breaking point from the continuity of the harmonious past.

Pia Kjærsgaard, the former leader of the DPP, once said that the popularity of old Danish TV series was an indication of people's longing for the peaceful, idyllic, good, old days when Denmark was ethnically homogenous. At first glance, her argument makes perfect sense: the movies and TV series do reflect a more homogenous Danish society. Longing for the "golden days" is a feeling that has probably always been expressed in reaction to change, for example, in reaction to modernization and industrialization at the beginning of the last century; the work of intellectuals, writers, and artists since the beginning of the twentieth century often reflects the same kind of longing after the good old days in which society is imagined to be a cohesive unity broken by industrialization. In this sense, "good old days" signify the "purity" or "absent unity of society" (Laclau and Mouffe 2001) caused by the antagonisms in society. Because ethnicity and culture today are divisive issues in Denmark (and throughout Europe), the longing is articulated in terms of ethnic (or cultural) homogeneity.

Although the popularity of old movies may reflect a longing after the good old days, the question is whether these old movies actually reflect an ethnically homogeneous, frictionless society. We have become so used to thinking of society in terms of ethnicity and culture that we do not see cultural differences in the past; we are automatically cued into thinking that what we had in the past was an ethnically and culturally homogeneous society. It is through the contemporary preoccupation with ethnic homogeneity that movies are interpreted as reflections of an ethnically homogenous, frictionless, innocent past.

Was society really frictionless, complete, and unified, even if we accept the suggestion that there was ethnic sameness? On the contrary, these movies reflect the social upheavals and conflicts of their own times; they deal with the problems of the postwar economic boom and the struggles of the 1960s and 1970s, which brought feminism, gays, and environmentalists to the forefront. Some films are concerned with the erasure of old, "authentic" Danish culture and of the social cohesion that belonged to the idyllic past (prior to their time). As Lucassen (2005: 18) explains, in this sense every society and nation-state is and has been automatically multicultural. The old movies that are ironically interpreted today as representing an ideal past (by today's standards) represent a fantasy; not about the past but about the future of Denmark that, according to populist forces, can be brought back to its original state by eliminating the thing (Muslim immigrant) that subverts the authenticity and unity of Denmark.

This is how the populist Right's vision has become hegemonic. Historical accounts do not merely describe historical facts. They (re)write history through significant elements of the contemporary discourse. If culture is one of the defining elements of contemporary discourse, then contemporary accounts will look at history through the lens of culture as if culture were also the defining feature of social divisions in the past. This seems to be a generic strategy for all narratives that attempt to articulate a vision for the future: if society is explained by class struggles, then "the history of hitherto existing society . . . [becomes] the history of class struggles" (Marx and Engels 1978: 1). If religious narratives are the focus, then the history of the society becomes a phantasmatic tale of divine creation. Any of these interpretations would indicate a past constructed from the particular perspective of a contemporary struggle on a given discursive terrain. Thus, the narrative that Denmark (or Europe) is becoming multiethnic and multicultural implicates a particular understanding of the past, that is, what was there before the change. My point is that it is the narrative on the nature of the change that constructs—in a reverse direction of causality—the past as if its ontology was imagined through the same categories. This narrative suggests that the popular reaction against foreigners is the "natural" result of the demographic changes. In other words, it is the presence of culturally alien immigrants that causes reactions among Danish people rather than the particular political mobilizations that shape the very nature of the reactions.

In conclusion, hegemonic projects universalize their particular political imaginary by projecting their vision of the ontological order back into the past as if that order had always constituted the social/political horizon. Once the new antagonistic identity categories become the "common sense" of the social structure, even those who argue against the policies of the populist (and now mainstream) Right draw upon the same epistemology of the social. In this sense, an epistemological collusion occurs between Right and Left. It is this shared epistemology of the social that is the basis for the new hegemony. Even criticism becomes straitjacketed by the vision of the culturalized ontology of the social.

The Present: The Populist Right's Vision Is the New Common Sense

The argument that Muslim immigrants pose a threat to the cohesiveness of the Danish people was recognized as a far-right argument in the mid-1980s. Although the most xenophobic expressions of this argument are still considered to be the property of the DPP, the more savvy articulations of the Muslim challenge to Danish culture are common to both sides of the political spectrum. What is more significant is that the ontological vision that originally belonged to the populist Right now informs even the arguments the oppose far-right positions. In this sense, the culturalized ontology of the social is the basic premise for the argumentative texture of discourse.

Denmark—Your Country, Your Choice . . . , for example, created an immediate controversy upon its release in 2001. The controversy, however, was not about its antagonistic picture of Muslim immigrants. The critics focused on the writer's dishonesty when interviewing people for the book rather than the vision it promoted. The basic premise of the book was never questioned. Rather, the focus of the debate was the different strategies for fending off that threat. The basic positions can be summarized as (*a*) a complete halt to further immigration from Muslim countries and a further marginalization of the present immigrants (the DPP line); (*b*) a more strict policy of tightening the borders; or (*c*) an assimilationist policy with the goal of transforming present and incoming immigrants from culture-bound peasants into modern subjects through a heavy-handed integration policy. There were, of course, also critics of the racist implications of the book.

What makes the antagonistic picture painted by the DPP hegemonic is the taken-for-granted status of its vision that characterizes mainstream discourse, institutions, and legal provisions about immigration. In August of the same year, a think tank released a report with the title *Immigration, Integration and Economy* (Danish Interior Ministry 2001). The report, commissioned by Karen Jespersen, set up a number of "core Danish norms and values" that foreigners should be expected to "endorse and live in accordance with." These norms and values included freedom of religion, freedom of speech, equality between men and women, and staying out of criminal activity ("Core Norms and Values in Denmark," *Politiken*, August 7, 2001). The authors of the report said that they would not consider the degree to which Danes endorsed or lived in accordance with these norms and values, but nevertheless concluded that in terms of these norms and values the integration of immigrants had failed.

The report illustrated the fact that immigration had come to be understood in terms of cultural values, and that Muslim immigrants were seen as a substantial challenge to the "core values of Danish society," which in turn were defined as values Muslim immigrants did not respect.

Politiken covered the report extensively and published a series of articles under the heading "Integration." Although many of the stories were critical of the report, the heading was illustrated with a logo picturing three young immigrant women with headscarves walking by a shop window in which there are three mannequins wearing lingerie and decorated with Danish flags. In other words, the newspaper approached the question of immigration and integration using the same epistemological perspective on the huge gap between Muslim and Danish culture(s).

Almost all the newspapers illustrated their coverage of immigration with similar images. For example, *Kristeligt Dagblad* (a Christian daily known for its immigrant-friendly stance) illustrated a commentary on freedom of religion with an image that contrasts a woman with headscarf with a billboard ad that pictured a modern young woman with sleeveless blouse ("Equality of Religion and Cultural Degradation," August 8, 2001). When the right-wing *Jyllands-Posten* published a prognosis about the future of the Danish population, forecasting an explosion in the number of Muslims a century hence,[2] the article was also illustrated with a picture of a Muslim woman with headscarf ("The New Denmark," July 15, 2001).

Jyllands-Posten's article deserves a bit more attention here because it did not merely reproduce the dichotomy between Muslim headscarves and Western nudity. The article was the main story of the paper that day and was based on a demographic prognosis that the newspaper commissioned from a well-known anti-immigrant demographer in order to provoke a new crisis around Muslim immigration. The article quoted Ole Feldbæk, who warned that "[the new] immigration will change the Danish national identity because it is fundamentally different from earlier immigration. Many people arrive here with a different culture and religion." As part of the typical journalistic strategy to create controversy, the paper asked politicians from both sides of the political spectrum to respond to the prognosis ("The Right-Wing Parties [*de borgerlige*] Are Scared by the New Prognosis," July 16, 2001). As expected, Birte Rønn Hornbech, a spokesperson for the Liberal Party, warned that "if the tendency continues, we will destroy our country." Lene Espersen from the Conservative Party also expressed concern over the development: "We are going to keep Denmark as a national state and the values that bind us together." Jytte Andersen from the SDP did not see the number of immigrants as a problem, but added that "no Islamic doctrine is going to define what Denmark is going to look like."

There were many commentaries explicitly arguing that immigration posed a threat to Danish culture. Even commentators who apparently opposed this view wrote assuming that Danish national identity was indeed at stake. A commentary in the left-wing intellectual daily *Information* argued, for example, that "the US is a bigger threat for Danish identity than immigrants" (August 17, 2001). In a *Politiken* commentary (August 14, 2005) entitled "The Threat to Danishness," a high school teacher proposed calming down about the threat and recommended that readers "let immigrants and their descendants keep their culture, as long as it lasts" because "they will develop a modern consciousness about a convenient, escapist life style similar to Danishness," that is, their traditional culture will eventually evaporate in the face of Danish modernity.

As these examples illustrate, the image of Muslim immigrants as a completely alien cultural category (either as a threat or, put more mildly, a challenge) to Danish national unity was already well anchored both in political discourse and in the general social imaginary, as reflected in the commentaries and in the newspapers' illustrations of their coverage before the 2001 elections. In Dyrberg's (2000) words, "The welfare state is largely legitimized by reference to this unity of nation, culture, and people. Both the political establishment and those who claim to challenge or resist it draw on this ideological figure" (2).

2001: The Populist Vision Moves into the Center of Political Discourse

As Laclau (2005) reminds us, the social imaginary is not something that takes place only at the level of words and images: it is also embedded in material practices that become institutionalized. In other words, "Any hegemonic displacement should be conceived as a change in the configuration of the state provided that the latter is conceived . . . in an enlarged, Gramscian sense, as the ethico-political moment of the community" (106–7).

What makes 2001 a turning point was not that the immigration debate descended into an inflammatory election campaign in the fall of that year during which almost all parties competed to appear tough on immigration. It was the beginning of the institutionalization of the new hegemonic system, or a "change of system," as Krarup called it ("Krarup: Denmark Has Become a Pioneering Country in Europe," *Politiken*, November 13, 2009). According to Krarup, the resistance against a self-righteous system based on "totalitarian humanism" had finally turned into a victory against the Left and "cultural radicalism,"[3] which had "forced Denmark to become an immigration country and subsequently cease to be a cohesive nation." Denmark was now a divided and conflict-ridden country and "it was a bullied Danish people who eventually enforced a system change that seeks to secure a cohesive force in Denmark" ("Politicians React to Objection [against blatant racism by twelve writers]," *Politiken*, December 15, 2005). In other words, the system change was about reinstating the idyllic past in the future.

It was the right-wing parties' election victory on November 20, 2001, that enabled the "system change." The elections in November 2001 were the first time since 1926 that right-wing parties had gained a pure majority in Danish parliament without the need for support from the "middle" parties. The DPP won a historic 12 percent of the votes and became the third largest party in the Folketing. For the first time since 1920, the Liberal Party had more seats than the Social Democratic Party.

The Liberal Party went into the elections with a rhetoric similar to that of the DPP, making the Muslim threat the focus of its campaign and election slogan, "Time for Change." For instance, one poster featured a well-known photograph of Muslim immigrant youths leaving court after being convicted of the gang rape of a white Danish girl. The only words on the poster were "Time for Change." As Hedetoft (2003) explained, "The opposition astutely capitalized on a debate climate pervaded by diffuse fears, moral panics and unspecified enemy images. They created the expectation that not only could they put a virtual stop to any further inflow of undesirable aliens, but also reinstate Denmark to its former status as a peaceful, ethnically homogeneous and politically sovereign welfare state." The coalition government led by the SDP was pushed into the defensive in spite of tightening immigration laws and provisions since it came to power in 1993.

The new hegemony—that society was no longer divided by class politics but united around common values—found its clearest expression in new prime minister Anders Fogh Rasmussen's inaugural speech on the opening day of the new parliament on December 4, 2001, in which he declared that Danes had been set free and that it had become old-fashioned to think in terms of class and social division:

> The elections on November 20 were historic. . . . First and foremost because the constituents sent a clear signal about the renewal of Danish society. The elections were a break with the old-fashioned political split between right and left. It was a break with the old-fashioned division of people according to their belonging to an occupational, educational, or social group. It was a break with the split between "them" and "us." It was a break with the class struggle. By their choice, the constituents voiced a demand for a new goal for Danish society, a society where the community is built upon solidarity around particular values and attitudes. (Rasmussen 2001; my translation)

But, as noted above, hegemony is not a question of the ideological domination of one group over others: it is the limits of the social imaginary that form the basis for further political debate. The SDP had tacitly accepted the centrality of immigration to political discourse in the mid-1990s (and for local politicians, this acceptance dates back to 1987; see chapter 3), but the SDP explicitly "admitted" that "class society" was over when new party leader Helle Thorning-Schmidt declared class struggle to be an anachronism in 2005:

> Let me say it straight: this is not about class struggle. It is not about somebody being forced to sell their labor to others who own the means of production. We can also put away the Marxist slogans because they mask the new inequalities our society. ("Helle Thorning-

Schmidt's Congress Speech," *Berlingske Tidende*, March 15, 2005; my translation)

What drives society forward in the new social imaginary is cultural cohesion. Whereas class solidarity is formed in a struggle against the other classes within the nation, the struggle for cultural cohesion brings together those who share core values against those who are seen to be threatening these values and therefore the cohesive force of society. Rasmussen explained in an interview that "it is the outcome of the cultural struggle that determines Denmark's future, not the economic policy. If you want to steer a society in a different direction, you have to take on the debate on values. The vital point is who is going to set the agenda in the value debate" (*Weekendavisen*, January 17, 2003). Putting cultural struggle at the center means a showdown with the cultural elite, who with their humanitarian ideas are responsible for continuing immigration that threatens the harmonious continuity of the nation. In his New Year speech right after elections, Rasmussen lashed out at "experts and taste arbiters" (i.e., the official councils, boards, commissions, and institutions) who told the public what is good and right and made decisions on behalf of the people. "People are not going to put up with raised fingers from the so-called experts who think they know the best" (*Politiken*, January 2, 2002). The "elite's tyranny" over its people was indeed Krarup's core message in his controversial newspaper ads in 1986. Less than two decades later, the leader of the Liberal Party was repeating this argument as one of the primary goals of the new government.

Moreover, the new government understood that the showdown with the cultural elite and their arrogant pedagogy had to center on immigration. Rasmussen articulated his vision of "a Danish society with a strong competitive ability and with a strong cohesive force" (Rasmussen's opening speech in the Folketing, February 24, 2005). The cohesive force of Danish society was under threat from "an aggressive practice of Islam as the greatest challenge" and the source of the problem was "some isolated groups of immigrants who challenged democratic values" (*Jyllands-Posten*, November 28, 2005). The Liberal Party had finally aligned its vision for the future of Denmark with that of Krarup and the DPP, whose support was vital for his government.

The first targets for the new government's showdown with the cultural elite were the Board for Ethnic Equality and the Danish Center for Human Rights, whose leaders were known for their antiracist remarks. The first was shut down, whereas the latter was restructured and the post of director removed. The government grant to the Documentation and Advice Center on Racial Discrimination was cut off, but the new government did not stop here. Its first legislative act was to prepare a new law that turned Denmark into the country with the strictest immigration laws in Europe: it removed de facto refugee status, leaving the door open only for those who fit the UN's Refugee Conventions and other human rights conventions. The new law also removed the immigrants' legal right to live together with their spouses in Denmark through a number of limitations: it created the twenty-four-year rule (nobody would be able to bring a spouse to Denmark before reaching the age of twenty-four; this rule was later softened for Danish citizens but stiffened for people with an immigrant background, even if they were citizens) and set a new requirement that those who wanted to bring their spouses into the country have at least about US$10,000 in savings. Becoming a citizen was also made much more difficult by the new law.

The sharp criticism of the new immigration law by European Union commissioner for human rights Alvaro Gil-Robles was dismissed, as were all criticisms by other international institutions. Bertel Haarder, the minister for refugees, immigrants, and integration called the new law "women progressive" because it was an effective tool against "arranged marriages." He accused Gil-Robles of not understanding cultural differences because Gil-Robles himself was a Spaniard from a similar culture of arranged marriages (*Politiken*, March 1, 2005).

The most significant act of the new government that placed immigration at the center of political discourse and value debate was the replacement of the Ministry of Interior[4] with a new Ministry for Refugees, Immigrants, and Integration, which was to be the originator of policy initiatives to revitalize the cohesive force of society, policies a *Politiken* editorial criticized for focusing on "ethnic purity" and "protecting the Danish tribe" ("Ethnic Purity," January 18, 2002). Within eighteen months of its establishment, the ministry published a vision and strategy paper for integration that called for "cultural transformation" as a precondition for social harmony. The main points in the paper were that the newcomers should not be "clientalized" (i.e., be dependent on welfare payments); they had to learn and respect "our values"; and their oppressive family traditions would not be tolerated just because they are "their culture." The linkages among "culture," "cohesion," "social functionality," and welfare, which until the mid-1990s were still mostly the property of the populist Right—despite the regular outbursts of similar statements by politicians from both sides of the political mainstream—became the official policy principle for the future of Denmark.

The revised integration law of 2006 is a revealing example of these linkages. According to the law (still in effect), all immigrants seeking a work and residence permit in Denmark have to sign a declaration[5] that sets up detailed but elusive criteria for earning the right to stay. The declaration makes explicit all of the points that I have been making about the articulation of an incommensurable gap between two fundamentally different cultures, one of which threatens the other. According to the law, a foreigner seeking a residency permit must declare allegiance to Danish laws, values, and democratic principles, promise not to beat his wife or children, become self-providing, pay taxes, respect gender equality and sexual orientation, not discriminate on the basis of gender or skin color, and, finally, not participate in terrorist activities. The penalty for not fulfilling the declaration ranges from a reduction in welfare payments (if one receives any), to diminished hopes for permanent residence (citizenship becoming almost impossible), to losing a residency permit altogether.

Gender and Sexuality as Core Danish Values

The interesting aspect of the declaration the new immigrants are forced to sign is the central position gender and sexuality in the so-called Danish core values.[6] Six of the sixteen norms and values listed in the declaration are directly related to gender equality:

1. I acknowledge that men and women have equal responsibilities and rights in Denmark and that both men and women are expected to contribute to society.
2. I know that it is illegal in Denmark to exert violence or force on one's spouse and others, including children.
3. I acknowledge that in Denmark there shall be equal respect and opportunities for development for all children, both girls and boys.
4. I respect every person's freedom and personal integrity, equality of the genders, freedom of religion, and freedom of expression, which are foundational in Denmark.
5. I know that female circumcision and forced marriages are illegal practices in Denmark.
6. I know that discrimination on the basis of gender or skin color, and threats or disdain toward groups on the grounds of faith or sexual orientation, are illegal in Denmark.

As these requirements show, gender, sexuality, and family relations have come to play a central role in defining the "core Danish values" that define "us" as opposed to the Muslim immigrants. As Christensen and Siim (2010) explain, "The official perception of gender equality has since the 1990s increasingly been associated with Danish values and constructed as something . . . which has already been achieved for the white majority" (13) and is now under threat. Petersen (2013) argues that homosexuality functions in the same way; sympathy for gays has become a symbol of Danish values. Its meaning has changed from being a threat to the nation's reputation to being part of the normal; it is now central to imagining Danishness.

The Liberal Party's equality spokesperson, Troels Lund Poulsen, declared in 2004 that the party would shift the focus in equality debate from the Danish women's problems to the (cultural) problems of immigrant women: female circumcision, forced marriages, and sharia laws ("Show-Down on Equality," *Politiken*, January 5, 2004).[7] He criticized women's movements for focusing too much on equal pay for women, which was but one issue, and could not be compared to the sufferings of Muslim women. The DPP has also increasingly adopted equality themes: "We must demand that the immigrants follow Danish laws, rules, and basic Danish values like gender equality, democracy, and freedom of expression—only by doing that . . . can we ensure that we also have a good Danish society in the future" (quoted in Andreassen 2012: 15). Never mind that according to a European Union report, 52 percent of Danish women experience sexual assault or harassment at workplace or home ("Report: Danish Men Are the Most Misogynist in EU," *Politiken*, March 5, 2014).

The cultural antagonism between a liberated Danish people and the oppressive practices of Muslim immigrants is echoed in the political discourse of the progressive parties and groups. For example, the SPP's leader, Villy Søvndal, "admitted" that the left had to acknowledge that the culture immigrants bring with them, often from Muslim countries, is a problem ("Villy Søvndal Settles with Immigration Politics," *Politiken*, March 6, 2008). In this sense, Denmark is a notable example of how sections of the Left have adopted approaches to immigration similar to those of the populist Right (Akkerman and Hagelund 2007: 212). As a result, "Traditional gender equality politics has waned from public agendas, to be replaced by a highly selective minority gender equality politics primarily targeting immigrant communities" (Siim and Skjeie 2008: 339). There is considerable academic research about the centrality of gender and sexuality not only in Denmark (e.g., Akkerman and Hagelund, 2007; Andreassen 2005, 2012; Borchorst and Teigen 2012; Christiensen and Siim 2010; Hervik 2011; Meret and Siim 2013; Siim and Skjeie 2008), but also in Europe (and in the West) in general (Bangstad 2011; Bracke 2012; Bredström 2003; Butler 2008; El-Tayeb 2012; De Leeuw and van Wichelen 2012; Göle 2011; Haritaworn 2012; Henkel 2012; Keskinen 2012, 2013; Lentin and Titley 2011; Kundnani 2012; Massad 2007; Petzen 2012; Pitcher 2009; Puar 2007; Siapera 2010; Stehle 2012).

It is important to emphasize the political and social implications of the articulation of gender equality and homosexuality as the core symbols of Danish culture. What happens when an achievement made possible by the struggle of progressive movements is appropriated by their opponents and presented as part of the "national core values" that bind us?

Gender equality has been one of the basic aspirations of women's movements regardless of the particular demands of specific historical periods. In addition, for left-wing movements, antisexism and antiracism have long been articulated as parts of the same struggle, and the extent to which gender equality is accomplished has been considered an important social and political achievement. However, the culturalized discursive environment in which immigrants, via their Muslim culture, are repeatedly described as oppressive to women creates tensions that are difficult to resolve within the given parameters of the progressive political identities. What happens here is that the old antagonistic frontier between traditional power structures and emancipatory movements is blurred by the hegemonic power incorporating some of the latter's demands into the system. Once immigrants are defined as a cultural category distinct from the nation rather than a part of the "oppressed classes," it becomes difficult to incorporate this culturalized social category into the traditional progressive paradigm. At the same time, the mobilization around traditional antiracist, antisexist, antihomophobic, and internationalist themes renders these progressive movements irrelevant to large sections of workers and others whose interests are now represented in nationalist terms by the populist Right, which has also adopted feminist and gay-friendly themes.

In the summer of 2001, the liberal daily *Politiken* initiated a fierce debate on feminism and immigrant women with a commentary that criticized the feminist movement for letting down oppressed immigrant women. The commentaries were illustrated with pictures of Muslim women in burkas as opposed to naked Danish women. The debate quickly spilled over into other newspapers. In a chronicle in *Jyllands-Posten*, Lone Nørgaard accused the feminist movement of being silent about the fact that some women live under the oppressive patriarchal norms from seventh-century Arabia and asked in the context of the debate on the headscarf if women's basic rights are not threatened by the religious dogmas permeated by patriarchal ideologies (July 25, 2001). Many of the commentaries followed this train of thought, but there were critical voices, too. In a commentary in *Politiken*, Annemette

Bach criticized feminists for being intolerant toward Muslim women by interpreting the headscarf as a sign of oppression without asking their Muslim sisters why they wear it. Her answer was that they wear it because of their religion, not because they are told so by their men. She argued that this was a contradiction for those feminists who would prefer that Muslim women conform to the oppressive ideals (of the West) that force women to dress in certain ways in order to please men (June 19, 2001). This was basically a debate on how to reconfigure the identity of the feminist movement in the face of the culturalized ontology of the social.

This tension creates factions within the feminist movement whose identity is shaped around the concept of emancipation. Emancipation in this context becomes what Laclau calls a "floating signifier."[8] Emancipation in this sense both signifies the feminist movement vis-à-vis the oppressive sexist system and Danishness vis-à-vis the Muslim immigrant with an oppressive culture. This kind of organic crisis often leads to radical conversions among feminists or left-wing radicals. Former interior minister Karen Jespersen (Social Democrat) is a good example: She was a member of the left-wing radical Left Socialist Party in the 1970s and describes herself as a feminist. In the 1980s, she joined the SDP and a decade later the right-wing Liberal Party. After joining the SDP, she gradually became one of the most vocal opponents of immigration within the party. In her meeting with Muslim immigrant women in August 2001, she called upon the women to riot against their husbands, who, according to Jespersen, confine them to the home. She also wanted to discuss issues such as "forced marriages" and "violence against immigrant women by their men" (*BT*, August 9, 2001). The women, on the other hand, would rather have talked about discrimination in the job market: they gave many concrete examples of discrimination against well-educated women. Yet, according to the *BT* reporter, who did not acknowledge these complaints or the women as agents of their own lives, the women shied away from talking about emancipation from their husbands because these issues were too difficult for them to discuss. Alas, the cultural category of "immigrant" predefines both the subject roles and the relevance of the issues to be discussed: "In other words, binaries delimit the outcome of proximity, if not prevent proximity itself, by predefining the reality before practice" (Diken 1998: 40).

The shared epistemology of the social has resulted in new alliances forged across the political spectrum around what are now (and usually tacitly) taken as core values such as democracy, gender equality, gay rights, freedom of speech, or even animal rights. The focus on such culturally coded signs (rather than, for example, rights) has unsettled traditional divides and realigned actors from across the political spectrum, forming what Gramsci (1971) called a new "historical bloc." The shift to culture led to the blurring of traditional structures of identification (e.g., left and right) and the displacement of well-established political identities based on class, gender, and other types of antagonisms that have had to be rearticulated onto the new ontology of the social.

"Cohesive Force of Society" and Democracy

One important signifier of the new hegemony is the concept of "cohesion" as the basis for the new welfare system, which itself has become a cultural construct, appearing as the product of national values, rather than as an outcome of class struggles and social democratic policies. The "cohesive force of society," interpreted as the force that is anchored in a cultural "value community," has replaced "solidarity," which traditionally refers to class. As Lykkeberg (2008: 260) argues, "While solidarity is connected with active engagement where the symmetry between rights and responsibilities is won in an ongoing struggle, the cohesive force is typically talked about as something handed down with fragility that is threatened."

The concern with social cohesion—which was originally put on the political agenda by Krarup's 1986 ad campaign (although he did not use the exact words: he "warned" against the destruction of the harmonious being of the nation) and was rejected as a racist idea—is not exclusive to the populist Right or the Liberal Party, which adopted a similar rhetoric in the second half of the 1990s;[9] it is a common concern for parties on both sides of the political spectrum. The concept was indeed used the first time by Karen Jespersen, when she was minister for social affairs in the 1990s, and Karen Hækkerup, the Social Democratic justice minister (2013–14), said at her inauguration, "It is important for Denmark's cohesiveness that we have a tough policy on immigration. The numbers matter for a small nation [if we want] to integrate the foreigners so they become Danes and part of Denmark" ("New Justice Minister to Continue Tough Immigration Line," *Copenhagen Post*, December 13, 2013). The Conservative Party's slogan is "Courage to make cohesion" (*Mod til at skabe sammenhæng*) and even Villy Søvndal did not refrain from presenting Muslim immigrants' culture as a problem for democracy (*Politiken*, March 7, 2008).[10]

Democracy, in the new parlance, is no longer a system of active participation, but a "value" to which one declares his or her allegiance, as is evident in Fogh Rasmussen's speech at his party's annual congress:

> We do not demand that everybody should be just like us or think the same way as us. But we do demand that if you want to live in Danish society, you must respect and acknowledge the core values. Freedom of speech. Equal rights for women and men. The separation of politics and religion. Can we do anything about it? It is not easy to make laws for. It is first and foremost a question of attitudes. It is our collective responsibility to say no, to set a limit. (*Berlingske Tidende*, November 24, 2004; my translation)

This chapter is not devoted to a detailed analysis of discourse, but this quote requires a brief comment. First, Rasmussen speaks about "us" as if "we" are a homogenous group of people who share the same ideas and values. "We" should demand from immigrants that they respect and obey these values as if "we" all share these values and as if the meaning of these values is given a priori. Implicit in its rhetoric is that those (i.e., Muslims) who do not share these values can be forced to respect them.

Clearly, not everybody believes in or shares these values, and not everybody agrees about what the "shared values" are and about the relationship between Islam and these values. The interesting aspect of the quote is the way the immigration debate structures the political discourse. As Lykkeberg (2008: 254) explains, when confronted by an alien force, "core values" need to be marked and defined; the existence of an external force requires a consciousness about an internal "belonging together." In a paradoxical way, the immigration debate produces the very "cohesion" claimed to be challenged by immigrants. The debate on democracy becomes a debate on the extent to which the alien immigrant can be integrated/assimilated into the welfare system. Democracy becomes identified with "core values," which secures the stability of the political community.

This understanding of democracy as a matter of the relationship between Danes and immigrants was mirrored in the commission that was tasked to write a canon of democracy by the second Rasmussen government in 2007. The government appointed no writers or artists but did include an integration counsel and a school inspector known for his dealings with immigrant children (Lykkeberg 2008: 254).

The centrality of culture and immigration and the articulation of the linkages among culture, cohesion, and welfare did not change when the right-wing government was replaced by a coalition led by the SDP in October 2011, as is evident in Hækkerup's statement about the necessity of a tough immigration policy to keep Denmark cohesive and the example of "meatball wars."[11] The debate about whether public institutions should serve halal meat was so heated that Yıldız Akdoğan, an "immigrant" member of the SDP, wrote: "Rhetorically, it feels as if Denmark's survival as a nation is at stake and the pork is the most essential cohesive force of society" (*Berlingske Tidende*, August 15, 2013). A few months after the debate in February 2014, Dan Jørgensen, the SDP minister of agriculture, fisheries, and food, banned so-called halal slaughtering (i.e., without numbing the animal).

It does not seem likely that the focus on immigration as a challenge to social cohesion will be vanishing from political discourse anytime soon. The elections on June 18, 2015, were once again all about immigration and resulted in a huge victory for the DPP, which is now the second biggest party and closely behind the SDP. The DPP needs to have the issue of immigration in focus to keep its popularity, and its growing popularity, in turn, incites even more discourse on immigration, and the other parties keep sharpening their rhetoric in an effort to match up in the toughness game. This is precisely what happened during the elections in June 2015. The DPP leadership knows that no party can match it when it comes to a harsh political rhetoric about immigration and it proposed a total end to Muslim immigration to Denmark, which set the bar higher for the other parties ("The DPP after the New Numbers: Immigration Itself Has to be Debated," *Ekstra Bladet*, January 5, 2015). SDP leaders matched this proposal with a new campaign promising even harsher policies on immigration with posters declaring that "immigrants who come to Denmark have to work and contribute to society" and "tighter asylum laws and more demands to immigrants."

The DPP received 21.1 percent of the votes following the SDP's 26.3 percent, while the Liberal Party lost 7.2 percent of its voters mostly to the DPP despite its wholehearted participation in the toughness game. It is ironic that a poll just before the 2015 elections showed that 13 percent of Danish voters (and 20 percent of right-wing voters) wish for a new right-wing party that is more anti-immigrant than the DPP. Ergo, Muslim immigration will remain at the center of political discourse for the foreseeable future.

The Transformation of the Political Parties

The incorporation of the populist demand for excluding immigrants from the welfare state is a sign of Denmark's transformed political landscape. The neoliberal approach demanding that immigrants become self-reliant, therefore ridding themselves of dependence on government aid,[12] is not untypical of the neoliberal, market-based approach to social issues. However, resentment against immigrants has never really been translated into support for dismantling the welfare state precisely because the immigration debate kept the focus on the question of access to welfare. The populist demand for making access to welfare conditional upon ethnicity implied that many welfare provisions need to be kept intact for Danes. To understand contemporary neoliberal anti-immigration discourse, one needs to understand the transformation of the main political actors.

In this sense, the transformation of the Liberal Party is interesting because it is intimately connected to the central role immigration has come to play in creating visions for the future of Denmark. A single example will illustrate this transformation. The leader of the party, Prime Minister Anders Fogh Rasmussen, forced one of his ministers, Eva Kjær, to renounce her statement that "inequality is the motivating power of society; it creates a dynamic" (*Jyllands-Posten*, September 18, 2005). According to Rasmussen, creating inequality could not be a goal itself; it would not create a more dynamic society. The goal was to create incentives to be employed and make the weakest in society do well enough (*Jyllands-Posten*, September 21, 2005). A decade earlier, however, the same Rasmussen wrote that inequality was a motivating power for society (1993). Making Muslim immigration the central political issue brought concepts such as community, cohesion, and state to the center of the Liberals' symbolic universe. In other words, Rasmussen's—and subsequently the Liberal Party's—transformation is about bringing community back into their political program and rearticulating the role of the individual as one who contributes to the community rather than being dependent on it.

Indeed, support for the welfare state had never been as great as under the Liberal-Conservative neoliberal government that came to power in 2001, although welfare now means something different. In its initial form, the welfare state was a state that took care of its citizens. Under the neoliberal governance, a welfare state means a state that maintains competitive abilities in a globalized world; it is by optimizing the competitive abilities that the state is said to secure the welfare of its citizens (Lykkeberg 2008). Because the class struggle is over, the oppressors are no longer the capitalist class—on the contrary, they provide jobs and consolidate wealth—but the cultural elite (i.e., leftist intellectuals, journalists, and human rights defenders) that conceive of themselves as superior to the ordinary Dane (cf. "the arbiters of taste"). The Liberal Party no longer sees "minimal state" as a possibility; rather, the social state creates the conditions for economic growth and flexibility. The conflict of interest between workers and employers is now replaced by common interests between them in a globalized world (hence the new right-wing hegemony). The antagonistic force is no longer the other end of the negotiation table but the global forces that attract capital and the immigrants, with their unorganized labor and low wages, who undermine the welfare system.

The transformation of the Liberal Party cannot be understood without understanding the transformation of the populist Right. The far-right populist movement has been transformed from the Progress Party's extreme economic liberalism (centered on an antitax struggle)[13] and Krarup's misogynistic and homophobic positions into a party that put the maintenance of the welfare system at the center of its political program (albeit as something threatened by Muslim immigration and Europeanization, i.e., the EU) while also defending women's rights and homosexuals (once again as values threatened by Muslims). Betz and Meret (2013: 118) explain that the DPP presented itself as the real inheritor of traditional social democratic values as opposed to "the Social Democrats, who were considered to have repudiated their role as protectors of welfare values and principles in the name of libertarian stances—on immigration, for instance—undermining the welfare state present and future."

The Crisis of the Center-Left

The culturalization of the entire political discourse, as evident in the so-called value debate, has paralyzed the center-left, which has not been able to produce an alternative vision. What paralyzes the Left is the hegemonic displacement that has changed the way the ontology of the social is imagined. In a new context, where the main threat is globalization and its incarnation in the form of culturally alien immigrants (rather than national and international capitalism), the Left has immense difficulty in finding its footing. The success of the center-left, particularly of the SDP, was based on an alliance between the "working class" and the progressive movements and the intelligentsia. The "working class," which no longer conceives itself and its struggle in class terms, has left the party for the populist DPP, which is now the biggest "workers' party"; the progressive intellectuals became tired of the SDP's (and the Socialist People's Party's [SPP]) explicit right turn and have left as well. The exodus of working-class voters resulted in the termination of reciprocal representation of the LO (the confederation of labor unions) and the SDP in each other's executive committees in 1996.

A *Politiken* editorial called it a historically exceptional situation that the party is backed by neither the working class nor the intelligentsia ("Thorning [SDP prime minister since 2011] Government Has No Friends," February 5, 2014). The editorial argued that the party had wasted the chance to mobilize popular frustration with perverted financial capitalism's greed. According to the editorial, the working class tilts to the right when it comes to the "value politics" and to the left when it comes to economic politics; when the SDP follows a right-wing economic policy, it pushes the working class to the ranks of the DPP while simultaneously pushing away the left-wing intelligentsia.[14]

The crisis of the SDP is mirrored in falling popular support for the party. The party has steadily been losing voters since the elections in 1990 where the party's support was at 37.5 percent (except a slight gain in the 2015 elections: a 1.5 percent increase to 26.3 percent). What is more interesting is that the SDP is no longer the biggest party among the "workers," a title the SDP lost to the DPP in recent years. The DPP was the biggest party with 26.6 percent of all votes in the European Parliament elections in May 2014, trailed by the SDP with 19.1 percent and the Liberals, who received only 16.7 percent.

The tacit acceptance of the neoliberal perspective in the 1980s (throughout Europe) had already blurred the line between left and right and led to a crisis of representation in which workers did not feel that their interests were being defended by the party that traditionally stood up for them. The hegemonic crisis opened up the political terrain for fringe forces who were able to articulate the workers' anxieties into a populist program.

What had been tacit acceptance in the 1980s became the main economic policy of the SDP leadership at the beginning of the 1990s (Mørch 2005; Betz and Meret 2013; Hemerijck 2013). Brian Croydon, the SDP minister of finance, expressed the party's abandonment of its original ideals about the welfare state by announcing that the social democratic goal was to create a "competitive state"[15] ("Corydon: Competitive State Is the New Welfare State," *Politiken*, August 23, 2013). Privatization and putting a cap on unemployment and social aid payments are central to this new neoliberal consensus, which makes it difficult for voters to see significant differences between mainstream parties in terms of economic policies. Once that difference is blurred, issues such as the role of immigration in sustaining/eroding social rights become central in the parties' appeals to voters, and here the SDP seems to have lost out to the populist DPP and the hardliners of the Liberal Party. After the party lost the elections again in 2005, Mogens Lykketoft resigned as the chairman of the SDP and admitted that it was difficult to detect ideological differences between the mainstream parties.

The "neoliberal" path, combined with a cultural focus, creates tension in SDP circles. Whereas parts of the Social Democratic movement criticize the party's right turn in economic and political (value) matters, others think that the party should focus even more on value politics. For example, the contributors to the book *Right-Wing Populism: The Left's Achilles' Heel* (Steen, Villermoes, and Jespersen 2013), published by the center-left think tank Cevea, argue that the path to renewal will entail an offensive built around a value-political response. The book argues that the Left must dissociate itself from "multiculturalism" (which, according to the authors, subverts social solidarity) and instead demand the liquidation of ghettos.

Others, however, argue that SDP cannot match the anti-Muslim rhetoric of the DPP, for whom immigration policy is the key issue. Every time the center-left agrees with the DPP's line, the DPP turns up the heat, putting the center-left into a defensive position (i.e., Brian Esbensen: "The DPP's New Restrictions Show That the SP and SPP's Course Is Completely Insane," *Politiken*, January 26, 2014).

The SPP, which is to the left of SDP, is no different in this regard. Villy Søvndal pulled the party to the right over the question of immigration with the argument that has become a cliché: we need to listen to people's concerns and stop the voter flight to the right. Søvndal drastically changed the party's course by turning the focus on the so-called value debate. He declared in 2008 that the integration efforts should focus on the "cultural struggle with the immigrants about our democratic values" ("Villy Søvndal Settles with Immigration Politics," *Politiken*, March 6, 2008). According to the same *Politiken* story, Søvndal and SDP leader Thorning-Schmidt entered into an agreement that meant that Social Democrats could sharpen their anti-immigration rhetoric to attract voters from the right without being criticized by the SPP. The right turn of the SPP seems to be closely connected to its acceptance of the SDP's neoliberal economic policy: once a party seems to accept neoliberal orthodoxy, the only path to appeal to the voters seems go through the debate on culture, cohesion, and immigration. The new path, however, has not helped the party that lost more than half of its voters (5 percent) in the 2015 elections down to 4.2 percent.

The crisis of the center-left is rooted in its inability to navigate in the new sociopolitical terrain, where social division is envisioned in cultural terms. The Left's humanitarian and internationalist traditions have been successfully presented by the populist Right as the main reason for the erosion of the welfare system. The Left is not equipped to fight on this new cultural terrain, a fight that would be necessary to regain strength and form a new "historical bloc."

The progressive parties and groups who have not accepted neoliberal dogma or populist-nationalist currents have been trying to rearticulate their identity around antiracist struggles. Without a new vision, however, they find themselves in an essentialist paradigm simultaneously promoting minority rights for immigrants while fighting the perceived traditional cultures of this group. Once immigrants are defined as cultural/ethnic groups rather than a part of the working class, it becomes difficult to incorporate this social identity into the classic paradigm of the Left. At the same time, their mobilization around traditional antiracist and internationalist themes renders them irrelevant to many workers and others whose interests are now represented by the populist Right. The culturalization of political discourse demands novel articulations between welfare commitments, gender equality, sexual freedom, and freedom of speech with new ontological entities.

As a *Politiken* editorial after the elections in 2005 predicted, the DPP's success has not been limited to making bloc politics (based on a left-right division) impossible by rendering the polarization between left and right irrelevant or to checkmating the SDP by splitting the old workers' party. "It seems as if the populism that has taken hold here will make it impossible to transform Denmark in the near future, regardless of which side of the Danish parliament, left or right, we are talking about" ("Ander Fogh's Big Victory—and Problem," *Politiken*, February 9, 2005). Whatever the differences, the basic antagonism, which produces its own culturally defined social division, makes it impossible to articulate alternative visions under the given political conditions. Nevertheless, both the political establishment and those who hope to challenge the Far Right's vision of Danishness draw on this epistemology. Unless a radical rearticulation of the political imaginary takes place, the movements of an oppositional party will be "limited by the straightjacket of the hegemonic formations whose parameters remain substantially unchanged" (Laclau 2005: 138).

The Transformation of Immigrant Organizations: From Worker to Muslim

In the introduction, I told a story about being interviewed by a journalist colleague from the Danish Broadcasting Corporation (DR). An older Turkish immigrant had killed his grandchild and injured his daughter-in-law with a cooking pan, and I was asked to comment on the background of the story. I said I could not comment on a case I did not know anything about and also remarked on the racist implications of being invited to talk about the case not because I had any expertise on crime or immigration, but because I was a journalist who had a "shared culture" with the murderer, which put me into a position to know his mind-set. It would be unimaginable to ask a Dane to explain a criminal act by another Dane merely because they share a culture (even though in the new discursive environment "shared culture" is what binds Danes into a community).

I was never again invited to give this type of interview: I was deemed irrelevant to the discussion. The media needed experts on immigrant (i.e., Muslim) culture and soon there were many of these, mostly with immigrant backgrounds, and they are widely used to explain every single phenomenon that could be associated with immigrants: criminality, murder, rape, misuse of the welfare system, even unemployment (i.e., they don't have the same modern work ethic as Danes).

Various Muslim religious figures and organizations now receive unprecedented attention in public discourse as expert speakers about the culture. This is a sign of the hegemonic change. When culture was not of primary concern in immigration matters, the people who were interviewed on immigration matters were representatives of immigrant organizations who denoted themselves in class and ethnic terms (e.g., the Turkish—or Moroccan—Workers' Association). Once immigrant workers became recast as Muslim immigrants whose culture (rather than their relationship to the labor market) came into focus, it created a need for "knowledge" about Islam and immigrants, and soon there was a proliferation of experts to explain Islam and Muslim immigrants to Danes (as discussed earlier).

If one effect of the need for cultural explanations is the production of experts with immigrant backgrounds (who often lacked any formal education in the topics on which they readily opined), the other effect was the relabeling of old representatives. İrfan Kurtulmuş, vice chair of the Turkish Religious Community, is a good example. He is a journalist who, since the early 1970s, had never presented himself as a religious person or been affiliated with any religious organization. In 2008, he entered the debate denouncing the authority of the Islamic Religious Community—a self-proclaimed umbrella organization for Muslims in Denmark—to represent Turkish Muslims (*Ekstra Bladet*, February 21, 2008).

Kurtulmuş's story is a good example of the more fundamental transformation of immigrants from workers to Muslims. Immigrant organizations were often associated with the host countries' political parties and labor unions. Parallel to the change in immigration discourse, which increasingly focused on immigrants' culture, immigrants' mobilization began to occur through ethnic and religious associations, and they began to articulate their political demands along religious lines. Yurdakul (2009: 66) describes a similar process in the German context: "As modes of production are transformed, neoliberal policies are strengthened, and the unions become weaker, the class struggle, indeed, the very notion of class, has become marginal to immigrant political representation."

In short, the transformation of immigrant worker to Muslim immigrant in mainstream political discourse dissolved the old workers associations, which were often affiliated with left-wing parties, and forced immigrants' political mobilization into the domain of religious organizations that have proliferated over the last two decades.

The Social Democratic MP Yıldız Akdoğan was a founder of Democratic Muslims, an organization formed after the Danish cartoon crisis in 2005 to represent so-called moderate Muslims (i.e., those not offended by the Mohammad cartoons), yet she does not normally define herself by religion. When she was new to the political scene in the early 2000s, *Ekstra Bladet* interviewed her but did not publish the story because the journalist found her to be "too much like us." The journalist had imagined the story would be about a young Muslim girl's emancipation from a backward Islamic culture into Danish modernity and the possibilities this created for her, but her story did not fit this narrative.[16] It is likely that she quickly learned that access to public discourse would be easier if she identified herself as a cultural subject and one who would be able to provide a counterweight of positive images of Muslims. In her role as a founder of Democratic Muslims, she complied with the narrative about cultural differences, not necessarily by confirming the insurmountability of the divide but by conforming to the basic ontological divide. One interesting feature of Democratic Muslims was the range of political affiliations among the members. The association brought together "Muslims" from opposite corners of the political spectrum—from the Red-Green Alliance on the radical left to members of the Conservative and Liberal Party—in the same way as the fear of an imminent Muslim threat leads to the convergence of Left and Right around "core values" (e.g., the huge demonstrations to support "freedom of speech" after the Charlie Hebdo murders in Paris).

The Hegemonic Effect: Imagining the Future

The main argument in this chapter has been that culture has become the key to the social imaginary in fundamental ways in political and everyday discourse through the figure of Muslim immigrant. I have demonstrated that not only has the category of Muslim immigrant become culturalized, the culturalized immigration debate has taken a central role in political discourse.

However, as already indicated, hegemony is not only a question of particular ideas becoming the dominant political discourse or the "dominant" ideology. Hegemony is also about how the ontological distinctions enable and constrain people in their dealings with social and political life.

"My Daughter Is Not Going to Pay the Price" was the title of an interview with a left-wing resident of an inner-city neighborhood in Copenhagen in *Politiken Weekly* (December 20, 2000). The interview illustrates the fine points of the hegemonic order from the perspective of an individual. The interview begins with a description of the interviewee: "She has all the immigrant-friendly views: Denmark is multicultural and Danish children should go to the same schools with [immigrant children] from other cultures." However, when it comes to sending her daughter to her local school where 80 percent of the children have an immigrant background, the interviewee has second thoughts. She does not think it is a good idea to have her daughter attend a school with too many immigrant children: "When [my daughter] asks why she is not going to attend the [local] school, I say that it is not a good school. I cannot tell her that there are too many immigrant children. . . . I am afraid that her education and her social life will suffer from it. How is it going to be with camping situations and birthday parties?" She expresses concern that there are too many cultures in the school:

> I don't know if it is a smart idea. I am not sure that the school can handle it. Besides, I expect more social problems in that school. Many immigrant families also choose not to send their children to local schools. On top of it, there are language problems, too. . . . I know my fear is not based on facts, but on what I hear from my friends and from the media. I don't know how the school really is. . . . I think it is totally necessary to meet other cultures in school in order to be able to manage in Danish society in the future. If the number of immigrant children in [the local] school equaled the percentage of the immigrants in local community, which is almost 50 percent, it would be okay.

Many discourse analysts would interpret the discrepancy between the speaker's ideals and her actual attitudes as a typical conflict between impression management techniques and sincere thinking, and the latter would be interpreted as the reflection of her prejudice toward immigrants (cf. van Dijk 1984, 1987, 1993).

The speaker's dilemma is real. She situates herself as belonging to the immigrant-friendly, multiculturalist left wing of the political spectrum. At no time does she utter a negative view about immigrants or their cultures, and she does not oppose a multiculturalist vision of Denmark. In this sense, her political standpoint can be described as opposed to the hegemonic articulation of ethnicity and culture in Denmark. On the other hand, she intuitively knows that "Danish culture" is an asset, an investment in a system that is now allocating resources along ethnic/cultural lines. She does not want her daughter "to pay the price" for her mother's political views because she knows the limits of her political vision. She assumes that in a school with 80 percent immigrant children, not only the literary and scientific skills necessary for further education but also the knowledge, rituals, and myths through which "Danish culture" is created may not be acquired properly, placing her daughter at a disadvantage later in life. The standards for a good education are defined according to the cultural resources one builds up. Not knowing or learning the rituals becomes nonproficiency—an obstacle to getting jobs, for instance.[17] The future of Denmark is produced in conformity with the current hegemonic articulations through her projections of what the future will bring. By sending her daughter to a private school where Danish children are in the majority and where she will become a culturally Danish subject, she reimposes the ethnic/cultural boundaries between immigrants and Danes. The politico-moral dilemma constrains her movements as a political subject and leads her to conform to the hegemonic vision of society even if she does not believe in it or agree with it.

The interview shows the limits that a hegemonic formation imposes on political subjects even if they oppose its ideological propositions. In Laclau and Mouffe's (2001) words, "A hegemonic formation also embraces what opposes it, insofar as the opposing force accepts the system of basic articulations of that formation as something it negates, but *the place of the negation* is defined by the internal parameters of the formation itself" (139).[18] The interviewee's opposition is formulated within the internal parameters of the hegemonic formation because the boundaries between cultures are her social reality. The irony is that she conforms to the basic premises of the hegemonic vision of society even as she negates the vision of Denmark's future as ethnically homogeneous. She sees a multicultural future in which her daughter is going to manage if she learns about the other cultures by attending the same schools as immigrant children. The interviewee contributes to the reproduction of the hegemonic order not because she believes in it but because her options are constrained by a hegemonic formation that defines social antagonisms in cultural terms and renders its definitions as the starting point for everyday practices and institutions.

It is easy for a scholar who analyzes other people's utterances to point to the discursive constraints a hegemonic articulation imposes upon subjects, as if the scholar himself is able to see beyond the hegemonic formation and able to articulate alternative visions. Nothing could be less accurate. In fact, I chose this example because I have many friends who have expressed similar concerns about their own children's education and future. They live in the same areas as immigrants but do not want to "sacrifice" their children's future for their political views. Could I give them any useful advice? Absolutely not. What constrains them constrains me, too. In a conversation about this issue, I was put into the same dilemma as the interviewee. I understood their dilemma because we all orient ourselves to public discourse in its broad sense, including spaces such as schools and housing projects in which subject positions are interpellated in particular ways. As the interview indicates, Danish schools and neighborhoods are slowly becoming ethnically segregated. In a different discursive environment where ethnicity and culture are not emphasized as constitutive of society, this might not be problematic. Here, however, the hegemonic mapping of subject positions is intensified by immigrant parents who send their children to Islamic-oriented schools and increasingly emphasize their "Muslim identity."

In short, the basic antagonism makes it difficult to articulate alternative visions under given conditions. It is impossible to think of society without thinking Muslim immigrants; they are indispensable, both politically and in general, whether one talks about big issues such as democracy, gender equality, and freedom of speech or everyday topics such as chocolate candy, pork, or choice of schools. The hegemonic ontological categories limit our horizon; even critique becomes imprisoned by the normalcy of these categories (Mahmud 2005: 940).

Conclusion

"I Can't Breathe"

If you come to Denmark, you must work.
Refugees and Immigrants on welfare must work.
I want a community where everybody contributes.

—Helle Thorning-Schmidt, the leader of the Social Democratic Party and the prime minister (March 2015)

If you come to Denmark, you have to pay taxes.
Many multinational corporations operate in Denmark without paying a dime in taxes.
I want a community where the richest also contribute.

—Stine Brix, the leader of the Red-Green Alliance (March 2015)

The epigraphs above are a good illustration of this book's main argument. Both quotes are from the election posters produced during the election campaign in 2015. The first poster by the SDP leader appeals to the popular anxieties about immigration as the threat to the welfare system and the second is a response by the Red-Green Alliance that attempts to shift the focus back to the "capitalist class" as the real problem.

The SDP's focus on immigration is a clear indication of the new right-wing hegemony that is formed through the debate on immigration which has been turned into a cultural threat. The recasting of immigrant *worker* as *Muslim* immigrant shifted the terrain for political struggle from economy (i.e., class struggle) to culture (i.e., cultural struggle), which has pushed the political discourse to the right during the last three decades. The populist Far Right successfully articulated immigration as the main threat to the nation.

In this articulation, the unity of the nation is the precondition for the welfare system whereas cultural diversity is seen to impede it. The mainstream Right and Left keep sharpening their anti-immigrant rhetoric to match up the Danish People's Party's popularity.

This has created a vicious circle that erases the differences between Right and Left. As a DPP convert explains it: "When I was at school, politics was divided into Left and Right: the Left—the social democrats—were for the poor and vulnerable, and the Right were for the big businessmen. But it's not that simple any more. Basically, our welfare state has created a beautiful society but we need to keep it that way" (quoted in Coman 2015). Despite the SDP's sharpened rhetoric against immigration, it becomes increasingly difficult for working people to vote for the SDP that talks about creating a "competitive state" to compete in the global era whereas the DPP's simple solution of isolating the nation from the ill effects of globalization and "protecting the Denmark we know" has a stronger appeal.

The rise of populist right-wing parties testifies to this conclusion. Their victory is wider and deeper than their electoral success might indicate. They have successfully transformed immigration into a cultural threat and pushed the culturalized immigration discourse to the center of political discourse which has brought mainstream Left and Right together around "core values."

The move to the right has been facilitated by endless chains of moral panics and controversies around Islam and Muslim immigrants' cultural and religious practices, which have been depicted as a threat to "common achievements" in such a way that political parties were forced to respond continually to ever fresh scandals and intentional provocations.

The reactions to the attacks on *Charlie Hebdo* in France on January 7, 2015, and to the attack on the public event "Art, Blasphemy and the Freedom of Expression" in Copenhagen a few weeks later illustrate the main thread of this book: the repeated crises around Muslims (i.e., "their" so-called culturally and religiously motivated practices and actions) are used to rally people from different political and social groups around some "core values" that "unite us." It is clear that these "core values" are defined by the nature of the imagined threat. Thus, a number of achievements and demands such as gender equality, gay rights, tolerance, nonviolence, and freedom of speech are turned into "shared cultural values" through moral panics and controversies around particular events. The events in Paris and Copenhagen are good examples of this culturalization process.

The day after the massacre in Paris, the headline of *Le Figaro* was "La liberté assassinée." *Le Parisien* and *L'Humanité* also used the word *liberté* in their headlines. French president François Hollande called the attacks "exceptional barbarism" against freedom of speech and added: "We have known we were threatened, *like other freedom-loving countries*, and it is for precisely this reason we are targets. We must all stand together at this difficult time. We must show *we are a united country*" (Hollande 2015; emphasis added). The reactions to Copenhagen attacks were similar. Prime Minister Helle Thorning-Schmidt said, "Nobody is going to get away with attacking the *open, free and democratic Danish society*" and "We know that there are forces in the world who think the *darkness is stronger than the light*" (Petersen 2015; emphasis added). In Paris, interior ministers from eleven European Union countries including France, Britain, and Germany issued the following statement:

> We reaffirm our unfailing attachment to the freedom of expression, to human rights, to pluralism, to democracy, to tolerance and to the rule of law: They are the foundation of our democracies and are at the heart of the European Union. By attacking *Charlie Hebdo*, police officers and Jewish community, the terrorists set out to tear down *these universal values*. They will not succeed. . . . In the face of a multiform terrorist threat directly *targeted against our values, we reaffirm our unfailing solidarity* and our determination to fight together against terrorism. (Joint Statement by Ministers of Interior 2015, emphasis added)

The irony that the statement by the EU interior ministers also proposed Internet censorship of online content "that aims to incite hatred and violence" and surveillance, including monitoring and storing information on air travelers' itineraries, was noted in a *New York Times* editorial (January 15, 2015). By the same token, the contradiction between what the French government says and does did not go unnoticed either: fifty-four people, including a stand-up comedian, were arrested for apologizing for terrorism while declaring "freedom of speech" and "the right to blaspheme" sacred. France was the first country to ban a pro-Palestinian rally; "attacks on the national anthem and flag" are punished with heavy fines or even imprisonment; even *Charlie Hebdo* fired one of its writers for refusing to apologize for making an anti-Semitic joke about President Sarkozy's son. People have been arrested for making antimilitary or antipolice comments on social media in the UK. "Hate speech" or "whistle blowers" about illegal programs are prosecuted in many countries.

The point, however, is not the hypocrisy of governments or political leaders. In the largest public rally since World War II, 3.7 million people joined demonstrations nationwide in France, and tens of thousands participated in commemorations of the victims of the Copenhagen attacks. In both cases, demonstrations in both countries included people from all corners of society, including many Muslims. The common perception for the participants was that democracy itself was under threat. This perception and the indignation over the attacks are understandable given the perverse nature of the attacks. How does one react to and act upon such unjustifiable atrocities?

What gets lost in the heat of indignation is the distinction between supporting the right to free speech—regardless of the content—and supporting the content of a particular speech. As Lordon (2015) explains, "'Je suis Charlie' was an injunction to identify ourselves with the paper *Charlie Hebdo.*" When the French daily *Libération* put this slogan into the first-person plural, "We are all Charlie," it became a celebration of free speech by suppressing all dissent "surreptitiously confusing the emotion of the tragedy with an implied political agreement with an editorial line . . . this unanimity-under-injunction was so perfect that all sorts of people jumped on it in order to recuperate it."

What is important here is that the slogan "Je suis Charlie" has come to signify a cultural commonality that would not otherwise be founded on a common cultural ground. In other words, freedom of speech would not be thought of as a shared cultural value if it was not considered to be under an "external" threat. Freedom of speech exists, like any other principle, precisely because of its limits; it cannot have an absolute existence. The limits to freedom of speech are generally set by the state within the nation; it cannot be equated to the nation. The principle would mean different things to different groups; what one group may consider the expression of freedom of speech would be "hate speech"—and therefore outside the limits of freedom of speech—for another group. To signify an entire nation's common value, it needs to be emptied of content and become an empty signifier. Only in this way does the principle of freedom of speech cease to signify a particular freedom (i.e., press freedom structured by legal rules) and becomes a "way of life" (culture) for an entire nation (or a larger entity such as "Western culture"). But a "way of life" cannot be a transparent state of being; or to use Laclau's (1996: 38) words, "It cannot signify itself in terms of any positive signified," that is, in terms of any positive content.

But what we are trying to signify is not just any way of life; it is "our way of life," and we can only know "our way of life" by its limits. What limits our way of life is the presence of a radically different way of life that excludes the values that define "our way of life." Freedom of speech is one value that no longer signifies particular practices, but is part of "our way of life," anchored in "shared values," because it is threatened by "the forces of darkness," as the Danish prime minister expressed it. The discourse on national unity excludes precisely those deemed to be Muslims and justifies not only harsh measures against "incitement to terrorism" but all kinds of dissent.

This is how the new populist right-wing hegemony is constituted. As my discussion of empty signifiers indicates, hegemony is not a question of producing shared meanings but of producing a new social vision characterized by a new ontological structure of society and reflected in legal provisions and institutions (e.g., there are ministries for Children Gender Equality, Integration and Social Affairs in Denmark, for Integration and Gender Equality in Sweden, for Immigration, Integration, National Identity, and Codevelopment in France—the latter was created by President Sarkozy to restore "national pride"). The new ontology enables certain ways of talking about and acting on the social and political problems while constraining how we navigate the new social landscape.

The new antagonism between the alien Muslims and the nation is produced through successive series of controversies and moral panics that were created around single acts of deviance described as instances of Muslim culture, for example, a murder categorized as "honor killing," an instance of gang violence, a report on female circumcision, an "investigative report" that "reveals" welfare fraud by an immigrant family, assassinations of journalists; a court case on gang rape; or an attack on a gay parade. It is obvious that none of these acts is specific to Islam but via cultural explanations and the tautological pairing of the act with an ontological category, a welfare fraud becomes the indication of the incompatibility of Muslim ethics with "our ethics." The ongoing sense of crisis around Islam produces "Muslims" as an antagonizing ontological category, which retrospectively produces our commonality in the face of the imminent threat. As Bhattacharyya (2008: 9) explains, "This grouping is linked tenuously through an appeal to shared values, through that most nebulous of ties, culture. And as with all cultural alliances, it can exist only through constant reaffirmation of key myths and narratives. Ideas about gender identity, sexuality and affective relations play a central role in this process." The new collectivity, however, is not a mere alliance of forces but a new hegemonic formation—a new historical bloc—anchored in the perception of common core values that bring us together. The new social horizon, structured by the new cultural antagonism, originates with the populist Far Right but has become the new common sense of the social order. The hegemonic force produces a moral, cultural, and symbolic order that forces social and political players to respond to the issues pressed onto the political agenda and therefore redefine their positions between the two poles of the culturalized ontological order. The new common sense is difficult to challenge except from a position of exteriority, which would be condemned to irrelevance.

Once this new vision becomes the new common sense, even the past is imagined in terms of the new order. The new vision of society is projected back into the past as if society has always been imagined as an organic entity united by common cultural values. The unity—the cohesive force—of society is said to be broken by the arrival of the alien Muslims, and a gap emerges in the harmonious continuity of the social. This vision was recognized as the far-right position in the mid-1980s, but has slowly become the new common sense in political, vernacular, and academic discourse, and is often expressed in terms of "challenges to the cultural homogeneity of European societies."

Hegemony, however, is a contingent, incomplete relation. A principle such as freedom of speech or gender equality cannot continuously be emptied of content because of the heterogeneity of discourse. In the cacophony of public discourse, these principles will have particular meanings in concrete contexts, stripping them of the universality that signifies a collective identity. This is why a general sense of anxiety about an antagonistic force must be in constant production. The ongoing sense of crisis ontologizes differences, which in turn organizes discourse along the antagonistic divide. The continuing crisis also sustains the sense of unity around what seems to be challenged or under threat, suspending internal frictions until the crisis is over. The threat, therefore, must be constantly reproduced through crises.

The attacks on *Charlie Hebdo* or in Copenhagen will normally recede into the background when new events, debates, and controversies take over. The attacks will cease to signify the "dark forces" as a constant threat to "our way of life." It is in this context that the provocation of continuous controversies and moral panics has been a main right-wing populist strategy. As Bail (2015: 11) also notes, "Such events provide fringe voices with the opportunity to exploit the emotional bias of the media" that amplifies the significance of fringe voices even if covered in a negative light. Populist actors on the fringe become the main protagonists in the debates because of their controversial utterances, and the media's disproportionate coverage of populist messages bestows legitimacy on them and pushes them into the mainstream debate (Ellinas 2010; Mondon 2013). The mainstream parties' angry denunciations of the populists contribute to their profile. Ostracizing far-right populists makes them appear as a potent alternative with clean hands compared to corrupt politicians (Benson 2013; Mondon 2013).

The successive controversies produce a general sense of crisis—a crisis of representation, which allows the populist Far Right to successfully articulate popular anxieties about globalization, immigration, and the erasure of welfare systems as "concerns about the future of the nation." These articulations rhetorically move populist forces into the role of the daring representatives of the "people" (described as silent majority), as opposed to oppressive political and cultural elites. Once the idea that the "people" are worried about the future of their nation in the face of a culturally alien immigration becomes, through repeated crises, established as the tacit depiction of the popular sentiment,[1] mainstream forces generally respond by adopting populist rhetoric about the alien threat with the argument that "we have to listen to people's concerns" while attacking right-wing populists. Once the populist articulation becomes the commonsense definition of people's concerns, populist actors become the "natural" representatives of these concerns because they are the main protagonists.

The articulation of these concerns in terms of an alien cultural threat has slowly displaced the old class structure of society, undermining the voter basis of traditional parties. This is not a simple case of the working class changing its allegiance from the left to the right (as many political scientists would argue). Rather, what we have been experiencing is the transformation of the very ontology of the social in which the old working class no longer conceptualizes the main antagonism in society in class terms, thereby transforming itself into a new entity: a populist "people" who are free of class frictions, but whose cohesive force is challenged by the presence of people from incompatible cultures. Coupled with the Left's failure to articulate an alternative vision, "the people" has become a construction not based on class or shared political principles but that of common cultural values; as a result, the understanding of politics has shifted from class struggle to a cultural struggle (Mondon 2013: 159). This is why it is no surprise that even the mainstream Left speaks of cultural cohesion and shared values regardless of whom they include in these collectivities (e.g., including "good" Muslims while excluding "bad Muslims"). The culturalization of political discourse through the immigration debate has paralyzed the mainstream Left, which has been in a deep crisis the last two decades.

This transformation did not occur in a vacuum. The mainstream Left's tacit acceptance of neoliberal orthodoxies, coupled with its inability to firmly address the Far Right's jeremiads about the Muslim threat created a hegemonic crises in which large segments of the populace increasingly lost faith in the traditional system of representation. The populist Right's Manichaean claims and simplifications of the problems with the neoliberal order stifled the possibility of the mainstream Right to appear as an alternative without being branded unpatriotic or elitist. As Mondon (2013: 161) notes, in the context of France, "It became increasingly common to see the mainstream left support the right, and even at times push further into populist territory. As a consequence, right-wing populism and the necessity to construct an exclusionary people to retain a semblance of 'common sense' became increasingly hegemonic in mainstream politics, both on the left and the right."

The Hegemonic Displacement Is a Pan-European Phenomenon

Although this book is based on an analysis of data from Denmark, the process of the hegemonic displacement in which political discourse is culturalized and pushed to the right can be found throughout Europe, as the rapid rise of populist right-wing parties testifies. Even though one may note different trajectories, actors, and terminologies across the continent, debates on national identity coalesce around events similar to those I have described. Thus, many of my conclusions can be generalized to other European countries, as my discussion of the reactions to the attacks in Paris and Copenhagen indicates: the association of critical social and political issues such as democracy, the welfare system, national security, freedom of speech, gender equality, and gay rights with the impact of Muslim immigration and Islam; and the focus on social cohesion, core values, and national unity; the widespread concerns about the Muslim threat—be it terrorism, parallel societies (e.g., ghettos), misogyny, homophobia, intolerance, violence/criminality, or numbers/birthrates. Fekete (2009: 2) notes,

> In the Netherlands, the theme of the national debate has been "standards and values"; in Sweden and Norway, cultural barriers to inclusion; in the UK, "community cohesion"; in France, the principle of *laïcité* (state secularism); in Germany, the primacy of "*Leitkultur*" (leading culture) . . . in Spain, public safety and crime. But even though the terms through which the debate is entered differ, it is always linked back to immigrant communities and cultures and the threat that multicultural policies pose to core values, cultural homogeneity and social cohesion.

Benson (2013) observes a similar shift in the French immigration debate from humanitarian concerns with wages, working conditions, and slum housing to cultural issues in the early 1980s when the "focus on immigrant workers was quickly being displaced by a concern with the 'second generation' and their relationship to French culture" (112). This focus shift led to a preoccupation with a national cohesion frame, "which portrays immigrant cultural differences (customs, religion, language) as a threat to national unity and social harmony," beginning in the early 1980s and intensifying in the 1990s (7, 112). As in Denmark, the entire media were allied against the rise of the far-right National Front in the 1970s and early 1980s, but when the political winds turned against diversity politics in favor of national cohesion, the media's coverage also shifted. Benson also notes "the ways that typical categories of left and right are scrambled in immigration politics, producing a number of 'strange bedfellows' alliances" (7).

Other scholars who have been following the French debates also note that there has been an increasing emphasis on the idea of the unity of the nation since the 1980s (Scott 2007: 117). Olivier Roy (2007) points to the blurring of traditional divisions (e.g., between left and right, between secularists and religious sectors) in the face of the intense focus on Islam and Muslim immigrants as a category incompatible with Frenchness. It is the intense focus on Muslims and Islam that unites political, journalistic, and intellectual opinion in an apparent confirmation of France's universal values, because, as Roy (2007: 1), explains, "Islam seems to call into question the very identity of the country, or at least the nature of its institutions. People mobilize for the defense of 'republican values' and '*laïcité*.'" National unity is threatened by "the stubborn refusal of Muslims to integrate, on the inherent 'foreignness' of their 'culture'" (Scott 2007: 120).

Mondon (2013) argues that the National Front's rhetoric, which was considered extreme and undemocratic, has become hegemonic as mainstream politicians on the left and right responded to its popularity by legitimizing "ethno-exclusivist and neo-racist ideas," rendering these ideas as "common sense" (157). Coupled with the Left's failure to articulate alternatives, the new hegemony shifted "the understanding of politics in the minds of the *classes populaires* from a class struggle, in the Marxist sense of the term, to a struggle of race and 'civilization'" (159).

The trajectory of the culturalization of discourse has been slightly different in Britain, the only country in Europe that had an official policy of multiculturalism, albeit coupled with tight immigration control after the formation of Commission for Racial Equality. Nevertheless, the focus on so-called parallel societies as evidence of the failure of multiculturalism pushed British immigration discourse into the terrain of culture where (especially Muslim) immigrants are considered to be a threat to national culture and social cohesion (Fekete 2009; Kundnani 2007; Lentin and Titley 2011; Siapera 2010; Pitcher 2009). Stolcke (1995), for example, explains that the controversy over immigration was, until the late 1970s, predominantly phrased in racist terms, but "when the Tory government took up the banner of curbing immigration it began to rationalize it, invoking, by contrast with earlier racist arguments, national-cum-cultural unity and calling for the cultural assimilation of immigrant communities 'in our midst' to safeguard the British 'nation' with its shared values and lifestyle" (11). Since 2001, multiculturalism has been attacked by the Right and the Left for threatening "community cohesion" (Pitcher 2009; Kundnani 2007; Fekete 2009). As in other European countries, "fundamental values of Britishness" are "thought to coalesce [around] sexual equality, tolerance, freedom of speech and the rule of the law" (Kundnani 2007: 126).

Although Germany, for historical reasons, never really had a huge far-right party since World War II, the discourse on immigration in Germany is similar to the rest of Europe: anxieties about "ethnic ghettos" and "parallel societies" are taken to be indicators of a failed experiment with multiculturalism. Partly to keep the Far Right at bay and partly to justify their attempts to dismantle welfare system, successive center-right governments made immigration and immigrants' culture the centerpiece of their politics. In the early 1980s, German chancellor (and CDU politician) Helmut Kohl was already claiming that cultural differences between foreigners and Germans were unbridgeable (Lucassen 2005: 156). Since, then the term *Leitkultur* has been popularized and employed by Chancellor Angela Merkel in the debate on national identity, which is invariably connected to immigration. Stehle (2012: 167) demonstrates that in the German imagination, "'Europe' functions simultaneously as an example for the failures of multiculturalism and as a bastion of western values in need of protection." Likewise, sexual tolerance and gender equality have become central to the debate on immigrants, who since the mid-1980s were transformed from "foreign workers" to "Muslim immigrants" (Lucassen 2005; Petzen 2012; Spielhaus 2010; Yıldız 2009, 2011; Yurdakul 2009). Ewing (2008) examines the role of moral panics around gender issues in the construction of Turkish immigrants as a threat in the German national imaginary. Ireland (2004: 51) notes that the Left and the Right unite in expressing concerns about women's rights under Islam.

In the Netherlands, new applicants for immigration are forced to watch a video in which women are topless and men are kissing one another and asked whether they are offended by the images. They are also asked whether they are willing to live in a democracy and respect the Dutch values à la the Danish integration contract (Butler 2008: 3). These exams, often only required from immigrants of non-Western origin, have spread throughout Europe (e.g., Britain, Germany). In many ways, Dutch discourse on Muslim immigration is similar to Scandinavian discourse (Andreassen 2012; Bangstad 2011; Bracke 2012; De Leeuw and van Wichelen 2012; El-Tayeb 2012).

In almost every case, a debate about national values and social cohesion is opened up through a specific event taken up first by populist far-right actors and then by mainstream politicians and the media, whose disproportionate coverage of the populists render them central figures in the debate. The event often quickly turns into a moral panic about Islamic values or Muslim cultural practices because the preceding moral panics had already established the framework. The debate generally results in the institutionalization of discriminatory practices toward Muslim immigrants (e.g., the ban on headscarves in France and Germany; integration contracts, civics tests, and loyalty oaths in Austria, France, Denmark, the Netherlands, Germany, and the UK). Mainstream parties across the European political spectrum have incorporated national identity themes into their programs and "issues such as immigration, citizenship, asylum, and historical memory have become a constant source of partisan rivalry" (Ellinas 2010: 2).

The controversies often focus on sexuality, particularly Muslims' view of gender equality, so much so that most integration contracts or civics tests seek to measure immigrants' beliefs on issues of sexuality. Articulation of gender equality or sexual tolerance as "core national values"—as opposed to Muslim immigrants' "cultural practices"—brings together people from across the political spectrum and therefore unsettles the traditional divide between left and right.

In this process, the Far Right, too, is transformed: far-right parties present themselves as true representatives of working class, albeit in classless terms; they defend feminist causes albeit only in cases where Muslims are thought to subvert them; the neo-Nazi English Defense League has even a gay section because, as they explain, Muslims do not tolerate homosexuality. Many far-right parties have dropped their previous pure neoliberal views (e.g., their stand against taxes) and adopted welfare-friendly stances, albeit only for those who belong to the nation.

The centrality of cultural values to political discourse and the presentation of Muslims and Islam as a threat to the "core values of the West," moral panics, and controversies around Muslims and Islam are not unique to Europe. Especially since 9/11, these phenomena seem to spread in the Western world through the discourse on the "war on terror" and the Muslim threat (Bail 2015; Ellinas 2010; Kundnani 2014; Massad 2015; Mondon 2013; Morgan and Poynting 2012; Puar 2007). As Massad (2015) argues, popular anxieties about violence, autocracy, intolerance, misogyny, and homophobia are projected onto Islam, and the West emerges as democratic, tolerant, feminist, and pro-LGBT rights—in short, Islam-free. This image, as Bhattacharyya (2008) elaborates, is used to create an alliance through an appeal to shared values and culture that can only exist though constant reaffirmation of key myths and narratives about gender identity and sexuality.

Populism, Neoliberalism, and Democracy

"I can't breathe" became a common slogan for protests in the fall of 2014 against the killing of unarmed African Americans in the United States, but it has since taken a larger meaning, challenging a discriminatory system and calling for greater equality. The inability to breathe is a global sentiment that transcends the United States or the West; it describes a widespread dissatisfaction with an increasingly authoritarian global neoliberal political and economic system with high levels of inequality. As Badiou (2013) noted, while most of these protests have been sporadic, disorganized, and largely unsuccessful because of the lack of a unifying language for "situated discussion of the future of emancipatory actions . . . the forces of fascism . . . against the illusory backdrop of a xenophobic and racist nationalism, now claim to lead the opposition" to the system (44).

In other words, "I can't breathe" represents the driving force behind the rise of populist forces globally: left populism in Latin America (and lately in Greece and Spain), right-wing populism in Europe, and Islamist populism in Turkey and Malaysia. The difference is the way they articulate the frontier: they establish who the enemies of the "people" are in different ways, which also determines the identity of the popular formation. In other words, the content of a given populist appeal depends on how the antagonistic relationship is defined. In one conjuncture, the defense of "the little guy" may be articulated against the corrupt economic and political power elites and their supporters in the form of imperialist or global capital, which causes poverty and oppression; in another conjunction, the ordinary Dane (or Frenchman, Dutchman, etc.) may be posed against the corrupt, treasonous political and cultural elites who let alien Muslim immigrants or deviant minorities destroy "our way of life" from within. In the Turkish case, the Islamist populist response has been articulated against the old secularist guard of the republic and their cosmopolitan (i.e., urban, educated) supporters with a deviant lifestyle, all of whom are said to be in the service of Western powers that intend to destroy the Muslim way of life. Populism, in this sense,

> is the language of politics when there can be no politics as usual: a mode of identification characteristic of times of unsettlement and de-alignment, involving the radical redrawing of social borders along lines other than those that had previously structured society. It is a political appeal that seeks to change the terms of political discourse, articulate new social relations, redefine political frontiers and constitute new identities. (Panizza 2005: 9)

In general, scholars agree that populist rhetoric typically gains audibility when the existing order loses its ability to absorb discontent and economic transformations dislocate the established political and social divisions (i.e., the established way of life; Laclau 2005; Mondon 2013; Mouffe 1995; Mudde 2004; Panizza 2005).

If we accept the premise that populist voices break through when there is a sense that existing social and political institutions fail to confine and regulate the discontent within the existing system, we may also say that there is a huge democratic deficit and the populist attraction is a clear indication of this deficit. The established parties throughout Europe seem to have accepted the neoliberal dogma that the old politics of left-right rhetoric is an obstacle to the modernization of economic and political systems and that politics is now about managing the resources in the most efficient way. European political systems have been "transformed into 'depoliticized democracies' in which administration has replaced politics (in modern parlance: governance instead of government). Not surprisingly, it is here that the populist call for the 'repoliticization of the public realm' and their role as taboo breaker have found the most receptive audience" (Mudde 2004: 555). As Mouffe (1995) warned two decades ago, when popular discontent with the way things are done cannot find channels of expression within the traditional political system, a crisis of representation occurs and popular discontent becomes susceptible to the simplistic solutions that populist far-right parties provide.

I started this project to understand the dynamics of social change: how certain political forces gain access to mainstream discourse and change the basic premises. My goal was to understand how progressive and democratic movements could intervene and challenge far-right populism. My analysis of the Danish case illuminates the way hegemonic displacement has taken place through controversies and moral panics about Muslim immigration. These ongoing controversies and panics (1) present Muslim immigrants as the "folk devils" of our time; (2) ontologize Muslim immigrants as an antagonistic force by keeping a constant focus on them; (3) create the impression that the future of the nation is under imminent threat from Muslim immigration; (4) push populist voices from the fringes into the center of mainstream discourse; (5) enable populists to present popular discontent with the breakdown of an established way of life as a protest against the "corrupt political and cultural elite" and their treasonous immigration policies; (6) allow populists to claim that they represent the oppressed "silent majority" because their "concerns" (as articulated by the populists) are dismissed as nationalistic, racist, and primitive; (7) convince the mainstream parties, through the media's amplification of controversial populist claims, that people are concerned with the future of the nation in the face of Muslim immigration; (8) and thus make the populist vision the new common sense; and (9) through this new "common sense" create a new unity among groups from the left and the right in defense of threatened "shared values." The unity around "shared values" implies that important achievements (e.g., such as a better distribution of wealth or a better level of gender equality) are embedded in, and reflective of, cultures. The cultural view of these achievements is based on a denial of a past that was characterized by major conflicts over these demands. The populist imagination presents the current state of crisis as a break from the culturally homogeneous past that was a precondition for social cohesion. This is how the new populist right-wing hegemony is formed by the premises of the populist Far Right.

So, what have we learned?

First, that it is the result of a political intervention by far-right populist forces that draws the contours of the new hegemony; it is not a necessary endpoint of a structural development. If, however, we accept the premise that populist far-right forces were able to articulate the general discontentment with the neoliberal framework by presenting immigration as the main problem and by advocating the closing of borders so that we can return to the idyllic, harmonious past where life was simpler as the solution (in the absence of an alternative articulation—because of the presumed collusion between the mainstream Left and Right), the question is, therefore, how to rearticulate the discontent with the neoliberal framework in new and creative ways without blaming the weakest for all the problems. The second question is, If support for the populist Right can be read as an indication of democratic deficit, can the populist logic that creates popular identity around sameness be made compatible with democratic thought with space for diversity and plurality?

Laclau (2005) answers this question positively. He is interested in revindicating populism as a politics par excellence where large segments of the populace are mobilized to participate in politics at a time when the distinction between left and right is blurred and politics has been reduced to the administration of austerity policies. Populism is about dichotomizing the political space and drawing a new border across the political battlefield. Populist politics creates a new "them" against which a popular identity is produced. The identities of the antagonistic camps are not given a priori but defined in the process of constituting the antagonism. If this is the case, the ideological significance of populism depends on how this border is drawn, and an inclusionary leftist populism would aim at drawing the border differently than exclusionary right-wing populism. The main difficulty for the Left, according to Laclau, is that they rarely engage in the hegemonic struggle by producing a new kind of political imaginary but rely on a rationalist discourse about rights. Thus, they look down at any populist imaginary as a simplistic appeal to basic instincts, hitting the lowest common denominator in the name of short-term success.

Laclau seemed to believe that the heterogeneity of the popular demands (i.e., difference) that are articulated as parts of the same struggle against political power would secure the democratic potential of populism, which would only be exclusionary toward the parasitic minority that clings to power. The democratic potential of populism is embedded in the fact that the logic of difference always subverts the logic of equivalence (sameness) and vice versa. In other words, the differences among the demands of various groups brought together in a popular identity would keep the identity open and contestable. The new populist political movements on the left (e.g., *Syriza* in Greece, *Podemos* in Spain) can be seen as democratic left-wing experiments in the creation of a new political mobilization against the increasingly oppressive neoliberal capitalist elites that have created unprecedented levels of inequality. These populist movements have envisioned a popular identity that is not ethnonationalist and exclusionary in the same way as the far-right populists of Europe.

Laclau would argue that a popular identity consists of fragmented groups with neglected demands but their demands have no logical connection to one another except the articulatory logic. The demands are brought together through their shared antagonism to "the enemy" who prevents the fulfillment of the particular demands. But because the demands are not necessarily connected to one another, the totality of the demands cannot be represented positively by a single slogan that can stand for all of the neglected demands, there has to be a synecdochic operation whereby a single slogan stands for the whole. This could be a demand such as "equality," which would mean different things for different groups in the opposition (e.g., racial equality, gender equality, economic equality, religious equality). The term "equality" needs, therefore, to be emptied of content so much that it is no longer attached to a particular demand (e.g., gender equality); it becomes an empty signifier that signifies the totality of the demands that make up the opposition. In other words, it would signify the identity of the opposition.

However, alongside the metonymic logic, there is another logic in operation in populism: the idea that constituting the popular identity "necessitates the political defeat of 'the other' that is deemed to oppress or exploit the people and impede its full presence" (Panizza 2005: 3). Populism externalizes the enemy into a "positive" ontological entity whose annihilation (it claims) would restore balance and cohesion. If antagonism, and annihilation of the enemy, is the necessary logic of populism, it needs to keep the external threat alive. In the absence of such a threat, those who claim to represent the popular will have the potential of turning their gaze inward in order to clean up the remnants of the threat—in the form of any kind of dissent. This would mean that the heterogeneity of the popular identity cannot guarantee its democratic potential; rather, the heterogeneous elements that do not align with the power can be quickly relegated to the exterior, therefore presenting them as new threats (or a continuation of the old threat), which are often depicted as the henchmen of external global powers. This is path the Islamist populists in Turkey chose after consolidating their grip on power, although they were, in their early days, praised for democratizing the political arena by including the disenfranchised sectors of the population in the political process and breaking down the influence of the military in politics. A similar criticism has been leveled against the populist left-wing government of Venezuela, which perceives any criticism or expression of dissatisfaction as an intrinsic threat organized by external, imperialist powers against the survival of the popular will (which may have some validity considering the United States' involvement in the coup against Hugo Chávez in the early days of his government). These examples of populists in power indicate that the heterogeneity of the social is far from being a guarantee for plurality. In short, populism has the potential of becoming fascism. Was Nazism not a populist movement that took the logic of antagonism to its extreme?

It seems to fall on left-wing European populist movements such as *Syriza* and *Podemos* (and in Latin American countries such as Uruguay) to demonstrate the democratic potential of left-wing populism.

APPENDIX I

Declaration of Integration and Active Residency in Danish Society

I hereby declare that I will actively work to secure my own and my resident children's and spouse's or partner's integration and active citizenship in Danish society.

I therefore declare the following:

1. Under all circumstances, I will uphold Danish law and protect Danish democratic principles.
2. I acknowledge that the Danish language and familiarity with Danish society are the key to a good and active existence in Denmark. I will therefore learn Danish and build knowledge about Danish society as quickly as possible. I know that I can learn Danish in Danish courses offered by the municipal ministry.
3. I acknowledge that individual citizens and families are responsible for providing for themselves. I will therefore work toward becoming self-sufficient as quickly as possible. I know that to become self-sufficient it helps to participate in activities that are described in my integration contract with the municipality.
4. I know that if I am seeking a job and participating in the Danish educational system and in activities that are described in my integration contract with the municipality, I am entitled to temporary economic help until I can provide for myself.
5. I acknowledge that men and women have equal responsibilities and rights in Denmark and that men and women should contribute to society through education, employment, payment of taxes, and par-

ticipation in the democratic process and to take care of parental responsibilities toward their own children.

6. I know that in Denmark it is forbidden to exert violence or apply illegal duress on one's spouse.
7. I acknowledge that in Denmark there shall be equal respect and opportunities for development of all children, both girls and boys, so they can grow up to become active and responsible citizens who are capable of making their own decisions. I will ensure that my children receive the best possible upbringing, attend school, and become integrated into Denmark. I will also make sure that my children learn Danish as early as possible and complete their homework through their school term, and I will actively participate with my children's institution or school.
8. I know that, in Denmark, it is illegal to strike your children.
9. I know that circumcision of girls as well forced marriages are illegal activities in Denmark.
10. I respect every person's freedom and personal integrity, equality of the genders, freedom of religion, and freedom of expression, which are foundational in Denmark.
11. I know that discrimination on the basis of gender or skin color, and threats or disdain toward groups on the grounds of faith or sexual orientation, are illegal activities in Denmark.
12. I acknowledge that Danish society has a strict policy against terrorism and that each citizen has a duty to fight terrorism, including assistance to the authorities in preventative and follow-up work.
13. I acknowledge that active engagement in Danish society is a requirement for a good existence in Denmark, regardless of how long that may be.
14. I know that extension of my residency permit depends on meeting the requirements of my residency permit.
15. I know that the requirements to receive permanent residency include that I have fulfilled my integration contract by participating in ongoing activities, preferably by being involved in education or employment early in my residency; that I have passed the Danish language exam; and that I do not owe a debt to the public sector. I know that criminal activities could delay or hinder receiving a permanent residency permit.

16. I know that if I am a refugee, I no longer have asylum if the situation in my home country changes so I can return home. I know that refugees and their families can receive economic support for traveling home to their country of origin or previous residency if they need it.

Date: Signature:

APPENDIX 2

Krarup's First Advertisement, *Jyllands-Posten*, September 21, 1986

No, not a single dime![1]

On Sunday, October 5, my doorbell will ring. The bell will also ring at your door. That Sunday the bells will ring at all Danish doors, for it is a national donation day under the motto "Refugee 86."

If I am at home, I will answer the door myself. And I will kindly greet the nice collector who rang the bell, and I will do my best to make my tone lovely and my actions polite, because I do not want to annoy the collector. The collectors are without doubt driven by the best intentions and motivations. The collectors should be received with friendliness. But I will tell them: No, not a dime!

It is not because I cannot afford to help. Neither is it because I am against helping refugees, who are, in my opinion, in one of the worst situations a human being can face. Rather, it is simply and solely because "Refugee 86" benefits the Danish Refugee Council.

And I will not support this organization with so much as a dime. On the contrary, I consider each dime given to the Refugee Council a dime given to the ruin of the fatherland. This so-called aid work has in recent years established itself as a state within the state, which imposes its law in the parliament, terrorizes public debate, drains the Treasury for millions, and acts as a bailiff among the farmers [*fæstebønder*: tenant farmer]. Do you remember the case in Øster Højst?[2]

Do you remember how the chairman of the Refugee Council ordered around the anxious villagers? And do you remember when Mogens Glistrup[3] allowed himself to express his opinion, and the same chairman, Thor A. Bak, commented on it: "Coop him up!" he hissed in the press. And do you remember in Ho? And in Blokhus? Each time it is the same scene: a dictatorial Refugee Council, which speaks to us as if we were dogs, demands our tax money, constantly requests more staff members, and brushes off our concerns.

For there is a real problem that the Refugee Council wants to forbid us Danes to speak about and utter publicly: if an uncontrolled and unconstrained mass migration of Mohammedan and Oriental refugees comes through our borders, then we cannot be here ourselves—in any case not in naturalness and peace. The disaster the Danish Refugee Council has caused to Denmark's future is immeasurable and will not be forgotten. Is Copenhagen going to be a Danish city in 50 years? Can Danes continue to be a people when there is no longer a common language, history, and religion? Or is it a fate such as Lebanon's that awaits us—torn apart by wars between incompatible minority groups? The Danish Refugee Council has tremendously damaged our fatherland with its proud and self-righteous pharisaism and its—by virtue of its "noble" purpose—unconstrained power over lawmaking and social life, and that politicians such as Bernhard Baunsgaard, Preben Wilhjelm, and Ole Espersen[4] have contributed does not lessen the Refugee Council's guilt. They have acted as an occupying power in a foreign country. They have deliberately taken a position against Danes who are concerned with good reason.

And now they beg for money in order to continue terrorizing us. . . .

No, not a dime!

That I will not support the Danish Refugee Council with so much as a dime does not mean that I will not help refugees, and the day after, on Monday, October 6, when the post office is open, I will send 100 kroner to the Danish Afghanistan Committee [account number]. There the helpful work is done by people who do not trample on their own to demonstrate their great goodness toward aliens. Here we can open both our doors and wallets. The Danish Refugee Council is not going to be endowed but to be put on its place.

It can happen on Sunday, October 5.

Say no to the Refugee Council and thereby to refugee policy!

P.S.: I chose to insert the article above as an ad to give it greater impact. The ad is unfortunately not free, and since I am the only one who is paying for it, I am asking for help from those who share my views. If there is an economic possibility, I will insert a similar appeal in the same place next Sunday. It will emphasize that "Refugee 86" in reality gives us a chance for a referendum on the present refugee policy that the politicians have denied us.

A possible surplus will be used toward other actions to change the present refugee law—I am considering a national petition (signature collection). The rest of the surplus will be paid to the Danish Afghanistan Committee.

APPENDIX 3

Krarup's Second Advertisement, *Jyllands-Posten*, September 28, 1986

We have chance now!

When your doorbell rings next Sunday and you get up to open the door, you have the chance.

What chance?

The chance to set bounds. The chance to say no to the way the Danish Refugee Council has treated Danes each time we have expressed doubts about the uncontrolled invasion of the country. The chance to tell the politicians that we are not going to put up with the refugee policy they force upon us.

It is a collector from the Danish Refugee Council who will ring the doorbell next Sunday, and the collector will ask for donation to "Refugee 86." And we have no reason to be anything but friendly toward the collector. We have also a reason to help refugees in distress.

But by saying no to "Refugee 86" we have at last the chance that we have been missing so long, to express our opinion with all our heart.

Because it is not about helping. The Danish Refugee Council is no longer a humanitarian and neutral aid organization. It has become a politicizing and power-conscious state within a state that has ordered us around and bullied us to have its own way in the last few years.

When people grouched, they were put on the rack. If it were about showing consideration for Danes who live in the country, the Refugee Council shouted with indignation and called it "racism." Just look at Chairman Thor A. Bak's comment on the government's latest plans to put the brakes on: "It is an outright step back for democracy" (*Berlingske Tidende,* October 9, 1986).

Now we have the chance to tell the Danish Refugee Council that in a democracy there must be respect for people whose lives and country are at stake.

We have also the chance to tell our politicians the simple truth. In 1983, they enacted alien legislation has abolished our borders. The door to Denmark is wide open. And in the years after 1983, we have seen the result. In 1985, 10,000 asylum-seekers came. Will 50,000 come in 1986?

Under these circumstances, Danes asked for permission to express their opinion through a referendum. It was refused to us. Flatly. The politicians did not want to lose face, and their face is more important than Denmark's future.

By boycotting "Refugee 86," we can express our opinion about both the Danish Refugee Council and refugee policy. A no to the Refugee Council's aid collection will be a popular protest that can set things and bounds in their place. Use the chance!

Boycott "Refugee 86!"

P.S.: I am thankful for the overwhelming support and approval that has flowed to me during the week and made it possible to insert this announcement. It is, as I had assumed: the public feels terrorized by the refugee policy's powerful advocates in the press and the public domain and is looking for a chance to demonstrate a No to the catastrophic developments in our country.

On this occasion, the following independent Danes formed a committee for changing the refugee law: Dr. Phil. Sune Dalgård, Copenhagen; parish priest Søren Krarup, Seem; parish priest Jesper Langballe, Thorning; parish priest Olval Lilleør, Virum; teacher Steen Steensen,

Ranum; and [. . .] Jens Toldstrup, Malling. The purpose is to start a nationwide signature collection for a petition against the refugee law and refugee policy. If we do not obtain the economic means to this end, the incoming contributions will be used toward other activities for the same purpose, primarily in the form of publications.

We are asking for help! Without economic help, we will not have capability.

Boycott Refugee 86!

Notes

Introduction

1. For Saussure, language was a closed system of a structural space, and it was only within that system that the meaning of a sign could be fixed. He subsequently distinguished between *langue* and *parole*—the latter being the individual speech act or utterance. For Saussure, it was *langue,* the underlying structure of rules and codes, that could be studied scientifically because of its closed nature. *Parole* lacked those structural properties and was therefore difficult to study. This notion of a closed system of rules and codes that produce meaning is clearly in conflict with my approach, according to which there is no meaning unless there is actual speech act, and as Saussure recognized, it is a terrain that does not obey scientific rules and codes, which is why it is easier to "fix" the meaning of a sign at an abstract level.

2. In other words, an articulation of different demands as parts of a coherent political movement.

3. Laclau and Mouffe (2001) draw heavily on Foucault's notion of discourse but reject Foucault's distinction between the discursive and the nondiscursive as a form of mentalism.

4. It does not mean "culture" has not previously been associated with immigrants. Immigrants have been presented as threats to the nation since the nineteenth century (see, e.g., Lucassen 2005). Immigrants were, however, even as a cultural category, configured within a different ontology of the social. This book investigates the broader process of the culturalization of the entire social and political life that has displaced the ontological distinctions.

5. Except for the distinction between discourse and reality that Foucault maintains.

6. The Royal Library has microfilms of all newspapers, but they are categorized chronologically, so one would have to look at all the newspapers to find the relevant articles. Photocopying from microfilms was also a practical problem.

7. According to Denmark's official website (www.denmark.dk), "With the Constitution of 1849, Denmark gained a free press, which quickly became an opinion-shaping press in close consonance with the major political and social conflicts following in the

wake of the change from an agrarian to an industrial society. The opinion-shaping press took the form of party-political organs, the so-called 'four-paper system.' Each of the four major political parties, The Right (*Højre*), from 1915 The Conservative Party (*Det Konservative Folkeparti*), The Social Liberal Party (*Det Radikale Venstre*), The Social Democratic Party (*Socialdemokratiet*), and The Liberal Party (*Venstre*), established a nationwide network of newspapers that mobilized the various social groups they represented." *Jyllands-Posten* was associated with the Liberals, *Berlingske Tidende* with the Conservatives, and *Politiken* with the Social Liberals (the Radicals), while the Social Democratic Party had its own party newspapers with different names, the last being *Aktuelt* (not included in my sample as it was closed down in the mid-1990s and therefore did not exist during the period of my research).

8. Circulation numbers are from 2005. There has been a considerable decline in the readership of all of the papers since the mid-1980s.

9. The publishers of *Politiken* and *Jyllands-Posten* joined forces economically in the first half of the 2000s but this merger has not (so far) influenced the political leanings of the newspapers.

Chapter 1

1. The "silly season," as it is called in some other countries, is the summer months when the media are filled with frivolous news stories.

2. Examples include Bangstad 2011; Bracke 2012; El-Tayeb 2012; Fekete 2009; Göle 2011; Haritaworn 2012; Henkel 2012; Hervik 2012; Horsti 2008; Jacobsen et al. 2012; Jensen 2009; Kundnani 2012; Lentin and Titley 2011; Petzen 2012; Pitcher 2009; Siapera 2010; Stehle 2012; and Wren 2001.

3. This is the general definition of "class"; "working class" may be defined by its cultural characteristics in actual discourse depending on the context in which it is used.

4. See Edwards (2003) for an intriguing analysis of commonsense discourse in race talk.

5. It is not that both sides articulated Germany as a clear-cut threat that had to be kept at a distance. Some argued that a "yes" vote involving Germany in a tighter European community would prevent Germany from returning to its bad old ways.

6. It is clear that cultural homogeneity itself is a myth. A mere two decades ago, homosexuality was not part of the allegedly homogenous Danish culture, but it is now included in the cultural narrative (Andreassen 2012; Keskinen 2012; Petersen 2013). Such examples show that the idea of cultural homogeneity has been a persistent part of the discourse on a Danish national identity always under threat by some other group.

7. Discursive psychology is not a single approach to discourse analysis but includes a number of methods. For examples, Michael Billig's (1991) analysis of ideology implies looking at larger structures of discourse, whereas Derek Edwards and Jonathan Potter's (1992) approach is closer to Schegloff's notion of conversation analysis focused on talk-in-interaction and how people use categories in concrete settings rather than how those categories function across settings in a more stable manner.

8. A growing number of studies across disciplines demonstrate that the dichotomy between "us" (the "nation" or the "people") and "them" (immigrants, Muslims) has

become a pervasive feature of European political discourse (e.g., Delanty, Wodak, and Jones 2008; Fekete 2009; Krzyżanowski and Wodak 2009; Kundnani 2007; Lentin and Titley 2011; Pitcher 2009; Reisigl and Wodak 2001; Scott 2007; Triandafyllidou 2001). The Danish context has been studied by Andreassen 2005, 2012; Betz and Meret 2009; Diken 1998; Hervik 2004, 2011, 2012; Hussain, Yılmaz, and O'Connor 1997; Jacobsen et al. 2012; Jensen 2008; Keskinen 2012; Meret 2011; Sampson 1995; Schierup 1993; Siim and Mokre 2013; and Wren 2001.

9. The introduction discusses data and analytical methods. Also, Potter and Wetherell (1987) produce a similar table, showing that attributes have wide variations across their own interviews with white New Zealanders about Maoris.

10. The noticeable pauses are marked with a dot in parentheses: (.); longer pauses are stated as such. Interruptions or restarts (self-repair) are indicated with a dash (—).

11. The second statement about immigrants calling themselves with Danish names to avoid discrimination indicates that they speak without an accent, so that only their names give them away.

12. I leave "prejudice" in quotations marks to deny a direct access to reality without the intermediation of language, against which a "prejudiced" version could be assessed. In my theoretical universe, where language constructs versions of reality relative to rhetorical function, the distinction between discourse and reality does not make sense. I use the term "prejudice" as understood in its vernacular sense: adverse judgment formed beforehand or without knowledge of the facts, people, or culture.

13. See Khosravinik 2010; Blommaert and Bulcaen 2000; and Phillips and Jørgensen 2002 for a more critical treatment of this point. For an interesting discussion about whether larger constructs can be analyzed in discourse, see Billig 1999; Schegloff 1997, 1999; and Wetherell 1998.

14. This designation is routinely applied even to those born and raised in Denmark.

15. The respondents in my sample never use the terms "racism" or "racist," confirming the common observation among scholars of race and immigration discourse in Denmark.

16. Although Khader, in this utterance, is treated as an uncontroversial figure, he is, in fact, quite controversial and has often been criticized for focusing on immigrants and their culture as the root of the problem, not unlike the Turkish-German sociologist Necla Kelek or the Somalian-Dutch politician Ayaan Hirsi Ali, who was controversial before she left politics for a job in the United States in May 2006. Treating Khader as uncontroversial helps Birgitte construct him as an authority who can testify to the nature of the reality she describes. I am sure she knows he is controversial and that her argument only works if it is not challenged by the interviewer (me). But this is how it works: if each premise is challenged in each case, no conversation or interview would be possible. Some definitions have to be treated as tacit facts if the participants are going to be able to interact and talk about things. Without this, communication would be even more interrupted and disjointed than it already is and would lack common ground on which people could communicate.

17. I am not sure that this issue could be solved with a more precise transcription that shows intonation since intonation is often lost in translation or can be misunderstood by speakers of another language.

18. There is an inherent tension in this kind of analysis in that I may sound critical

of Birgitte for doing what she is doing in her context of speech. First, these are generic rhetorical strategies common in all kinds of discourse and available to all kinds of people. Attributing them to her in this context may seem to identify them as strategies to justify racist discourse. A deeper moral and ethical tension arises around my position as an analyst, which situates me as an expert who appears to know more about the person than she does herself. Most discourse analyses are open to this criticism. It is a difficult tension to resolve. Some analysts (i.e., conversation analysts) attempt to counter it by rejecting the use of any category not used by respondents, therefore avoiding imposing ideas, categories, intentions, or ideologies onto speakers.

19. According to the dictionary in my Lotus program, a mammal is "any of various warm-blooded vertebrate animals, including human beings, marked by a covering of hair on the skin and in the female, milk-producing glands." One can argue that whales do not exactly fit into this taxonomy of mammals.

20. Since this is an argument analysis, I have not numbered the lines.

21. As long as it is possible to reconstruct a proposition from its linguistic context, that proposition can be considered to have been communicated (Quasthoff 1978: 25).

22. For Laclau (2014), the relationship between ontic content and ontological signification is not related to the relationship between actual statements and the category they describe but the relationship between a privileged signifier—a particularity—and a universality whereby the name of that particularity stands for an absent universality. It is, he proposes, a "movement from metonymy to metaphor, from contingent articulation to essential belonging," as when trade unions engage in antiracist struggle for a long period and antiracism "becomes a part of the central meaning of the term 'trade-union'" (63). For Laclau, the statements about "us," although contingent, are articulated in a chain of equivalences opposed to the antagonistic chain of equivalences linked to "them." I use the ontic/ontological distinction in a more flexible way. I argue that it is not the particular content of what is attributed to a category that comes to signify the category but the act of articulating these inherently contingent (and at times contradictory) statements *as if* they signify antagonistic ontological categories.

23. As Andreassen (2012) and Jensen (2008) note, immigrants and Muslims have come to be used synonymously even though there are any number of non-Muslim immigrant groups.

24. "Perceived" here refers to the rhetorical treatment of difference as if difference is given prior to discourse. It is difficult to know how people actually perceive things because expressions of perceptions vary according to context.

25. Discriminatory practices that rely on justifications other than race (e.g., religious, biological, and cultural categories of difference) have been conceptualized as neoracism (Balibar 1991), differential racism (Taguieff 2001), and cultural racism (Blaut 1992; Stolcke 1995). Because my focus in this chapter is not on racism as such but how a culturalized ontology of the social can be analyzed in discourse that is inherently fragmented and disjointed, I use the term heuristically to refer to discriminatory practices in general.

26. See Edwards 2003; Gotsbachner 2001; Khosravinik 2010; Reisigl and Wodak 2001; Wetherell and Potter 1992; van Dijk 1984, 1987.

Chapter 2

1. Akkerman and Hagelund 2007; Andersen 2002, 2004; Andreasen 2005; Larsen 1997; Borchorst and Teigen 2012; Diken 1998; Hjarnø and Jensen 1996; Schierup 1993; Gaasholt and Togeby 1995; Hervik 1999, 2002, 2004; Hussain, Yılmaz, and O'Connor 1997; Madsen 2000; Necef 2000; Rydgren 2004; Togeby 2004; Wren 2001; Østergaard 2007.

2. "Indvandring og Islam splitter danskerne," *Jyllands-Posten*, August 16, 2010.

3. These scholars are usually political scientists who study the far/radical/extreme/populist Right and therefore describe the political world using political science terminology. Their terminology does not always correspond to my terminology informed by discourse theory.

4. The coalition government consisted of the two major mainstream right parties, the Conservative Party, the Liberal Party, and the two small middle-right parties, the Centrum Democrats and the Christian People's Party. The prime minister was Poul Schlüter from the Conservative Party.

5. These austerity politics were branded the "potato cure."

6. This argument has also been transformed from a neoliberal argument to an argument for an ethnicized politics: since 2001, the Liberal/Conservative government has used this argument to cut immigrants from the welfare system with the argument that they need an incentive to find work and "integrate," completely ignoring the fact that discrimination is one of the reasons that immigrants are three and one-half times as unemployed as Danes. The incentive argument is now rarely used regarding the unemployed.

7. "Culturalization of discourse" is my phrase.

8. Or whatever various scholars call it: dislocation of political identities; the prevalence of sociocultural cleavages; transformation of the social structures. There is a general agreement that a tectonic shift has occurred in Denmark (and in other Western European societies) since the mid-1980s.

9. An election threshold is a rule that requires that, to elect representatives, for example to the national parliament, a party must receive a specified minimum percentage of votes.

10. The Progress Party's rhetoric was populist; it tried to mobilize "the people" against "the corrupt elites" and demanded more referenda.

11. The technically correct term is "asylum seekers"; a substantial number of asylum seekers never receive asylum and technically become refugees. However, I use the term "refugee" for both categories.

12. In the twenty-five years before the surge, ten thousand refugees were accepted to Denmark.

13. The term "politicization" does not do justice to the more fundamental transformation of foreign/immigrant workers into Muslim immigrants, a process I call "culturalization."

14. One may point to the cultural "similarities" between Poland and the rest of Europe as the reason for the relative absence of the controversy. However, the prospect of receiving Polish workers was used as an argument against the European Union in Denmark in 1990s.

15. For instance, stories that merely described the incoming number of immigrants or governments' allocation of extra resources were coded as neutral even though they effectively contributed to the creation of a moral panic.

16. Manifest positivity or negativity: explicit arguments for or against immigrants, immigration, or immigration law.

17. Again, repeating the news/editorial divide, only four out of nineteen commentaries (21.1 percent) were negative (against the immigration law), whereas fourteen (73.7 percent) of them were very positive (up to arguing for Denmark's ability to receive even more refugees than the actual numbers coming in).

18. Letters to the editor and commentaries were the two genres where it was easy to determine the tone of the single story.

19. "Quota refugees" are refugees who come to Denmark through the United Nations Commission on Human Rights according to an annual quota. Ninn-Hansen had proposed an increase in the annual quota as a way of closing off the border for other refugees who came to Denmark on their own.

20. Of course, controversy also exists around crime, but the counterarguments would usually be represented by reform groups who share with the authorities basic definitions of the problem (e.g., pedophilia). Alternative views are repressed within this consensual view. The discussion of crime would then be pushed onto the terrain of the pragmatic: Given that there is a problem about crime, what can we do about it?

21. I admit that numbers alone do not say much. Each instance is grounded in concrete stories and events, each enlisting a particular set of explanations, arguments, and rhetorical and generic devices that are difficult to express in numbers. My conclusions about the dominance of cultural perspective in later periods involves more than quantitative content analysis.

22. No news story in this period (1984) focused on refugees' culture, and there were only two letters to the editor emphasizing cultural difference as a problem.

23. As noted above, I did not include local papers in content analysis, although there were more stories from local papers in my data sample than from national newspapers. They may have had a more direct influence on public perceptions of the issues because they often illustrated general information about numbers and problems with local details. Many Danes read at least one local paper besides a national one.

24. "Unemployed" is not a general category of people without employment but a particular category of people who are considered as being temporarily out of work. They are entitled to maintain their membership in labor unions and receive so-called unemployment insurance during the unemployment period.

25. The cultural elite was also included because they were the main promoters of the humanitarian approach to refugees.

26. Berezin (2009), for example, is one of the few scholars who argues that immigration is not a sufficient condition for the contemporary Right. She argues that Europeanization is the driving force for the right-wing populist parties.

Chapter 3

1. Public opinion research shows us that there are a number of problems associated with the aggregation of "individual opinions" as an expression of public opinion or

will. For conceptual problems, see Blumer (1948), Bourdieu (1979), and Potter and Wetherell (1987); for measurement problems, Glynn et al. (1999), Herbst (1993, 2011), and Goidel (2011); for an overall view, see Moore (2008) and Lewis (2001). It has never been clear to me what Habermas's (1971) notion of deliberative rationality would look like in actual discourse.

2. I translated the text of both ads. See appendixes 2 and 3.

3. It is ironic that his ideas about the threat to Danish culture by alien cultures are now adopted by some members of the feminist movement against whom he raged.

4. He did not use the terms "silent majority" or "Upper Denmark" in his ads, but the terms were a key part of his rhetoric in the entire controversy.

5. I do not read rhetorical effects out of a particular text, insofar as the effect of a text is not so much embedded in the text itself as meaning, but in its interaction with other texts and utterances. It is possible to analyze rhetorical moves that present a particular version of reality as the reality itself, but any rendering of reality is fragile once put forward, and it does not necessarily have an influence outside the boundaries of the text. As noted in the introductory discussion of Bakhtin's ideas about language, I take discourse to be inherently responsive to other utterances in text or speech. The effects of Krarup's rhetorical strategies can therefore be read in the reactions to his intervention.

6. The positioning has some rhetorical resonance with what Gramsci (1971) called an "organic intellectual," one distinguished by the ability to direct the ideas and aspirations of the working class to which he structurally belongs (3). Krarup, of course, is no Marxist. He occupies a position of privilege relative to most Danes, but creates for himself a kind of organic identity emerging from the naturally Christian, antagonism-free, and culturally exclusive nation of Danish people constructed in the ad.

7. Content analysis is a limited tool for making sense of his access to the discourse. The numbers, as coded, do not do his influence justice. According to my statistics, he was the main source for 12.7 percent of the stories on Refugee 86. The problem is that the stories on Refugee 86 were not only about Krarup's call for boycott but included many other topics, such as how many volunteers had registered as collectors. These stories do not have Krarup as the source or the subject of the story, but even a story about the number of volunteers would implicitly be about Krarup's boycott campaign in the sense that the number of volunteers was taken to be indicative of the success of the boycott. Content analysis cannot register this kind of contextual information.

8. It was well known that the official line of the Danish government was to collaborate with Nazis during the occupation and that the authorities sent Danish communists and Jews to Nazi concentration camps. The number of "resistance fighters" was relatively small; and after the war ended, there were instances of people beating up Danes who had worked for Germans or had slept with German soldiers, which indicates that Danish people were not united against German occupiers. It is only after the war that this small number of resistance fighters was made to signify the "entire" Danish people.

9. As is often the case with fundraising, it later became clear that contributions had not reached the pledged amount, despite the intense campaign. There were also several comments and letters to the editor from collectors who described people's reception of them as hostile or at best cold.

10. A "war of maneuver" is a frontal attack on one's enemies, whereas "war of

position" refers to a slow process of preparing for a "system change," which Krarup declared had been achieved by the mid-2000s. Thus, "war of position" involves a long-term "ideological" struggle for setting the agenda and changing the perceptions.

11. Krarup characterized leftists as people who cared more about their image than about knowing what was going on. The evil character of the political Left and the mainstream had more to do with their ignorance and self-obsession than any desire to destroy the country. Arrogant in their "noble" naïveté, they think evil can be prevented by silence. He offers typical right-wing discourse applied to immigration, race, and ethnicity: the tolerant liberals are naive; their arguments may sound noble but do not address reality, so their naïveté makes them dangerous (van Dijk 1991, 1993).

12. For example, in live debate in TV, he represented the "negative" side together with Ole Hasselbach, the chairman of the Danish Association, Pia Kjærsgaard of the DPP, and Per Madsen against the "positive" side, Jacques Blum, Ebba Strange, MP for the Socialist People's Party, Thorkild Høyer, a lawyer for refugees, and Ann Pedersen from Friends of Refugees. Even this constellation indicates the hegemonic position Krarup's claims were acquiring: the contenders were continuously being forced to contend with his claims.

13. Shared Path (*Fælles Kurs*) was a small party formed in 1986 by breakaway members of the Communist Party. The party's election campaign was also based on populist rhetoric, the main elements of which were limiting immigration and withdrawal from the European Community (later the European Union).

14. The Left Socialists later formed an alliance with other small left-wing groups call the "Unity List," and entered the Folketing again in 1990s. Having learned their lesson, this time their election campaign was purely anti–European Union, speaking to the nationalist sentiments that had always been strong among Danes.

15. A decade later, another immigrant/Muslim expert, Naser Khader, who enlightened Danes about the importance of religion in Muslims' lives in his book *Honor and Shame* (1996), became one of the most influential politicians in Denmark and was an MP for the most "immigrant friendly" party, the Social Liberal Party (*Det Radikale*) until his right-wing leanings became clear; he left the party in 2007 to form a new party, New Alliance (now Liberal Alliance). He left that party in early 2009 and joined the Conservative Party a couple of months later. It is not surprising that he became a senior fellow at American right-wing think tank, the Hudson Institute. He followed a path similar to that of the Dutch politician Ayaan Ali Hirsi, who was an MP for an "immigrant friendly" party in the Dutch parliament only to end as a fellow at the American Enterprise Institute.

Chapter 4

1. A systematic analysis would show that many of the crises were provoked by the same actors. Kåre Bluitgen, who provoked the Danish cartoon crises by postulating that he could not find a caricaturist who dared to draw an illustration of the prophet Mohammed, provoked several controversies and crises around Muslim immigrants in collaboration with the daily *Jyllands-Posten*.

2. The prognosis was challenged by scholars who argued that a prognosis that spans

more than a century could not be made in any rational way and that this was a deliberate act on the part of the right-wing *Jyllands-Posten* in its ongoing efforts to create crises around Muslim immigration. The paper asked some economists from the Danish Statistical Institute to produce a population prognosis for the newspaper for the next century. They published it in the midst of a slow news period when the debate would not be drowned out by other news, and the story was published immediately before the publication of an official report that discussed the values upon which the future of Denmark should be built (and an assessment of the actual state of immigrants' integration into these values).

3. "Cultural radicalism" is a specific Danish phenomenon that describes the progressive cultural elite's criticism of the old cultural norms. They were critical of religious thought and Victorian sexual morality; they were known for their humanism, internationalism, and antimilitarism. They were considered to belong to the Left.

4. Some of the responsibilities of the old minister for internal affairs were moved over to the health minister.

5. See appendix 1.

6. See appendix 1 for a full list of the values and norms to which immigrants must declare allegiance.

7. The party's spokespeople had criticized Muslims several times for their gender practices in the early 1990s. Liberal Party MP Inge Dahl Sørensen: "It is a huge problem that there are some Muslims in Denmark who go for selling of brides, forcing young girls into marriage, female circumcision, polygamy and other forms of women subjugation, child abuse, child rearing and punishment traditions that belong to the Middle Ages, and much more that is in conflict with Danish laws and current moral values" (*Politiken*, February 23, 1994).

8. A floating signifier is a demand that receives "structural pressure of *rival* hegemonic projects": positioned between two equivalential articulations, its meaning remains indeterminate. The "floating dimension becomes most visible in periods of organic crisis, when the symbolic system needs to be radically recast" (Laclau 2005: 131–2).

9. Claus Hjort Frederiksen, the minister for employment from the Liberal Party, admitted that the Liberals and the DPP share core values: "We are all concerned with the cohesive force of Danish society. We are concerned with what it means to be Danish and the core values such as freedom of speech and democracy. We were in the same struggle against the experts who in fact spoke with political motivations" ("The Liberals and the DPP Share Values," *Politiken*, September 22, 2006).

10. See http://www.humanisme.dk/hate-speech/ for a list of people who have made xenophobic statements.

11. See chapter 1.

12. The operative word here is "clientalization," which is used by Rasmussen and in official government documents, not only about immigrants but in general.

13. The leader of the party, Kristian Thulesen Dahl, who replaced Pia Kjærsgaard in 2012, was himself an "ultraliberal" who defended open borders and zero public spending while he was the chair of the youth section of the Progress Party in the 1980. His resistance against the European Community (EC) was more about the "socialist bureaucracy" of the EC.

14. The editorial was specifically referring to the government's sale of the public energy company DONG to Goldman Sachs, tax relief for corporations, and the government's tribute to the "competitive state" (see below).

15. The political goal for a competitive state is to enable the nation to powerfully compete in the global economic competition; a politics based on the neoliberal dogma that the optimization of the private sector's competitive position in the global markets is the only way to sustain the welfare state (Hemerijck 2013).

16. Personal conversation with Yıldız Akdoğan.

17. Andreassen reports on similar interviews in the television news in which parents complain that public schools do not teach Danish children about Danish culture any more (Andreasen 2005, chapter 7).

18. This notion is usually misinterpreted as if hegemony is a system that incorporates its opponents in its differential system in an ever-expanding manner. This is a misunderstanding of hegemony theory: a hegemonic project needs some kind of constitutive antagonism that leaves out certain social groups outside its boundaries.

Conclusion

1. I remember the feeling in mid-1980s Denmark, where repeated crises around immigrants had created the feeling that the actions of the alien immigrants had become indefensible. One must also note that the left was repeatedly criticized for being naive and ignorant of the real problems, which were constantly on the agenda in cycle after cycle of moral panic concerning immigrants' deviant behavior.

Appendix

1. "Nej, ikke en krone!" translates literally as "No, not one krone!"

2. Øjster Højst, Ho, and Blokhus are small towns where the inhabitants did not want Iranian refugees to be housed and were criticized by the chairman of the Danish Refugee Council.

3. Gilstrup was the leader of the only anti-immigrant party at the time, the Progress Party.

4. All three prominent defenders of refugee rights: Baunsgaard was an MP for the social-liberal *Det Radikale Venstre*, Wilhjelm for the Left Socialists, and Espersen for the Social Democrats.

References

Akkerman, Tjitske, and Anniken Hagelund. 2007. "'Women and Children First!' Anti-immigration Parties and Gender in Norway and the Netherlands." *Patterns of Prejudice* 41, no. 2: 197–214.

Alderman, Liz, and Dan Bilefsky. 2015. "Huge Show of Solidarity in Paris against Terrorism." *New York Times*, January 11, accessed March 10, 2015. http://www.nytimes.com/2015/01/12/world/europe/paris-march-against-terror-charlie-hebdo.html.

Andersen, Jørgen Goul. 2002. "Danskernes Holdninger Til Indvandrere: En Oversigt." AMID Working Paper Series no. 17. Aalborg, Denmark: Akademiet for Migrationsstudier i Danmark, Aalborg University.

Andersen, Jørgen Goul. 2004. "The Danish People's Party and New Cleavages in Danish Politics." Working paper, Centre for Comparative Welfare Studies, Aalborg University.

Andreassen, Rikke. 2005. "Mass Media's Construction of Popular Memory, Gender, Sexuality, and Nationality." PhD diss., University of Toronto.

Andreassen, Rikke. 2012. "Gender as a Tool in Danish Debates about Muslims." In *Islam in Denmark: The Challenge of Diversity*, edited by Jørgen S. Nielsen, 143–60. Plymouth, England: Lexington Books.

Badiou, Alain. 2013. "Our Contemporary Impotence." *Radical Philosophy* 181: 43–47.

Bail, Christopher. 2015. *Terrified: How Anti-Muslim Fringe Organizations Became Mainstream*. Princeton: Princeton University Press.

Bakhtin, M. M. 1981. *The Dialogic Imagination: Four Essays*. Edited by Michael Holquist. Translated by Caryl Emerson and Michael Holquist. Austin: University of Texas Press.

Balibar, Etienne. 1991. "'Is There a 'Neo-racism?'" In *Race, Nation, Class: Ambiguous Identities*, edited by Etienne Balibar and Immanuel Wallerstein, 17–28. New York: Verso.

Bangstad, Sindre. 2011. "The Morality Police Are Coming! Muslims in Norway's Media Discourses." *Anthropology Today* 27, no. 5: 3–7.

Baumann, Andreas, and Anna F. Schefte. 2014. "Halvdelen Af Danskerne Skammer Sig over Udlændingedebatten." *MandagMorgen*, December 15, accessed

December 16, 2014. https://www.mm.dk/halvdelen-danskerne-skammer-sig-over-udlaendingedebatten.

Benson, Rodney. 2000. "Shaping the Public Sphere: Journalistic Fields and Immigration Debates in the United States and France, 1973–1994." PhD diss., University of California, Berkeley.

Benson, Rodney. 2013. *Shaping Immigration News: A French-American Comparison.* Cambridge: Cambridge University Press.

Berezin, Mabel. 2009. *Illiberal Politics in Neoliberal Times.* Cambridge: Cambridge University Press.

Berggren, Erik, Branka Likic-Brboric, Gülay Toksöz, and Nicos Trimikliniotis. 2007. *Irregular Migration.* Maastricht, the Netherlands: Shaker.

Betz, Hans-Georg. 1994. *Radical Right-Wing Populism in Western Europe.* New York: St. Martin's Press.

Betz, Hans-Georg, and Stefan Immerfall, eds. 1998. *The New Politics of the Right: Neo-populist Parties and Movements in Established Democracies.* New York: St. Martin's Press.

Betz, Hans-Georg, and Susi Meret. 2009. "Revisiting Lepanto: The Political Mobilization against Islam in Contemporary Western Europe." *Patterns of Prejudice* 43, nos. 3–4: 313–34.

Betz, Hans-Georg, and Susi Meret. 2013. "Right-Wing Populist Parties and the Working-Class Vote: What Have You Done for Us Lately?" In *Class Politics and the Radical Right,* edited by Jens Rydgren, 107–21. London: Routledge.

Bhattacharyya, Gargi. 2008. *Dangerous Brown Men: Exploiting Sex, Violence and Feminism in the "War on Terror".* London: Zed Books.

Billig, Michael. 1991. *Ideology and Opinions: Studies in Rhetorical Psychology.* London: Sage.

Billig, Michael. 1996. *Arguing and Thinking: A Rhetorical Approach to Social Psychology.* Cambridge: Cambridge University Press.

Billig, Michael. 1999. "Whose Terms? Whose Ordinariness? Rhetoric and Ideology in Conversation Analysis." *Discourse and Society* 10, no. 4: 543–82.

Billig, Michael, Susan Condor, Derek Edwards, and Mike J. Gane. 1988. *Ideological Dilemmas: A Social Psychology of Everyday Thinking.* London: Sage.

Bjørklund, Tor, and Jørgen Goul Andersen. 2002. "Anti-Immigration Parties in Denmark and Norway: The Progress Parties and the Danish People's Party." In *Shadows over Europe: The Development and Impact of the Extreme Right in Western Europe,* edited by Martin Schain, Aristide Zolberg, and Patrick Hossay, 107–36. New York: Palgrave Macmillan.

Blaut, James M. 1992. "The Theory of Cultural Racism." *Antipode* 24, no. 4: 289–99.

Blommaert, Jan, and Chris Bulcaen. 2000. "Critical Discourse Analysis." *Annual Review of Anthropology* 29: 447–66.

Blum, Jacques. 1986. *Splinten I Øjet: Om Danskernes Forhold Til de Fremmede.* Århus, Denmark: Stavnsager.

Blumer, Herbert. 1948. "Public Opinion and Public Opinion Polling." *American Sociological Review* 13, no. 5: 542–49.

Borchorst, Anette, and Mari Teigen. 2012. "Political Intersectionality: Tackling Inequalities in Public Policies in Scandinavia." *Kvinder Køn & Forskning* 2–3: 19–28.

Bornschier, Simon. 2010. *Cleavage Politics and the Populist Right: The New Cultural Conflict in Western Europe*. Philadelphia, PA: Temple University Press.

Bourdieu, Pierre. 1979. "Public Opinion Does Not Exist." In *Communication and the Class Struggle*, edited by A. Mattelart and Armand Siegelaub, 124–30. New York: International General.

Bowman, Paul. 2007. *Post-Marxism versus Cultural Studies: Theory, Politics and Intervention*. Edinburgh: Edinburgh University Press.

Bracke, Sarah. 2012. "From 'Saving Women' to 'Saving Gays': Rescue Narratives and Their Dis/continuities." *European Journal of Women's Studies* 19, no. 2: 237–52.

Bredström, Anna. 2003. "Gendered Racism and the Production of Cultural Difference: Media Representations and Identity Work among 'Immigrant Youth' in Contemporary Sweden." *NORA: Nordic Journal of Feminist and Gender Research* 11, no. 2: 78–88. doi:10.1080/08038740310002932.

Brink, Angela. 2014. "En Profesor Taler Ud." *Jyllands-Posten*, October 21, accessed December 7. http://jyllands-posten.dk/blogs/angelabrink/ECE7130252/En-professor-taler-ud/.

Butler, Judith. 2008. "Sexual Politics, Torture, and Secular Time." *British Journal of Sociology* 59, no. 1: 1–23.

Chanock, Martin. 2000. "'Culture' and Human Rights: Orientalising, Occidentalising and Authenticity." In *Beyond Rights Talk and Culture Talk: Comparative Essays on the Politics of Rights and Culture*, edited by Mahmood Mamdani, 15–36. Cape Town, South Africa: David Philip.

Christensen, Ann-Dorte, and Birte Siim. 2012. "Citizenship and Politics of Belonging: Inclusionary and Exclusionary Framings of Gender and Ethnicity." *Kvinder Køn & Forskning* 2–3: 8–17.

Cohen, Stanley. 1972. *Folk Devils and Moral Panics*. London: Routledge.

Coman, Julian. 2015. "How the Nordic Far-Right Has Stolen the Left's Ground on Welfare." *The Guardian*, July 26. Accessed July 27, 2015, at http://www.theguardian.com.

Danish Interior Ministry. 2001. *Immigration, Integration and Economy*. Copenhagen: Danish Interior Ministry.

Delanty, Gerard, Paul Jones, and Ruth Wodak. 2008. *Identity, Belonging, and Migration*. Liverpool, England: Liverpool University Press.

De Leeuw, Marc, and Sonja van Wichelen. 2012. "Civilizing Migrants: Integration, Culture and Citizenship." *European Journal of Cultural Studies* 15, no. 2: 195–210.

De Leon, Cedric, Manali Desai, and Cihan Tuğal. 2009. "Political Articulation: Parties and the Constitution of Cleavages in the United States, India, and Turkey." *Sociological Theory* 27, no. 3: 193–219.

Diamond, Jeremy. 2015. "Jindal: Some Muslims Trying to 'Colonize' West." *CNN*, January 21, accessed April 19, 2015. http://www.cnn.com/2015/01/21/politics/bobby-jindal-no-go-zones-fox/index.html.

Diken, Bülent. 1998. *Stranger, Ambivalence and Social Theory*. London: Ashgate.

Dyrberg, Torben Bech. 2000. "Racisme Som En Nationalistisk Og Populistisk Reaktion På Elitedemokrati." In *Diskursteorien På Arbejde*, edited by Torben Bech Dyrberg, Allan Dreyer Hansen, and Jacob Torfing, 221–46. Copenhagen: Roskilde Universitetsforlag.

Edwards, Derek. 1995. "A Commentary on Discursive and Cultural Psychology." *Culture and Psychology* 1, no. 1: 55–65.

Edwards, Derek. 2003. "Analyzing Racial Discourse: The Discursive Psychology of Mind-World Relationships." In *Analyzing Interviews on Racial Issues: Multidisciplinary Approaches to Interview Discourse*, edited by H. van den Berg, H. Houtkoop-Steenstra, and M. Wetherell, 31–48. Cambridge: Cambridge University Press.

Edwards, Derek, and Jonathan Potter. 1992. *Discursive Psychology*. London: Sage.

Eliasoph, Nina. 1998. *Avoiding Politics: How Americans Produce Apathy in Everyday Life*. Cambridge: Cambridge University Press.

Ellinas, Antonis. 2010. *The Media and the Far Right in Western Europe*. Cambridge: Cambridge University Press.

El-Tayeb, Fatima. 2012. "'Gays Who Cannot Properly Be Gay': Queer Muslims in the Neoliberal European City." *European Journal of Women's Studies* 19, no. 1: 79–95.

Engelbreth Larsen, Rune. 2001. *Det Nye Højre I Danmark*. Copenhagen: Tiderne Skifter.

Esmark, Anders, and Peter Kjær. 1999. "Mediernes Politiske Rolle: Tre Gamle Myter Og En Ny." In *Magt Og Fortælling: Hvad Er Politisk Journalistik?* edited by Erik Meier Carlsen, Peter Kjær, and Ove K. Pedersen, 116–34. Århus, Denmark: Center for Journalistik og Efteruddannelse.

Ewing, Katherine. 2008. *Stolen Honor: Stigmatizing Muslim Men in Berlin*. Stanford, CA: Stanford University Press.

Fadel, Ulla Holm. 1999. "Skik Følge Eller Land Fly: Danske Fortåelser Af Kulturel Forkel-Lighed." In *Den Generende Forskellighed: Danske Svar På Den Stigende Multikulturalisme*, edited by Peter Hervik, 214–61. Copenhagen: Hans Reitzels Forlag.

Fantz, Ashley. 2015. "At Least 3.7 Million Rally against Terrorism in France." *CNN*, January 11, accessed March 19, 2015, http://www.cnn.com/2015/01/11/world/charlie-hebdo-paris-march/index.html.

Fekete, Liz. 2009. *A Suitable Enemy: Racism, Migration and Islamophobia in Europe*. New York: Pluto Press.

Fernando, Mayanthi L. 2014. *The Republic Unsettled: Muslim French and the Contradictions of Secularism*. Durham, NC: Duke University Press.

"François Hollande Condemns 'Cowardly' Attack on Satirical Magazine Charlie Hebdo." 2015. *Euronews*, January 7, accessed February 17, 2015. http://www.euronews.com/2015/01/07/francois-hollande-condemns-cowardly-attack-on-satirical-paper-charlie-hebdo/.

Gaasholt, Øystein, and Lise Togeby. 1995. *I Syv Sind: Danskernes Holdninger Til Flygtninge Og Indvandrere*. Århus, Denmark: Forlaget Politica.

Geertz, Clifford. 1973. *The Interpretation of Cultures: Selected Essays*. New York: Basic Books.

Givens, Terri E. 2005. *Voting Radical Right in Western Europe*. Cambridge: Cambridge University Press.

Glynn, Carroll, Susan Herbst, Garret O'Keefe, Robert Shapiro, and Mark Lindeman. 1999. *Public Opinion*. Boulder, CO: Westview Press.

Goffman, Erving. 1959. *The Presentation of Self in Everyday Life*. New York: Doubleday.

Goidel, Kirby, ed. 2011. *Political Polling in the Digital Age: The Challenge of Measuring and Understanding Public Opinion*. Baton Rouge: Louisiana State University Press.

Göle, Nilüfer. 2011. "The Public Visibility of Islam and European Politics of Resentment: The Minarets-Mosques Debate." *Philosophy and Social Criticism* 37, no. 4: 383–92.

Goode, Erich, and Nachman Ben-Yehuda. 2009. *Moral Panics: The Social Construction of Deviance*. West Sussex, England: Wiley-Blackwell.

Gotsbachner, Emo. 2001. "Xenophobic Normality: The Discriminatory Impact of Habitualized Discourse Dynamics." *Discourse and Society* 12, no. 6: 729–59.

Gramsci, Antonio. 1971. *Selections from the Prison Notebooks*. Edited and translated by Quintin Hoare and Geoffrey Nowell Smith. London: Lawrence and Wishart.

Gramsci, Antonio. 2000. *The Antonio Gramsci Reader*. Edited by David Forgacs. New ed. London: Lawrence and Wishart.

Gullestad, Marianne. 2002. "Invisible Fences: Egalitarianism, Nationalism and Racism." *Journal of the Royal Anthropological Institute* 8, no. 1: 45–63.

Habermas, Jürgen. 1971. *Toward a Rational Society: Student Protest, Science, and Politics*. Translated by Jeremy J. Shapiro. Toronto: Beacon Press.

Hainsworth, Paul. 2008. *The Extreme Right in Western Europe*. London: Routledge.

Hall, Stuart. 1977. "Culture, the Media and the 'Ideological Effect.'" In *Mass Communication and Society*, edited by James Curran, Michael Gurevitch, and Janet Woolacott, 315–48. London: Routledge.

Hall, Stuart. 1988. *The Hard Road to Renewal: Thatcherism and the Crisis of the Left*. New York: Verso.

Hall, Stuart. 1993. "Culture, Community, Nation." *Cultural Studies* 7, no. 3: 349–63.

Hall, Stuart, Chas Crithcer, Tony Jefferson, John Clarke, and Brian Roberts. 1978. *Policing the Crisis: Mugging, the State, and Law and Order*. London: Macmillan.

Hallin, Daniel. 1989. *The Uncensored War: The Media and Vietnam*. Berkeley: University of California Press.

Haritaworn, Jin. 2012. "Women's Rights, Gay Rights and Anti-Muslim Racism in Europe: Introduction." *European Journal of Women's Studies* 19, no. 1: 73–78.

Hedetoft, Ulf. 2003. "How Denmark Faces Immigration." *Open Democracy*, October 30, accessed April 19, 2015. http://www.opendemocracy.net/people-migrationeurope/article_1563.jsp.

Hemerijck, Anton. 2013. *Changing Welfare States*. Oxford: Oxford University Press.

Henkel, Heiko. 2012. "The Political Anthropology of Scandinavia after July 22, 2011." *American Anthropologist* 114, no. 2: 353–55.

Herbst, Susan. 1993. *Numbered Voices: How Opinion Polling Has Shaped American Politics*. Chicago: University of Chicago Press.

Herbst, Susan. 2011. "Un(numbered) Voices? Reconsidering the Meaning of Public Opinion in a Digital Age." In *Political Polling in the Digital Age: The Challenge of Measuring and Understanding Public Opinion*, edited by Goidel Kirby, 85–98. Baton Rouge: Louisiana State University Press.

Hervik, Peter, ed. 1999. *Den Generende Forskellighed; Danske Svar På Den Stigende Multikulturalisme*. Copenhagen: Hans Reitzels Forlag.

Hervik, Peter, ed. 2002. *Mediernes Muslimer: En Antropologisk Undersøgelse Af Mediernes Dækning Af Religioner I Danmark*. Copenhagen: Nævnet for Etnisk Ligestilling.

Hervik, Peter, ed. 2004. "The Danish Cultural World of Unbridgeable Differences." *Ethnos* 69, no. 2: 247–67.

Hervik, Peter, ed. 2011. *The Annoying Difference: The Emergence of Danish Neonationalism, Neoracism, and Populism in the Post-1989 World*. New York: Berghahn Books.

Hervik, Peter, ed. 2012. "Ending Tolerance as a Solution to Incompatibility: The Danish 'Crisis of Multiculturalism.'" *European Journal of Cultural Studies* 15, no. 2: 211–25.

Hiro, Dilip. 1992. *Black British, White British: A History of Race Relations in Britain.* London: Paladin.

Hjarnø, Jan, and Torben Jensen. 1996. *Diskrimineringen Af Unge Med Indvandrerbaggrund Ved Jobsøgning.* Esbjerg, Denmark: Sydjysk Universitetsforlag.

Horsti, Karina. 2008. "Overview of Nordic Media Research on Immigration and Ethnic Relations: From Text Analysis to the Study of Production, Use and Reception." *Nordicom Review* 29, no. 2: 275–93.

Hussain, Mustafa, Ferruh Yılmaz, and Tim O'Connor. 1997. *Medierne, Minoriteterne Og Majoriteten: En Undersøgelse Af Nyhedsmedier Og Den Folkelige Diskurs I Danmark.* Copenhagen: Nævnet for Etnisk Ligestilling.

Hvenegård-Lassen, Kirsten. 1996. *Grænseland: Minoriteter, Rettigheder Og Den Nationale Idé.* Copenhagen: Danish Center for Human Rights.

Ignazi, Piero. 2003. *Extreme Right Parties in Western Europe.* Oxford: Oxford University Press.

Ireland, Patrick. 2004. *Becoming Europe: Immigration, Integration, and the Welfare State.* Pittsburgh, PA: University of Pittsburgh Press.

Iyengar, Shanto, Mark D. Peters, and Donald R. Kinder. 1982. "Experimental Demonstrations of the 'Not-So-Minimal' Consequences of Television News Programs." *American Political Science Review* 76, no. 4: 848–58.

Jäckel, Eberhard. 1981. *Hitler's World View: A Blueprint for Power.* Boston: Harvard University Press.

Jacobsen, Brian A. 2009. "Muslims on the Political Agenda." *Nordic Journal of Religion and Society* 22, no. 1: 15–35.

Jacobsen, Sara Jul, Tina Gudrun Jensen, Kathrine Vitus, and Kristina Weibel. 2012. *Analysis of Danish Media Setting and Framing of Muslims, Islam and Racism.* Copenhagen: Danish National Centre for Social Research.

Jameson, Fredric. 1991. *Postmodernism; or, the Cultural Logic of Late Capitalism.* Durham, NC: Duke University Press.

Jenkins, Richard. 1997. *Rethinking Ethnicity: Arguments and Explorations.* London: Sage.

Jenkins, Richard. 1999. "Why 'Danish Identity' Doesn't Explain Much about Denmark's Rejection of the Maastricht Treaty in 1992." *Folk* 41: 117–37.

Jensen, Bent. 2000. *De Fremmede I Dansk Avisdebat: Fra 1970'erne Til 1990'erne.* Copenhagen: Spektrum.

Jensen, Bent. 2001. *Foreigners in the Danish Newspaper Debate from the 1870s to the 1990s.* Copenhagen: Rockwool Foundation Research Unit.

Jensen, Tina Gudrun. 2008. "To Be 'Danish,' Becoming 'Muslim': Contestations of National Identity?" *Journal of Ethnic and Migration Studies* 34, no. 3: 389–409.

Jensen, Tina Gudrun. 2009. "The Cartoon Affair and the Question of Cultural Diversity in Denmark." *E-Cadernos Ces* 3: 64–73.

Karpantschof, René. 2002. "Populism and Right Wing Extremism in Denmark 1980–2001." Sociologisk Rapportserie no. 4. Department of Sociology, University of Copenhagen.

Keskinen, Suvi. 2012. "Limits to Speech? The Racialised Politics of Gendered Violence in Denmark and Finland." *Journal of Intercultural Studies* 33, no. 3: 261–74.

Keskinen, Suvi. 2013. "Antifeminism and White Identity Politics." *Nordic Journal of Migration Research* 3, no. 4: 225–32.

Khader, Naser. 1996. *Ære Og Skam*. Copenhagen: Borgen.

Khosravinik, Majid. 2010. "Actor Descriptions, Action Attributions, and Argumentation: Towards a Systematization of CDA Analytical Categories in the Representation of Social Groups." *Critical Discourse Studies* 7, no. 1: 55–72.

Kitschelt, Herbert. 1995. *The Radical Right in Western Europe: A Comparative Analysis*. Ann Arbor: University of Michigan Press.

Klandermans, Bert, and Nonna Mayer. 2006. *Extreme Right Activists in Europe: Through the Magnifying Glass*. London: Routledge.

Körmendi, Eszter. 1986. *Os Og de Andre: Danskernes Holdninger Til Indvandrere Og Flygtninge*. Copenhagen: Socialforskningsinstituttet.

Krinsky, Charles. 2013. "Introduction: The Moral Panic Concept." In *The Ashgate Research Companion to Moral Panics*, edited by Charles Krinsky, 1–14. London: Ashgate.

Krzyżanowski, Michal, and Ruth Wodak. 2009. *The Politics of Exclusion: Debating Migration in Austria*. New Brunswick, NJ: Transaction.

Kundnani, Arun. 2007. *The End of Tolerance: Racism in 21st-Century Britain*. London: Pluto Press.

Kundnani, Arun. 2012. "Multiculturalism and Its Discontents: Left, Right and Liberal." *European Journal of Cultural Studies* 15, no. 2: 155–66.

Kundnani, Arun. 2014. *The Muslims Are Coming: Islamophobia, Extremism and the Domestic War on Terror*. New York: Verso.

Laclau, Ernesto. 1996. *Emancipation(s)*. New York: Verso.

Laclau, Ernesto. 2005. *On Populist Reason*. New York: Verso.

Laclau, Ernesto. 2008. "Articulation and the Limits of Metaphor." In *A Time for Humanities: Futurity and the Limits of Autonomy*, edited by James Joseph Bono, Tim Dean, and Ewa Plonowska Ziarek, 61–83. Bronx, NY: Fordham University Press.

Laclau, Ernesto. 2014. *The Rhetorical Foundations of Society*. New York: Verso.

Laclau, Ernesto, and Chantal Mouffe. 2001. *Hegemony and Socialist Strategy: Towards a Radical Democratic Politics*. 2nd ed. New York: Verso.

Larsen, John Aggergaard. 1997. "Bosniske Krigsflygtninge I Dansk Offentlighed. Forestillinger Og Politisk Virkelighed." University of Copenhagen.

Lentin, Alana, and Gavan Titley. 2011. *The Crises of Multiculturalism: Racism in a Neoliberal Age*. London: Zed Books.

Lewis, Justin. 2001. *Constructing Public Opinion: How Political Elites Do What They Like and Why We Seem to Go Along with It*. New York: Columbia University Press.

Lordon, Frédéric. 2015. "Charlie at Any Cost?" *Verso Books Blogs*, January 20, accessed January 19, 2015. http://www.versobooks.com/blogs/1813-frederic-lordon-charlie-at-any-cost.

Lowndes, Joseph. 2005. "From Founding Violence to Political Hegemony: The Conservative Populism of George Wallace." In *Populism and the Mirror of Democracy*, edited by Francisco Panizza, 144–71. New York: Verso.

Lucassen, Leo. 2005. *The Immigrant Threat: The Integration of Old and New Immigrants in Western Europe since 1850*. Champaign: University of Illinois Press.

Lucassen, Leo, David Feldman, and Jochen Oltmer. 2006. *Paths of Integration: Migrants in Western Europe (1880–2004)*. Amsterdam: Amsterdam University Press.

Lykkeberg, Rune. 2008. *Kampen Om Sandhederne*. Copenhagen: Gyldendal.

Madsen, Jacob G. 2000. *Mediernes Konstruktion Af Flygtninge- Og Indvandrerspørgsmålet*. Århus, Denmark: Magtudredningen, University of Aarhus.

Mahmud, Tayyab. 2005. "Limit Horizons and Critique: Seductions and Perils of the Nation." *Villanova Law Review* 50, no. 4: 939–61.

Marrus, Michael R. 1988. "The Strange Story of Herschel Grynszpan." *American Scholar* 57, no. 1: 69–79.

Marx, Karl, and Friedrich Engels. 1978. *The Marx-Engels Reader*. Edited by Robert Tucker. New York: Norton.

Massad, Joseph. 2007. *Desiring Arabs*. Chicago: University of Chicago Press.

Massad, Joseph. 2015. *Islam in Liberalism*. Chicago: University of Chicago Press.

McCombs, Maxwell. 2005. "The Agenda-Setting Function of the Press." In *The Press*, edited by Geneva Overholser and Kathleen Hall Jamieson, 156–68. Oxford: Oxford University Press.

McIntosh, Laurie. 2015. "Impossible Presence: Race, Nation and the Cultural Politics of 'Being Norwegian.'" *Ethnic and Racial Studies* 38, no. 2: 309–25.

Mercer, Kobena. 1990. "Powellism: Race, Politics and Discourse." PhD diss., Goldsmiths College, University of London.

Meret, Susi. 2011. "From the Margins to the Mainstream? The Development of the Radical Right in Denmark." In *Is Europe on the "Right" Path? Right-Wing Extremism and Right-Wing Populism in Europe*, edited by Nora Langenbacher and Britta Schellenberg, 243–65. Berlin: Friedrich-Ebert-Stiftung Forum Berlin.

Meret, Susi, and Birte Siim. 2013. "Gender, Populism and Politics of Belonging: Discourses of Right-Wing Populist Parties in Denmark, Norway and Austria." In *Negotiating Gender and Diversity in an Emergent European Public Sphere*, edited by Birte Siim and Monika Mokre, 78–96. New York: Palgrave Macmillan.

Mikkelsen, Flemming. 2001. *Integrationens Paradox: Indvandrere Og Flygtninge I Danmark Mellem Inklusion or Marginalisering*. Copenhagen: Catinet.

Ministers of the Interior, European Commission. 2015. Paris, January 11, accessed February 17, 2015. http://ec.europa.eu/dgs/home-affairs/what-is-new/news/news/docs/20150111_joint_statement_of_ministers_for_interrior_en.pdf.

Modood, Tariq. 2005. *Multicultural Politics: Racism, Ethnicity, and Muslims in Britain*. Minneapolis: University of Minnesota Press.

Moffitt, Benjamin. 2015. "How to Perform Crisis: A Model for Understanding the Key Role of Crisis in Contemporary Populism." *Government and Opposition* 50, no. 2: 189–217.

Mondon, Aurélien. 2013. *The Mainstreaming of the Extreme Right in France and Australia: A Populist Hegemony?* London: Ashgate.

Moore, David William. 2008. *The Opinion Makers: An Insider Exposes the Truth behind the Polls*. Boston: Beacon Press.

Mørch, Søren. 2005. *Poul Nyrup Rasmussen*. Copenhagen: Gyldendal.

Morgan, George, and Scott Poynting, eds. 2012. *Global Islamophobia: Muslims and Moral Panic in the West*. London: Ashgate.

Mouffe, Chantal. 1995. "The End of Politics and the Rise of the Radical Right." *Dissent*, Fall, 498–502.

Mouffe, Chantal. 2005. *On the Political*. London: Routledge.

Mouillot, Miranda Richmond. 2015. "I Won't Fear Muslims." Salon.com, January 24, accessed January 27, 2015. http://www.salon.com/2015/01/24/no_amount_of_argument_seems_to_deter_those_who_insist_i_should_be_afraid_of_muslims/.

Mouritsen, Per. 2006. "The Particular Universalism of a Nordic Civic Nation: Common Values, State Religion and Islam in Danish Political Culture." In *Multiculturalism, Muslims, and Citizenship*, edited by Tariq Modood, Anna Triandafyllidou, and Ricard Zapata-Barrero. London: Routledge.

Mudde, Cas. 2004. "The Populist Zeitgeist." *Government and Opposition* 39, no. 4: 542–63.

Mudde, Cas. 2007. *Populist Radical Right Parties in Europe*. Cambridge: Cambridge University Press.

Mudde, Cas, and Cristobal Rovira Kaltwasser. 2013. "Populism." In *The Oxford Handbook of Political Ideologies*, edited by Michael Freeden, Lyman Tower Sargent, and Marc Stears, 493–512. Oxford: Oxford University Press.

Necef, Mehmet Ümit. 2000. "Den Danske Debat Om Indvandrere Og Flygtninge 1964–2000: Synspunkter I Og På Forskningen." *Den Jyske Historiker* 89: 133–59.

Necef, Mehmet Ümit. 2001. "Indvandring, Den Nationale Stat Og Velfærdsstaten." In *Ubekvemme Udfordringer*, edited by Peter Seeberg, 31–64. Odense, Denmark: Odense Universitetsforlag.

Noble, Greg. 2012. "Where Is the Moral in Moral Panic?" In *Global Islamophobia: Muslims and Moral Panic in the West*, edited by Scott Poynting and George Morgan, 215–31. London: Ashgate.

Norris, Pippa. 2005. *Radical Right: Voters and Parties in the Electoral Market*. Cambridge: Cambridge University Press.

Orsi, Robert A. 2003. "Is the Study of Lived Religion Irrelevant to the World We Live in? Special Presidential Plenary Address, Society for the Scientific Study of Religion, Salt Lake City, November 2, 2002." *Journal for the Scientific Study of Religion* 42, no. 2: 169–74.

Østergaard, Bent. 2007. *Indvandrerne I Danmarks Historie: Kultur-Og Religionsmøder*. Odense, Denmark: Syddansk Universitetsforlag.

Panizza, Francisco, ed. 2005. *Populism and the Mirror of Democracy*. New York: Verso.

Petersen, Malene Lembcke. 2015. "Statsministeren: Ingen Skal Slippe Afsted Med at Angribe Det Danske Samfund." *Politiken*, February 15, accessed February 17, 2015. http://www.dr.dk/Nyheder/Politik/2015/02/15/082902.htm.

Petersen, Michael Nebeling. 2013. "Somewhere, over the Rainbow: Biopolitiske Rekonfigurationer Af Den Homoseksuelle Figur." PhD diss., University of Copenhagen.

Petzen, Jennifer. 2012. "Contesting Europe: A Call for an Anti-modern Sexual Politics." *European Journal of Women's Studies* 19, no. 1: 97–114.

Phillips, Louise, and Marianne Jørgensen. 2002. *Discourse Analysis as Theory and Method*. London: Sage.

Pitcher, Ben. 2009. *The Politics of Multiculturalism: Race and Racism in Contemporary Britain*. New York: Palgrave Macmillan.

Polakow-Suransky, Sasha. 2002. "Fortress Denmark?" *American Prospect*, May 13, accessed November 22, 2012. http://prospect.org/article/fortress-denmark.

Potter, Jonathan. 1998. "Discursive Social Psychology: From Attitudes to Evaluative Practices." *European Review of Social Psychology* 9, no. 1: 233–66.

Potter, Jonathan, and Margaret Wetherell. 1987. *Discourse and Social Psychology: Beyond Attitudes and Behaviour*. London: Sage.

Puar, Jasbir K. 2007. *Terrorist Assemblages: Homonationalism in Queer Times*. Durham, NC: Duke University Press.

Quasthoff, Uta. 1978. "The Uses of Stereotypes in Everyday Argument." *Journal of Pragmatics* 1, no. 2: 1–48.

Rasmussen, Anders Fogh. 1993. *Fra socialstat til minimalstat*. Copenhagen: Samleren.

Rasmussen, Anders Fogh. 2001. "Statsminister Anders Fogh Rasmussens Redegørelse I Folketinget Tirsdag Den 4. December 2001." December 4, accessed on March 14, 2015. http://www.statsministeriet.dk/_p_7327.html.

Reisigl, Martin, and Ruth Wodak. 2001. *Discourse and Discrimination: Rhetorics of Racism and Antisemitism*. London: Routledge.

Roy, Oliver. 2007. *Secularism Confronts Islam*. New York: Columbia University Press.

Roy, Oliver. 2010. *Holy Ignorance: When Religion and Culture Part Ways*. Oxford: Oxford University Press.

Rydgren, Jens. 2004. "Explaining the Emergence of Radical Right-Wing Populist Parties: The Case of Denmark." *West European Politics* 27, no. 3: 474–502.

Rydgren, Jens. 2010. "Radical Right-Wing Populism in Denmark and Sweden: Explaining Party System Change and Stability." *SAIS Review of International Affairs* 30, no. 1: 57–71.

Rydgren, Jens, ed. 2013. *Class Politics and the Radical Right*. London: Routledge.

Sampson, Steve. 1995. "The Threat to Danishness: Danish Culture as Seen by Den Danske Forening: Taking the Xenophobic Right Seriously." In *Multi-culturalism in the Nordic Societies (Proceedings of the 9th Nordic Seminar for Researchers on Migration and Ethnic Relations)*, edited by Jan Hjarnø, 59–69. Copenhagen: Nordic Council of Ministers.

Saunders, Doug. 2012. *The Myth of the Muslim Tide: Do Immigrants Threaten the West?* New York: Vintage.

Schain, Martin, Aristide Zolberg, and Patrick Hossay, eds. 2002. *Shadows over Europe: The Development and Impact of the Extreme Right in Western Europe*. New York: Palgrave Macmillan.

Schegloff, Emanuel A. 1997. "Whose Text? Whose Context?" *Discourse and Society* 8, no. 2: 165–87.

Schegloff, Emanuel A. 1999. "'Schegloff's Texts' as 'Billig's Data': A Critical Reply." *Discourse and Society* 10, no. 4: 558–72.

Schierup, Carl-Ulrik. 1993. *På Kulturens Slagmark: Mindretal Og Størretal Taler Om Danmark*. Esbjerg, Denmark: Sydjysk Universitetsforlag.

Schwarz, Bill. 1996. "'The Only White Man in There': The Re-racialisation of England 1956–1968." *Race and Class* 38, no. 1: 65–78.

Scott, Joan Wallach. 2007. *The Politics of the Veil*. Princeton: Princeton University Press.

Shotter, John. 1993. *Conversational Realities: Constructing Life through Language*. London: Sage.

Siapera, Eugenia. 2010. *Cultural Diversity and Global Media: The Mediation of Difference*. West Sussex, England: Wiley-Blackwell.

Siim, Birte, and Monika Mokre, eds. 2013. *Negotiating Gender and Diversity in an Emergent European Public Sphere*. New York: Palgrave Macmillan.

Siim, Birte, and Hege Skjeie. 2008. "Tracks, Intersections and Dead Ends: Multicultural Challenges to State Feminism in Denmark and Norway." *Ethnicities* 8, no. 3: 322–44.

Smith, Anna Marie. 1994. *New Right Discourse on Race and Sexuality: Britain, 1968–1990*. Cambridge: Cambridge University Press.

Smith, Stephen. 2002. "Copenhagen Flirts with Fascism." *Guardian*, June 4, accessed April 19, 2015. http://www.theguardian.com/politics/2002/jun/05/thefarright.uk.

Soysal, Levent. 2009. "Introduction: Triumph of Culture, Troubles of Anthropology." *Focaal* 55: 3–11.

Spielhaus, Riem. 2010. "Media Making Muslims: The Construction of a Muslim Community in Germany through Media Debate." *Contemporary Islam* 4, no. 1: 11–27.

Statistics Denmark. 2015. *Denmark in Figures 2015*. Copenhagen, DK: Statistics Denmark. http://www.dst.dk/pukora/epub/upload/19006/denmark2015.pdf.

Stavrakakis, Yannis. 2005. "Religion and Populism in Contemporary Greece." In *Populism and the Mirror of Democracy*, edited by Francisco Panizza, 224–49. New York: Verso.

Steen, Jens Jonatan, Søren Villemoes, and Niels Henrik Jespersen, eds. 2013. *Højrepopulismen: Venstrefløjens Akilleshæ*. Copenhagen: Frydenlund.

Stehle, Maria. 2012. "White Ghettos: The 'Crisis of Multiculturalism' in Post-unification Germany." *European Journal of Cultural Studies* 15, no. 2: 167–81.

Stolcke, Verena. 1995. "Talking Culture: New Boundaries, New Rhetorics of Exclusion in Europe." *Current Anthropology* 36, no. 1: 1–13.

Taggart, Paul A. 2000. *Populism*. Buckingham, England: Open University Press.

Taguieff, Pierre-André. 2001. *The Force of Prejudice: On Racism and Its Doubles*. Minneapolis: University of Minnesota Press.

Thalhammer, Eva, Vlasta Zucha, Edith Ezenhofer, Birgitte Salfinder, and Günther Ogris. 2001. *Attitudes towards Minority Groups in the European Union: A Special Analysis of the Eurobarometer 2000 Survey*. Vienna: European Monitoring Centre on Racism and Xenophobia.

Thompson, Kenneth. 1998. *Moral Panics*. London: Routledge.

Togeby, Lise. 1997. "Er vi Ved at Vænne 'Os' Til 'Dem'? Ænderinger I Danskernes Holdninger Til Flygtninge Og Indvandrere 1993–96." *Politica* 29, no. 1: 70–88.

Togeby, Lise. 2003. *Fra Fremmedarbejdere Til Etniske Minoriteter*. Århus, Denmark: Universitetsforlag/Magtudredningen.

Torfing, Jacob. 2005. "Discourse Theory: Achievements, Arguments and Challenges." In *Discourse Theory in European Politics: Identity, Policy and Governance*, edited by Jacob Torfing and David Howarth, 1–32. New York: Palgrave Macmillan.

Toulmin, Stephen. 1958. *The Uses of Argument*. Cambridge: Cambridge University Press.

Triandafyllidou, Anna. 2001. *Immigrants and National Identity in Europe*. London: Routledge.

Van Dijk, Teun A. 1984. *Prejudice in Discourse*. Amsterdam: John Benjamins.

Van Dijk, Teun A. 1987. *Communicating Racism: Ethnic Prejudice in Thought and Talk.* London: Sage.

Van Dijk, Teun A. 1991. *Racism and the Press.* London: Sage.

Van Dijk, Teun A. 1993. *Elite Discourse and Racism.* London: Sage.

Waddington, P. A. J. 1986. "Mugging as a Moral Panic: A Question of Proportion." *British Journal of Sociology* 37, no. 2: 245–59.

Wetherell, Margaret. 1998. "Positioning and Interpretative Repertoires: Conversation Analysis and Post-structuralism in Dialogue." *Discourse and Society* 9, no. 3: 387–412.

Wetherell, Margaret, and Jonathan Potter. 1992. *Mapping the Language of Racism: Discourse and the Legitimation of Exploitation.* London: Harvester Wheatsheaf.

Williams, Michelle Hale. 2006. *The Impact of Radical Right-Wing Parties in West European Democracies.* New York: Palgrave Macmillan.

Wren, Karen. 2001. "Cultural Racism: Something Rotten in the State of Denmark?" *Social and Cultural Geography* 2, no. 2: 141–62.

Yıldız, Yasemin. 2009. "Turkish Girls, Allah's Daughters, and the Contemporary German Subject: Itinerary of a Figure." *German Life and Letters* 62, no. 4: 465–81.

Yıldız, Yasemin. 2011. "Governing European Subjects: Tolerance and Guilt in the Discourse of 'Muslim Women.'" *Cultural Critique* 77, no. 1: 70–101.

Yılmaz, Ferruh. 2011. "The Politics of the Danish Cartoon Affair: Hegemonic Intervention by the Extreme Right." *Communication Studies* 62, no. 1: 5–22.

Yurdakul, Gökçe. 2009. *From Guest Workers into Muslims: The Transformation of Turkish Immigrant Associations in Germany.* Newcastle, England: Cambridge Scholars.

Žižek, Slavoj. 1999. "The Matrix, Or, the Two Sides of Perversion." Paper presented at "Inside the Matrix: International Symposium." Center for Art and Media, Karlsruhe, Germany, October 28.

Index